MW00512092

McDougal Littell

Grammar for Writing

McDougal Littell

Grammar for Writing

- GRAMMAR
- USAGE
- MECHANICS

McDougal Littell
A HOUGHTON MIFFLIN COMPANY

ISBN 13: 978-0-618-56620-4 ISBN 10: 0-618-56620-1

Printed in China

Acknowledgments begin on page 365.

2 3 4 5 6 7 8 9–DSC–12 11 10 09 08

Contents Overview

Grammar, Usage, and Mechanics

Student Resources

Grammar, Usage, and Mechanics

3 Using Phrases

Pierre DuPont
World-class rock climber
Don't be left hanging without
DuraTwine Rope

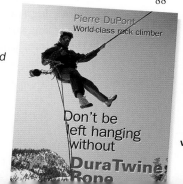

9 Using Modifiers

Mechanics

10 Capitalization

11 Punctuation

Quick-Fix Editing Machine

Fixing Errors

Improving Style

Special Features

Real World Grammar

Grammar in Literature

Quick-Fix Editing Machine

Student Resources

Grammar, Usage, and Mechanics

A Closer Look

Open the back of an old-fashioned clock, and you'll uncover tiny gears, levers, and pins. You can watch them work together, performing their functions perfectly and predictably. Similarly, if you look closely at the parts of a sentence, you will see how they, too, work together to bring about meaning—even more amazing than the appearance of the right time on the face of the clock.

Chapter 1

The Parts of Speech

A sorbish of
bilm and churvy
filbs krimmed
beside a
snarfy dorge.

Theme: Travel Stories

Now Guess This

What color were the filbs?

Can you answer this question? If you can, you have decoded a nonsense sentence solely on the basis of the forms and arrangement of its words. Clues like the ending *-ed* and the placement of a word after *a* can help you decide what kinds of words you are looking at. The categories of words—nouns, verbs, adjectives, adverbs—are called **parts of speech.**

Write Away: Decoder Game

Write the nonsense sentence shown above. One by one, cross out the nonsense words and write in real words that could replace them. Then try to label each word in the sentence with its part of speech. Save your work in your **Working Portfolio.**

Diagnostic Test: What Do You Know?

Write the letter of the term that correctly identifies each underlined word.

Many explorers (1) have been drawn to Antarctica (2), even though the continent has the harshest environment in the world. It (3) is dry, windy, and extremely cold. Ninety-eight percent of its surface is (4) a sheet of ice. In the summer of 1911–1912, two groups of explorers actually reached (5) the South Pole. The English group, led by Robert Falcon Scott, picked their way carefully (6) across the dangerous (7) ice with its deep crevasses. When they finally reached the pole, however, they found that another team had been there before (8) them. The Norwegian (9) group, led by Roald Amundsen, had reached the pole one month before Scott, and (10) they had left their flag to mark the spot.

1. A. proper noun
   B. common noun
   C. action verb
   D. linking verb

2. A. proper noun
   B. common noun
   C. action verb
   D. linking verb

3. A. common noun
   B. preposition
   C. pronoun
   D. conjunction

4. A. pronoun
   B. conjunction
   C. action verb
   D. linking verb

5. A. common noun
   B. proper noun
   C. action verb
   D. linking verb

6. A. linking verb
   B. action verb
   C. adjective
   D. adverb

7. A. common noun
   B. action verb
   C. adjective
   D. adverb

8. A. preposition
   B. pronoun
   C. conjunction
   D. adverb

9. A. common noun
   B. linking verb
   C. proper adjective
   D. adverb

10. A. preposition
    B. conjunction
    C. pronoun
    D. adjective

Nouns

CHAPTER 1

Here's the Idea

A noun is a word that names a person, place, thing, or idea.

Things: cameras, vehicle, cheetah

Persons: tourists, photographers, Chris

Ideas: surprise, suddenness, happiness

Places: Masai Mara Game Preserve, Kenya, lake, city

A **common noun** is a general name for a person, place, thing, or idea. Common nouns are usually not capitalized.

A **proper noun** is the name of a particular person, place, thing, or idea. A proper noun is always capitalized.

Common	river, mountain, pilot
Proper	Nile, Mt. Kenya, Charles Lindbergh

A **concrete noun** names an object that can be seen, heard, smelled, touched, or tasted.

An **abstract noun** names an idea, quality, or characteristic.

Concrete	shoe, car, perfume, thorn
Abstract	simplicity, beauty, truth, intention

A noun may be either **singular** or **plural** in form, depending on whether it names a single person, place, thing, or idea or more than one.

Singular	map, berry, deer, mouse
Plural	maps, berries, deer, mice

For more about spelling plural forms, see p. 341.

Every noun is either common or proper, concrete or abstract, and singular or plural. For example, *desert* is common, concrete, and singular. *Great Lakes* is proper, concrete, and plural.

A **collective noun** refers to a group of people or things. Examples include *herd, family, crew, team,* and *staff.* Even when a collective noun is singular in form, it can be used to refer to a group either as a single unit or as a number of individuals.

The herd (unit) **runs away as we get close.**

The herd (individuals) **find hiding places in the brush.**

A **compound noun** is formed from two or more words. Some compound nouns are written as single words, some as hyphenated words, and some as separate words.

Compound Nouns	
One word	toothbrush, backpack, watermelon
Hyphenated word	self-knowledge, sister-in-law
Separate words	duffel bag, South Carolina, Taj Mahal

PARTS OF SPEECH

A **possessive noun** shows ownership or relationship. Possessive nouns are spelled with apostrophes.

Ownership the tourist's passport
Relationship the tourist's companion

2 Why It Matters in Writing

The use of proper nouns in the description of a setting makes the setting seem more specific and real. How would the following passage differ if the writer had used common nouns, such as *plains* and *lake,* instead of the proper nouns she did use?

LITERARY MODEL

The **Serengetti Plains** spread from **Lake Nyaraza,** in **Tanganyika,** northward beyond the lower boundaries of **Kenya Colony.** They are the great sanctuary of the **Masai** . . . and they harbour more wild game than any similar territory in all of **East Africa.**

—Beryl Markham, *West with the Night*

3 Practice and Apply

CONCEPT CHECK: Nouns

Write the nouns in each sentence, identifying each as common or proper and as singular or plural. Use a chart like the one below.

Example: Swahili is one of Kenya's major languages.

Noun	Common	Proper	Singular	Plural
Swahili		✓	✓	
Kenya's		✓	✓	
languages	✓			✓

Life on Safari

1. Life on safari offers a new perspective on humans and animals.
2. Many camps in Kenya's game parks are surrounded by fences.
3. Here the humans live inside the fences while the herds of elephants, giraffes, and gazelles wander freely.
4. Animals have the right of way on all roads.
5. At the Sarova Mara Camp in the Masai Mara Game Preserve, visitors are taught how to lock their tents.
6. The problem here is a troop of clever monkeys who unzip and raid the camp's unlocked tents.
7. At one lodge near the Samburu Game Preserve, a young boy patrols the dining area and chases away monkeys.
8. Endangered species, such as rhinos, are often moved to sanctuaries where they are protected.
9. Rhinos at the Lewa Downs Wildlife Conservancy roam 55,000 fenced acres.
10. Armed guards patrol on foot, in jeeps, and in airplanes to count and protect these rhinos.

→ **For a SELF-CHECK and more practice, see the EXERCISE BANK, p. 306.**

CHALLENGE

Use the sentences above to do the following.

1. Find two possessive nouns.
2. Find two collective nouns.
3. Find two abstract nouns.
4. Find two compound nouns.

Personal Pronouns

1 Here's the Idea

A pronoun is a word used in place of a noun or another pronoun. The word that a pronoun stands for is called its **antecedent.**

Malcolm waved as he boarded the bus to the airport.
(Malcolm: ANTECEDENT; he: PRONOUN)

An antecedent can consist of two or more words, and it may be in a sentence other than the one in which the pronoun occurs.

Malcolm and Hal shared a sandwich. They munched on it.
(They STANDS FOR Malcolm and Hal; it STANDS FOR sandwich)

The forms of the personal pronouns are shown below.

Personal Pronouns

	Singular	Plural
First person	I, me (my, mine)	we, us (our, ours)
Second person	you (your, yours)	you (your, yours)
Third person	he, him, she, her, it (his, her, hers, its)	they, them (their, theirs)

Like possessive nouns, **possessive pronouns** show ownership or relationship. In the chart above, possessive pronouns are in parentheses.

Hal almost left his backpack on the bus.
(his: OWNERSHIP of backpack)

Calvin and Hobbes by Bill Watterson

PARTS OF SPEECH

❷ Why It Matters in Writing

Pronouns help writers to achieve coherence. Notice how the personal pronouns in the following passage link the two sentences and link the second half of each sentence to the first half.

LITERARY MODEL

The next day the young sportsman hovered about the woods, and Sylvia kept **him** company, having lost **her** first fear of the friendly lad, who proved to be most kind and sympathetic. **He** told **her** many things about the birds and what **they** knew and where **they** lived and what **they** did with themselves.

—Sarah Orne Jewett, "A White Heron"

CHAPTER 1

❸ Practice and Apply

CONCEPT CHECK: Personal Pronouns

Write each pronoun and identify its antecedent.

Journey to Scotland

1. Malcolm and his family flew to Scotland to see where their ancestors had come from.
2. They took a ferry to Lewis Island, where Malcolm's mother's grandmother had once lived with her family.
3. There they found her house, complete with its original furnishings.
4. "You must be my relatives, too," said Mrs. Morrison, opening the door to their knock.
5. "We are related to your great-aunt," said Malcolm.
6. "She was my great-grandmother," he added.
7. "I remember your grandmother," Mrs. Morrison said to Malcolm's mother. "She was younger than mine."
8. "In fact, you remind me of her," she added.
9. Mrs. Morrison showed the family the house and served them lunch.
10. They enjoyed the baked potato, but when she offered them haggis, only Malcolm ate it.

➜ **For a SELF-CHECK and more practice, see the EXERCISE BANK, p. 306.**

Other Kinds of Pronouns

1 Here's the Idea

Some kinds of pronouns are used to perform special functions in sentences.

Reflexive and Intensive Pronouns

A **reflexive pronoun** "reflects," or represents, the subject of the sentence or clause in which it appears.

REFLECTS

Soo-ni treats herself to a stroll through Chinese food markets.

An **intensive pronoun** is used to emphasize a noun or pronoun that appears in the same sentence.

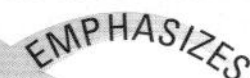

The merchants themselves enjoy sampling the goods.

Reflexive and intensive pronouns are formed by adding *-self* or *-selves* to forms of the personal pronouns.

Reflexive and Intensive Pronouns

	First Person	Second Person	Third Person
Singular	myself	yourself	himself, herself, itself
Plural	ourselves	yourselves	themselves

Reflexive pronouns should never be used alone. They must always have antecedents.

She buys souvenirs for herself and ~~myself~~ me.

Demonstrative Pronouns

Demonstrative pronouns point out specific persons, places, things, or ideas. They allow you to indicate whether the things you are referring to are relatively nearby (in time or space) or farther away. The demonstrative pronouns are *this, these, that,* and *those.*

The merchant tells Soo-ni, "My oranges are better than those in the other stall."

Indefinite Pronouns

Indefinite pronouns refer to persons, places, things, or ideas that are not specifically identified. Unlike other pronouns, they don't usually have antecedents.

Everyone in the market radiates energy.

Indefinite Pronouns	
Singular	another, anybody, anyone, anything, each, either, everybody, everyone, everything, much, neither, nobody, no one, nothing, one, somebody, someone, something
Plural	both, few, many, several
Singular or plural	all, any, more, most, none, some

Interrogative and Relative Pronouns

CHAPTER 1

An **interrogative pronoun** introduces a question.

A **relative pronoun** introduces a noun clause or an adjective clause; it connects an adjective clause to the word or words it modifies.

Interrogative and Relative Pronouns	
Interrogative	who, whom, whose, which, what
Relative	who, whom, whose, which, that

Interrogative and relative pronouns look similar, but they function differently.

Who would believe the crowds and excitement?
INTERROGATIVE PRONOUN

The merchants, who are eager for sales, shout to customers.
RELATIVE PRONOUN

2 Why It Matters in Writing

Notice how the writer of this sentence used relative pronouns to introduce clauses that add information in an economical way.

LITERARY MODEL

Maybe this man, **who** didn't believe in love, realized by the time his hair was white that in his heart was something **which** could be called love.

—Zhang Jie, "Love Must Not Be Forgotten"

CLAUSES

3 Practice and Apply

A. CONCEPT CHECK: Other Kinds of Pronouns

Write each pronoun and indicate what kind it is.

Tracking the Tibetan Ox

1. Travelers to Tibet are fortunate if they see wild yaks, because few of the large beasts remain today.
2. The furry animals, which may have 30-inch horns, weigh about a ton apiece.
3. Each of the animals can supply people with milk, fuel, wool, and transportation—or with meat.
4. Since the 1950s, most of the wild yaks on the Tibetan plateau have been killed for meat.
5. Hunters, who have used a new road to reach their prey, have reduced the herds to almost none.
6. The Chang Tang Reserve, which stretches across the plateau, provides protection for yaks today.
7. The Chang Tang Reserve itself covers 115,500 square miles, an area greater than that of Arizona.
8. Most of the yaks have deep black fur.
9. Occasionally, one appears whose coat is golden rather than black.
10. Travelers who have never seen a golden yak might ask themselves, What are we looking at?

→ **For a SELF-CHECK and more practice, see the EXERCISE BANK, p. 307.**

B. REVISING: Relative Pronouns

Combine these groups of sentences, using relative pronouns.

Wildlife of India

1. Travelers in India rarely see wild animals nowadays. India used to be famous for its wild animals.
2. Forests once covered over 40 percent of the country. They were the homes of all the wildlife. The forests have been cut down.
3. Now wild animals are protected in only 3 percent of the country. Wild animals are increasingly endangered.
4. Some visitors want to see the wildlife. These people have to go to game preserves.
5. Animals are abundant in some game preserves. Game preserves are home to numerous species, including elephants.

PARTS OF SPEECH

Verbs

1 Here's the Idea

A verb expresses an action, a condition, or a state of being. The two main types of verbs are action verbs and linking verbs. Both kinds can be accompanied by auxiliary verbs.

Action Verbs

An **action verb** expresses an action. The action may be physical or mental.

My family and I drove 500 miles to Montana. (PHYSICAL)

We wanted good weather for our vacation. (MENTAL)

When an action verb can take a direct object (that is, a word naming a person or thing that receives the action), it is called a **transitive verb.** When an action verb cannot take an object, it is called an **intransitive verb.**

Mom locked Dad's wheelchair into place.
TRANSITIVE VERB (locked) — OBJECT (wheelchair)

Uncle Lou snored loudly in the back of the van.
INTRANSITIVE VERB (NO OBJECT) (snored)

Linking Verbs

A **linking verb** links a word in the predicate to the subject.

We were happy to see the sign for Big Sky Country.
LINKED (happy — We)

The campsite appeared tiny beside the grand mountain.
LINKED (tiny — campsite)

There are two groups of linking verbs: forms of *be* and verbs that express conditions.

Forms of *Be*

is, am, are, was, were, been, being

Verbs That Express Conditions

look, smell, feel, sound, taste,
grow, appear, become, seem, remain

Some verbs can be either action or linking verbs.

Dad tasted the fresh water. It tasted wonderful.
(tasted ↑ ACTION; tasted ↑ LINKING)

Uncle Lou smelled skunks. They smelled awful.
(smelled ↑ ACTION; smelled ↑ LINKING)

If you can substitute a form of *be* for a verb, it is a linking verb.

Auxiliary Verbs and Verb Phrases

Auxiliary verbs, also called helping verbs, are combined with other verbs to form **verb phrases.** A verb phrase may be used to express a particular tense of a verb (that is, the time being referred to) or to indicate that an action is directed at the subject.

Small scraps of birch bark are crackling in the fire.
(are ↑ AUXILIARY; crackling ↑ MAIN)

Our muscles will be sore from chopping wood.
(will ↑ AUXILIARY; be ↑ MAIN)

At last all the wood has been chopped.
(has ↑ AUXILIARY; chopped ↑ MAIN)

Auxiliary Verbs

be		have	do	can	should
am	were	has	does	could	may
is	being	had	did	will	might
are	been			would	must
was				shall	

Some of these verbs can also function as main verbs. For example, notice how *had* stands alone in the first sentence below and is a helping verb in the second sentence.

At the end of the evening, we had no more energy. (MAIN)

We had exhausted ourselves. (AUXILIARY)

2 Why It Matters in Writing

Action verbs can be used to create strong images and metaphors. Notice how verbs in the following passage convey a picture of rain soaking into dry earth.

LITERARY MODEL

The rain **began** with gusty showers. . . . And at first the dry earth **sucked** the moisture down and **blackened.** For two days the earth **drank** the rain, until the earth was full. Then puddles **formed** . . . .

—John Steinbeck, "The Flood" from *The Grapes of Wrath*

3 Practice and Apply

CHAPTER 1

CONCEPT CHECK: Verbs

Write each verb or verb phrase and identify it as linking or action. Circle the auxiliary verbs.

Disabled Overcome Obstacles to Travel

1. Like everyone else, travelers with disabilities want fun vacations.
2. With a wide range of accessibility features available, travel seems easy.
3. Wheelchair travelers can choose rental cars with hand controls or transport in accessible taxis or vans.
4. Accessible tours are available for vacationers worldwide.
5. Cities such as Rome, with its hills and narrow cobblestone streets, appear manageable these days.
6. A tour to Nepal has featured a ride on an elephant's back through Royal Chitwan National Park.
7. Alaskan cruises expose people with mobility challenges to views of marine wildlife and scenic glaciers.
8. Various tour services provide communicators for deaf travelers and companions for the blind.
9. Skiers with disabilities can use special skis in a wide array of designs.
10. With careful arrangements, a traveler with special needs can experience adventure.

→ **For a SELF-CHECK and more practice, see the EXERCISE BANK, p. 307.**

LESSON 5

Adjectives

1 Here's the Idea

An adjective limits the meaning of a noun or pronoun. Words, like adjectives, that describe or give more specific information about the meanings of other words are said to **modify** those words.

We watched a terrific game on the outdoor field.

(MODIFIES; ADJECTIVE — terrific; MODIFIES; ADJECTIVE — outdoor)

An adjective answers the question *what kind, which one, how many,* or *how much.*

Adjectives

What Kind	Which One	How Many	How Much
fast ponies **green** field **steamy** afternoon	**this** seat **that** goal **these** friends	**four** players **most** fans **both** teams	**no** time **more** noise **enough** speed

PARTS OF SPEECH

Articles

The most common adjectives are the articles *a, an,* and *the.* *A* and *an* are **indefinite articles**. They are used to refer to unspecified members of groups of people, places, things, or ideas. Use *a* before words beginning with consonant sounds and *an* before words beginning with vowel sounds.

A fan yelled as we looked for an exit.

The is the **definite article,** used to refer to a specific person, place, thing, or idea.

The coach yelled as we left through the exit.

Proper Adjectives

Proper adjectives are formed from proper nouns. They are capitalized and often end in *n, an, ian, ese,* or *ish.*

Persian players originated the sport of polo.

British players popularized the game in India.

Proper Nouns	Shakespeare, Jamaica, Taiwan
Proper Adjectives	Shakespearean, Jamaican, Taiwanese

2 Why It Matters in Writing

Writers use adjectives to express feelings and to add important descriptive details.

LITERARY MODEL

Have you ever seen
anything
in your life
more **wonderful**

than the way the sun,
every evening,
relaxed and **easy**,
floats toward the horizon . . . ?

—Mary Oliver, "The Sun"

CHAPTER 1

3 Practice and Apply

A. CONCEPT CHECK: Adjectives

Write each adjective in these sentences, along with the word it modifies.

Riding Swimming Horses

1. An enjoyable way to travel in a new country is on a horse.
2. We had a unique horseback ride in Jamaica.
3. In Jamaica, formerly a British colony, polo is popular among English immigrants.
4. To exercise polo ponies in the hot country, trainers let them swim in deep water.
5. In swimsuits, we rode polo ponies bareback in ocean waters.
6. My very competitive pony swam up between two other ponies.
7. I gripped only a green strap and held on for dear life.
8. The two adjacent horses smashed against my bare legs.
9. Unlike its reluctant rider, my pony wanted to win this water race.
10. The experience was both frightening and exhilarating.

→ **For a SELF-CHECK and more practice, see the EXERCISE BANK, p. 308.**

B. REVISING: Adding Adjectives

Rewrite the following paragraph, adding adjectives and combining sentences to make it more interesting.

STUDENT MODEL

The Rough Sport of Polo

Today, polo is mostly played in England and the countries that were once British colonies. It is a sport for the rich. Only they can afford to maintain strings of ponies. At the same time, the sport is not for the faint-hearted. A match requires courage and daring. Ponies and players crash into each other. Players fall off their horses. That's why they wear helmets. Sometimes they accidentally hit each other with their mallets.

C. WRITING: Using Strong Adjectives

Choose one of the following postcard scenes and describe it fully, using sentences with strong adjectives. Try to be as exact as possible.

LESSON 6 Adverbs

1 Here's the Idea

▶ **An adverb modifies a verb, an adjective, or another adverb.**

Mike scrambled quickly from the icy pond.
MODIFIES — VERB

He was extremely cold.
MODIFIES — ADJECTIVE

He had fallen into the pond quite accidentally.
MODIFIES — ADVERB

An adverb answers the question *where, when, how,* or *to what extent.*

Adverbs	
Where	there, here, downstairs, northward
When	yesterday, soon, daily, never, again
How	slowly, happily, well, brightly
To what extent	almost, nearly, completely, somewhat

Many adverbs are formed by adding *-ly* to adjectives. Sometimes a slight change in spelling is necessary.

strong + *-ly* = **strongly** honest + *-ly* = **honestly**

true + *-ly* = **truly** happy + *-ly* = **happily**

Other Commonly Used Adverbs

afterward	forth	near	still
already	hard	next	straight
also	instead	not	then
back	late	now	today
even	long	often	tomorrow
far	low	slow	too
fast	more	sometimes	yet

CHAPTER 1

An **intensifier** is an adverb that defines the degree of an adjective or another adverb. Intensifiers always precede the adjectives or adverbs they modify.

Fortunately, Mike was an extremely fast thinker.

EMPHASIZES

INTENSIFIER

Intensifiers

almost	more	only	really	too
extremely	most	quite	so	truly
just	nearly	rather	somewhat	very

2 Why It Matters in Writing

PARTS OF SPEECH

Writers typically use adverbs to describe the ways things happen—slowly, for instance, or gradually or suddenly. Notice how the adverbs in the following passage not only describe the actions but convey information about the characters as well.

LITERARY MODEL

Gussie, in particular, fascinated me. He was spoiled, clever, casual; good-looking, with his mother's small clean features; gay and calculating. I saw that when I left and his mother gave me a sixpence. **Naturally** I refused it **politely**, but she thrust it into my trousers pocket, and Gussie dragged at her skirt, **noisily** demanding something for himself.

"If you give him a tanner, you ought to give me a tanner," he yelled.

"I'll tan you," she said **laughingly**.

—Frank O'Connor, "The Study of History"

❸ Practice and Apply

A. CONCEPT CHECK: Adverbs

Write each adverb in these sentences.

Fast, Fun, and Wet!

1. Quite often, when we travel anywhere, we go to water parks.
2. We have slid crazily down water slides at the Wisconsin Dells.
3. At the top of a slide, you sit carefully on a mat and nervously grip its edges.
4. Immediately, you start whizzing down, careening nearly uncontrollably from side to side.
5. When you finally reach the bottom, screaming happily, you splash suddenly into a pool of water.
6. You stand and want to repeat your ride again and again.
7. On top of a very tall water slide in Cincinnati, we waited anxiously while lightning crackled dangerously in the distance.
8. Luckily, we finally took our turn before the storm hit.
9. Once we even enjoyed an incredibly huge water park in Toronto, Canada.
10. Almost every big city has water parks, which are never empty during the summer.

➜ **For a SELF-CHECK and more practice, see the EXERCISE BANK, p. 308.**

For each adverb in sentences 1–5, identify the verb, verb phrase, adjective, or adverb it modifies.

B. WRITING: Using Adverbs to Describe Action

Write five sentences that describe the car race shown below, from the viewpoint of a driver. Use at least one adverb in each.

CHAPTER 1

Lesson 7 Prepositions

1 Here's the Idea

A preposition shows the relationship between a noun or pronoun and another word in a sentence.

Luis traveled to Guatemala with other teenagers.

Commonly Used Prepositions

about	before	down	of	throughout
above	behind	during	off	to
across	below	except	on	toward
after	beneath	for	onto	under
against	beside	from	out	underneath
along	between	in	outside	until
among	beyond	inside	over	up
around	but	into	past	upon
as	by	like	since	with
at	despite	near	through	within

Prepositions that consist of more than one word are called **compound prepositions.**

Because of his heavy pack, Luis had trouble hiking.

Commonly Used Compound Prepositions

according to	by means of	in place of	on account of
aside from	in addition to	in spite of	out of
because of	in front of	instead of	prior to

PARTS OF SPEECH

Prepositional Phrases

A **prepositional phrase** consists of a preposition, its object, and any modifiers of the object. The **object of a preposition** is the noun or pronoun that follows the preposition. Prepositional phrases are used as modifiers to express such characteristics as location, direction, duration, and time.

Beside a roaring river, Luis tripped and fell.
PREPOSITION OBJECT

His ankle started to swell during the afternoon.

The shoe on his left foot no longer fit.

A sentence may contain more than one prepositional phrase. Each preposition has its own object.

The group traveled by boat to a health clinic.

A nurse at the clinic put a bandage around Luis's ankle.

Use a comma to set off a series of prepositional phrases that comes at the beginning of a sentence.

From time to time during the day, Luis complained.

When a word that is commonly classified as a preposition is used without an object, it functions as an adverb. *Down* is used as an adverb in the first sentence below and as a preposition in the second.

Luis had trouble with his ankle after he fell down.

Luckily, no one else fell down the riverbank.

CHAPTER 1

2 Why It Matters in Writing

Because they help locate things in time and space, prepositional phrases are useful for describing a scene or giving precise directions. Notice how prepositional phrases help to make clear what is happening in the following passage.

LITERARY MODEL

We watched **on our screens** the footage captured **by his assistant's camera**, **in which** he was **up to his knees in muck**, a microphone **in his hand**, **in the midst of a bedlam of lost children, wounded survivors, corpses, and devastation**. The story came **to us in his calm voice**.

—Isabel Allende, "And of Clay Are We Created"

3 Practice and Apply

A. CONCEPT CHECK: Prepositions

Write the prepositional phrases in these sentences. Circle the prepositions.

Teens Making a Difference

1. Some organizations plan trips for students, combining education, service, and adventure.
2. These trips offer young people special opportunities in other countries.
3. These teens visit small villages instead of tourist attractions.
4. They get to know the people in addition to the countryside.
5. Sometimes they work with local teenagers on projects.
6. One group built a campground in the wilderness.
7. In another location young people painted a school.
8. Before the trip, teens receive training and raise funds.
9. You can find information about educational and service-based travel on the Internet.
10. Search under the keywords *travel, educational,* and *youth.*

➜ **For a SELF-CHECK and more practice, see the EXERCISE BANK, p. 308.**

B. WRITING: Using Prepositions in Directions

Imagine that you and a friend are going to an informational meeting about educational and service trips for teens. You will meet at your family's apartment. Use the map below to prepare written directions for your friend to use in getting from school to your home. Underline the prepositions you use.

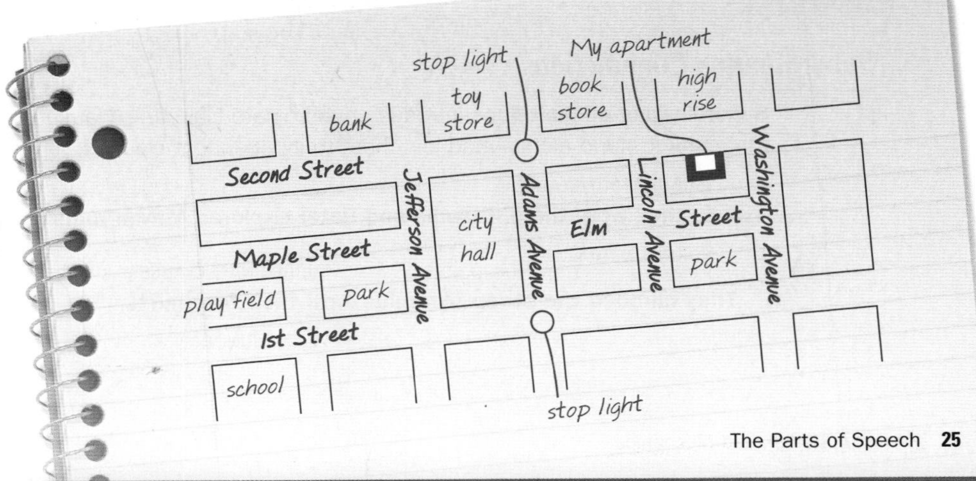

Conjunctions

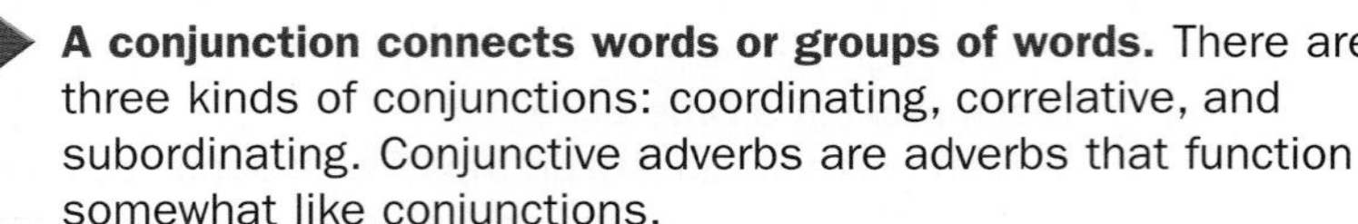

1 Here's the Idea

A conjunction connects words or groups of words. There are three kinds of conjunctions: coordinating, correlative, and subordinating. Conjunctive adverbs are adverbs that function somewhat like conjunctions.

Coordinating Conjunctions

Coordinating conjunctions connect words or groups of words of equal importance in a sentence.

Claudia and Peter visited the Yucatán Peninsula, but they stayed only a few days.

Coordinating Conjunctions						
and	but	for	nor	or	so	yet

Correlative Conjunctions

Correlative conjunctions are word pairs that serve to join words or groups of words.

Neither Claudia nor Peter had been to Mexico before.

They found it not only beautiful but also rich in history.

Correlative Conjunctions		
both . . . and neither . . . nor	whether . . . or either . . . or	not only . . . but also

Subordinating Conjunctions

Subordinating conjunctions introduce subordinate clauses—clauses that cannot stand alone—and join them to independent clauses.

SUBORDINATE CLAUSE

While they were there, Claudia and Peter explored Mayan ruins.

CONJUNCTION

SUBORDINATE CLAUSE

They climbed the steep pyramids until their feet hurt.

CONJUNCTION

CHAPTER 1

Subordinating Conjunctions				
after	as though	if	so that	when
although	because	in order that	than	where
as	before	provided	unless	whereas
as if	even though	since	until	while

Conjunctive Adverbs

Conjunctive adverbs are used to express relationships between independent clauses.

CONJUNCTIVE ADVERB

The Mayans did not have telescopes; however, they built and used astronomical observatories.

Conjunctive Adverbs		
accordingly	furthermore	otherwise
also	hence	similarly
besides	however	still
consequently	instead	therefore
finally	nevertheless	thus

PARTS OF SPEECH

2 Why It Matters in Writing

Writers use conjunctions to combine sentences in first drafts into smooth, more interesting sentences in later drafts. Notice how the second sentence below contains information that could have come from several sentences in an earlier draft.

LITERARY MODEL

On my first return visit to Texas, I stopped to hear a group of *mariachis* playing their instruments with proud gusto. I was surprised **and** probably embarrassed **when** my eyes filled with tears **not only** at the music, **but** at the sight of wonderful Mexican faces.

—Pat Mora, "The Border: A Glare of Truth"

❸ Practice and Apply

A. CONCEPT CHECK: Conjunctions

Write the conjunctions and conjunctive adverbs in the following sentences.

Opening a Mayan Pyramid

1. Many people visit Mexico or Central America to see the remains of the Mayan civilization.
2. The Mayan culture fascinates visitors because the Mayans achieved so much.
3. Mayans not only created a written language but also built many large pyramids.
4. In 1952, Mexican archaeologist Alberto Ruz climbed a 65-foot pyramid and made an important discovery.
5. While he was examining the inscriptions on top of the pyramid, he noticed a removable stone slab.
6. Beneath the slab, Ruz and his helpers found a stairway leading into the pyramid; however, it was filled with rubble.
7. They started to clear the stairway; still, it took them four field sessions to reach the bottom.
8. Not only did they find a chamber that contained human skeletons, but they also discovered another room.
9. When they entered that room, they found many objects made of jade.
10. Both the jade objects and the written inscriptions identified the chamber as the tomb of an important ruler.

➔ **For a SELF-CHECK and more practice, see the EXERCISE BANK, p. 309.**

Identify each of the words you listed as a coordinating conjunction, a correlative conjunction, a subordinating conjunction, or a conjunctive adverb.

B. WRITING: Using Conjunctions

Write conjunctions that can complete this passage.

Baja California

The Mexican peninsula called Baja California offers many kinds of recreation, including scuba diving ___(1)___ whale watching. In the Sea of Cortés, you might be lucky enough to see ___(2)___ blue whales ___(3)___ gray whales and sperm whales. Whale watchers also visit islands ___(4)___ they can observe many species of birds and land animals. They have their choice of going in motorboats ___(5)___ paddling in sea kayaks.

LESSON 9

Interjections

1 Here's the Idea

An interjection is a word or phrase that expresses a feeling. A strong interjection is followed by an exclamation point. A mild interjection is set off with commas.

> **Yikes! Have you ever seen such a tall building?**
>
> **Well, no, I guess I haven't.**

2 Why It Matters in Writing

Interjections can add realism to your writing, particularly to dialogue.

PARTS OF SPEECH

STUDENT MODEL

The sleepy group got off the bus after riding all night. Dragging their suitcases, they rounded the corner into the sunlight.

"**Wow!**" cried Rani, staring up at the skyscrapers.

"**Whew!**" sighed Holly, sitting down on her suitcase. "This bag is too heavy."

"**Uh-oh,** don't look now, but we have another block to go."

3 Practice and Apply

CONCEPT CHECK: Interjections

Write the interjections in these sentences.

Chicago Snapshots

1. Here we are in Chicago, and wow, is it cold!
2. Hey, is it always this cold here in the winter?
3. Oh, no! You left your gloves in the hotel room?
4. Well, we can always get you another pair.
5. Brrr! Better hurry; it's about to snow.

Real World Grammar

Lab Report

Using precise language is especially important when you are writing about science, because others may need to duplicate your experiments in order to verify your results.

In the report below, one student, Eric, described an experiment he conducted. His lab partner, Courtney, wrote the questions after she tried to follow the notes the next day. Because Eric didn't describe his work precisely, Courtney had trouble repeating the experiment.

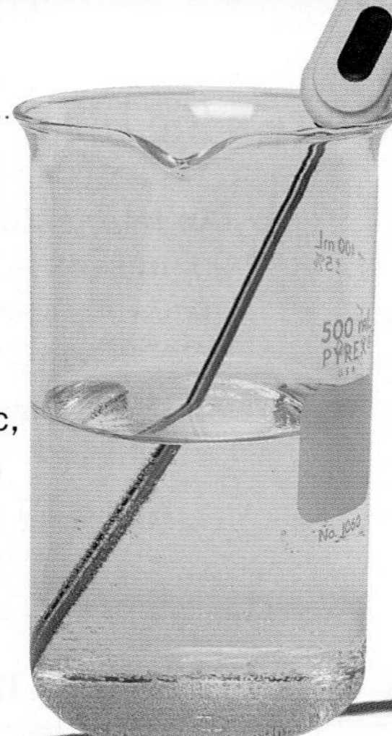

CHAPTER 1

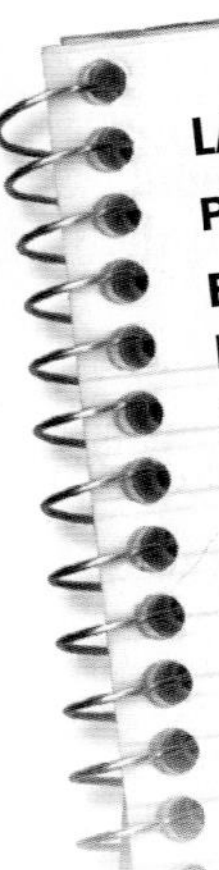

LAB REPORT

Purpose: To find the boiling point of a mixture of salt and water

Equipment:
lab stand with clamps
burner
one 1-liter container
one 500-milliliter container
thermometer that measures 0° to 200° Celsius
stopper
glass tube with a sharp bend

What kinds of containers?

This should be a 2-hole stopper, right?

Materials:
5 grams salt
200 milliliters water

Is tap water OK, or should I use distilled water?

Procedure:
Combine the salt and water in the large container. Stir the mixture with a glass rod until the salt dissolves. Put the container on the stand, with its base about 5 centimeters above the burner. Insert the thermometer and the glass tube. Insert the stopper assembly. Heat the solution. Record the time and temperature every two minutes, as well as when the solution just begins to boil and when it begins to boil rapidly.

How should I attach the container?

Where does the thermometer go? Where is the stopper inserted?

Should I heat the solution slowly or quickly?

Using Grammar in Writing	
Use specific nouns and verbs	Use specific words to make your meaning clear. Instead of the general word *container,* use the name of the kind of container, such as *flask* or *beaker.*
Include necessary modifiers	Use modifiers to make the meanings of other words more specific. Instead of simply writing *water,* tell what kind of water by using a modifier such as *distilled* or *tap.*
Use prepositions for clarity	Choose prepositions, such as *into* and *through,* that tell precisely how the pieces are to be connected.

REVISED LAB REPORT

Purpose: To find the boiling point of a mixture of salt and water

Equipment:

lab stand with clamps
burner
one 1-liter **flask**
one 500-milliliter **beaker**
thermometer that measures 0° to 200° Celsius
two-hole stopper
glass tube with a sharp bend

Materials:

5 grams salt
200 milliliters **distilled** water

Procedure: Combine the salt and water in the flask. Stir the mixture with a glass rod until the salt dissolves completely. **Clamp** the flask onto the stand, with its base about 5 centimeters above the burner. Insert the thermometer and the glass tube **through the holes in the stopper.** Insert the stopper assembly **into the neck of the flask.** Heat the solution **quickly.** Record the time and temperature every two minutes, as well as when the solution just begins to boil and when it begins to boil rapidly.

PARTS OF SPEECH

PRACTICE AND APPLY: Proofreading

Read the incomplete directions below. What else would you need to know before you could make biscuits? List your questions.

Ingredients:
1¼ cup sifted flour
½ salt
powder
4–6 chilled butter
¾ milk

Directions: Sift together flour, salt, and powder. Add chunks of chilled butter. Once the butter is combined well, stir in the milk. Cut with a cutter dipped in flour. Place on an ungreased baking sheet. Bake 12 to 15 minutes.

Mixed Review

A. Nouns, Pronouns, Adjectives, Adverbs Read this passage from *The Great Railway Bazaar* by Paul Theroux. Then answer the questions below it.

(1) The hooting of the train woke me early the next morning for the sight of camels grazing among brown bushes and great herds of sheep bunched together on sandy hillsides. **(2)** The villages were few, but their design was extraordinary; they were walled and low and resembled the kind of sand castles you see parents making for their children at the seashore, with a bucket and spade. **(3)** They had tiny windows, crumbling ramparts, and inexact crenellations; impressive at a distance, up close they were visibly coming apart, the fortifications merely a feeble challenge to intruders.

1. What part of speech is *train* in sentence 1?
2. What part of speech is *me* in sentence 1?
3. What type of noun is *herds* in sentence 1?
4. What part of speech is *sandy* in sentence 1?
5. What type of pronoun is *their* in sentence 2?
6. What part of speech is *extraordinary* in sentence 2?
7. What type of noun is *children* in sentence 2?
8. What type of pronoun is *They* is sentence 3?
9. What part of speech is *visibly* in sentence 3?
10. What part of speech is *feeble* in sentence 3?

B. Verbs, Prepositions, Conjunctions, Interjections Read the following passage. Then identify each underlined word as an action verb, a linking verb, a preposition, a conjunction, or an interjection.

PROFESSIONAL MODEL

Under (1) the lee of Child's Island they stopped (2) at a sheltered beach, since (3) Charley had promised the ladies a cup of tea at the first convenient spot. But when the men went (4) ashore for firewood, the wind veered (5) and breakers began rolling into (6) the bay. Captain and (7) crew had to strip and shove the boat out to (8) sea: "Oh! (9) It was cold. And the sight of all hands naked was (10) enough to make a cat laugh. We were red as lobsters and our teeth chattering."

—Bruce Chatwin, *In Patagonia*

CHAPTER 1

Mastery Test: What Did You Learn?

Write the letter of the term that correctly identifies each underlined word.

During the 1200s, Marco Polo, an Italian (1) traveler and trader, brought Westerners some of their (2) first substantial information about Chinese life and customs. Marco and his father, Niccolò Polo, spent several (3) years in the court of the Chinese Mongol ruler Kublai Khan, returning to Venice in 1295. Among (4) the Chinese customs (5) described by Polo were (6) the use of coal as fuel, the use of paper money, and Kublai Khan's extensive postal system. Polo dictated a (7) book, *Description of the World*. Because (8) printing had not been invented in Europe (a form of printing was already (9) in use in China), the book was available only in handwritten copies. The book had a widespread effect (10) in Europe and helped to introduce a number of Chinese innovations to the West.

1. A. proper adjective
   B. action verb
   C. proper noun
   D. common noun
2. A. demonstrative pronoun
   B. possessive pronoun
   C. proper noun
   D. common noun
3. A. adverb
   B. adjective
   C. preposition
   D. conjunction
4. A. conjunction
   B. interjection
   C. adverb
   D. preposition
5. A. verb
   B. adjective
   C. adverb
   D. noun
6. A. action verb
   B. conjunction
   C. linking verb
   D. preposition
7. A. adverb
   B. article
   C. preposition
   D. pronoun
8. A. subordinating conjunction
   B. correlative conjunction
   C. adjective
   D. preposition
9. A. preposition
   B. adverb
   C. adjective
   D. conjunction
10. A. conjunctive adverb
    B. preposition
    C. common noun
    D. adjective

Student Help Desk

Parts of Speech at a Glance

Oops! You carelessly left your old but useful hat in the rain.

Oops!	interjection
You	pronoun
carelessly	adverb
left	verb
your	pronoun
old	adjective
but	conjunction
useful	adjective
hat	noun
in	preposition
the	article
rain	noun

Kinds of Nouns — Nouns to Remember

Every noun is either
- common or proper
- concrete or abstract
- singular or plural

Some nouns are
- collective
- compound

Joni and her **family** kept their **memories** in **diaries** and **scrapbooks.**

Joni	family	memories	diaries	scrapbooks
proper	common	common	common	common
concrete	concrete	abstract	concrete	concrete
singular	singular	plural	plural	plural
	collective			compound

Types of Verbs — Verbs to Revisit

Every verb is either a linking verb or an action verb.

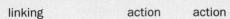

Malik looks thoughtful and sighs as he opens the box of photographs.

looks	sighs	opens
linking	action	action
	intransitive	transitive

Every action verb is either transitive or intransitive.

Adverbs

STORY TEMPLATE
Once upon a time.

Suddenly.

Luckily.
ACME

Happily ever after.
R. Chast

Types of Pronouns

Pronouns to Replay

You (personal) **have your** (personal (possessive)) **own favorite memories.**

What (interrogative) **are they** (personal)**?**

Those (demonstrative) **are the ones** (indefinite) **that** (relative) **you** (personal) **should give yourself** (reflexive) **time to ponder.**

PARTS OF SPEECH

The Bottom Line

Checklist for Parts of Speech

Have I . . .

____ chosen precise nouns?
____ used pronouns to avoid repeating nouns?
____ selected specific verbs?
____ added adjectives to identify nouns?
____ used adverbs to describe actions?
____ made good use of conjunctions to link ideas?
____ used prepositions to clarify relationships?
____ used interjections to show character in dialogue?

Chapter 2

The Sentence and Its Parts

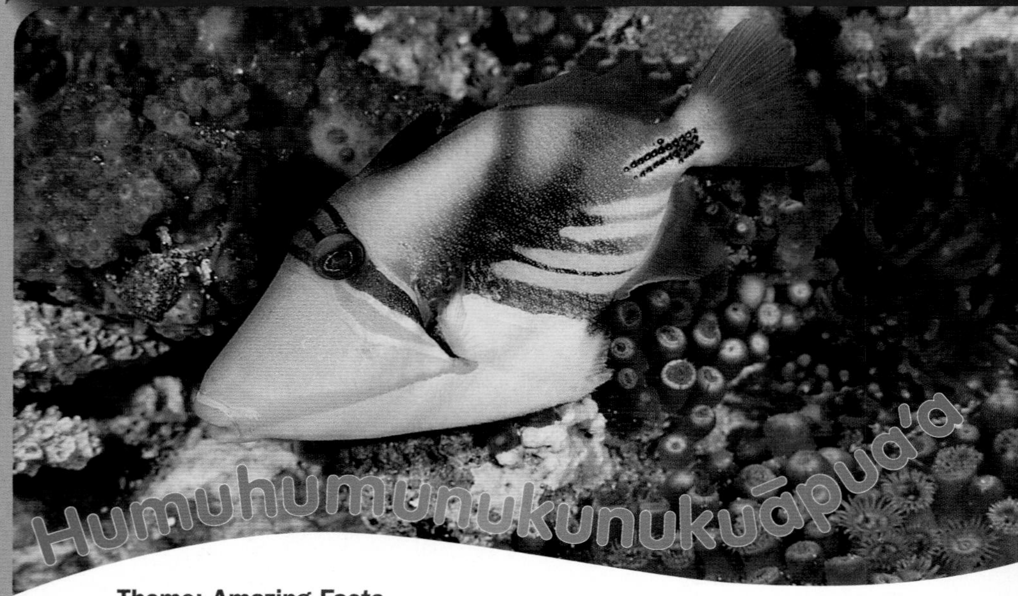

Theme: Amazing Facts

Amazing but True

The Hawaiian triggerfish is called *humuhumunukunukuāpua'a* in the Hawaiian language. Though the name seems long, it is actually very concise. *Humuhumu* means "to fit pieces together," and *nukunukuāpua'a* means "nose like a pig." Thus, one word takes the place of eight English words.

The English language has the largest vocabulary of any language, with 616,500 words and 400,000 technical terms. Amazingly, though, all of the possible sentences you can make with these words have only two basic parts: subjects and predicates. In fact, every day, as you think, talk, and write, you are forming hundreds of sentences with just these two components.

Write Away: Personal Best

In ten sentences, write ten amazing facts about your own life. Save the sentences in your **Working Portfolio.**

Diagnostic Test: What Do You Know?

Choose the letter of the term that correctly identifies each numbered part of this passage.

> In 1962, a brand-new baseball team (1) made sports history. The New York Mets earned baseball's worst win-loss record (2). Crusty manager Casey Stengel ranted and raved (3) at the young team. During one particularly bad game, he asked his players a rather sarcastic question. (4) "Can't anybody here play this game?" (5) There was only one thing (6) worse than a Mets game, according to Stengel. That was a Mets double-header (7). But Stengel did feel good (8) about the team's very first game. The officials canceled it (9) because of rain. Stengel's jokes won the hapless team (10) many loyal fans.

1. A. simple subject
   B. complete subject
   C. simple predicate
   D. complete predicate

2. A. simple subject
   B. complete subject
   C. simple predicate
   D. complete predicate

3. A. compound subject
   B. compound verb
   C. complete subject
   D. complete predicate

4. A. declarative sentence
   B. imperative sentence
   C. interrogative sentence
   D. exclamatory sentence

5. A. declarative sentence
   B. imperative sentence
   C. interrogative sentence
   D. exclamatory sentence

6. A. compound subject
   B. compound verb
   C. simple subject
   D. predicate nominative

7. A. direct object
   B. indirect object
   C. predicate adjective
   D. predicate nominative

8. A. direct object
   B. indirect object
   C. predicate adjective
   D. predicate nominative

9. A. direct object
   B. indirect object
   C. predicate adjective
   D. predicate nominative

10. A. direct object
    B. indirect object
    C. predicate adjective
    D. predicate nominative

Simple Subjects and Predicates

❶ Here's the Idea

Every sentence has two basic parts: the subject and the predicate.

The **subject** tells whom or what the sentence is about. The **predicate** tells what the subject is or does or what happens to the subject.

The world's tallest woman	stands almost eight feet tall!
SUBJECT	PREDICATE

The **simple subject** is the key word or words in the subject. The simple subject does not include modifiers, such as *The world's tallest* in the example above. To find the simple subject, ask who or what performs the action of the verb.

Sandy Allen wears size 22 sneakers.
Who wears size 22 sneakers? **Sandy Allen**

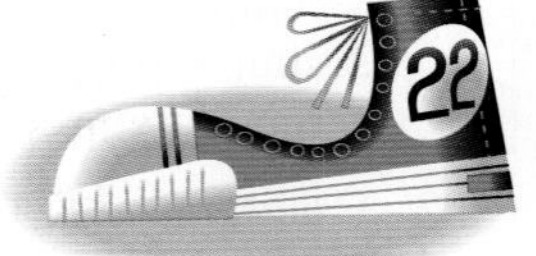

Stores do not carry her shoe size.
What do not carry her shoe size? **Stores**

The **simple predicate** is the verb or verb phrase that tells something about the subject. Modifiers are not part of the verb phrase, even if they interrupt the verb phrase.

People ask Allen about her height.
What do people do? **ask**

She does not mind their questions.
(Notice that the modifier *not* is excluded from the simple predicate.)

❷ Why It Matters in Writing

Both the subject and predicate are necessary for the meaning of the sentence to be clear. If the subject or predicate of a sentence is missing, the group of words is a **sentence fragment**. Sentence fragments do not express complete thoughts.

Allen gets her shoes from the National Basketball Association.

Without the subject, *Allen,* you wouldn't know whom the predicate refers to. Without the predicate, the only word left is *Allen*.

CHAPTER 2

3 Practice and Apply

A. CONCEPT CHECK: Simple Subjects and Predicates

Write the simple subject and simple predicate of each sentence.

Example: People have always enjoyed novelty acts.
Answer: People, have enjoyed

The Daring Young Flea on the Flying Trapeze

1. Maria Fernanda Cordoso runs an unusual small business.
2. She owns the Cordoso Flea Circus.
3. All the circus performers are fleas.
4. Samson lifts cotton-ball barbells high above his head.
5. Pierre crosses tinfoil swords with Pedro in a fierce duel.
6. Teeny floats through the air on a tiny trapeze.
7. Flamboyant fleas in colorful costumes dance to a Latin beat.
8. Harry Fleadini simply disappears.
9. The circus has been traveling all over the world.
10. People can hardly wait for the smallest show on earth.

➜ **For a SELF-CHECK and more practice, see the EXERCISE BANK, p. 310**

SENTENCE PARTS

B. EDITING: Complete Sentences

Write *S* if a group of words is a complete sentence or *F* if it is a sentence fragment. For each fragment, tell whether the simple subject or simple predicate is missing.

Example: Animal behavior unpredictable.
Answer: F, missing simple predicate

The Curious Case of the Parental Parrot

1. A story about a peculiar pet was reported in England long ago.
2. At night, a pet parrot slept in a large outdoor birdhouse.
3. During the day, the bird in the woods.
4. One day, a pregnant cat climbed into the birdhouse.
5. Had a litter of kittens in the parrot's nest.
6. Then the new mother in the woods for food.
7. The parrot home early that day.
8. Must have been surprised by the uninvited kittens.
9. Was not at all frightened, however.
10. The motherly parrot adopted the kittens for her own.

Complete Subjects and Predicates

1 Here's the Idea

The complete subject includes the simple subject and all the words that modify it. The complete predicate includes the verb and all the words that modify it.

Every generation **develops its own foolish fads.**

COMPLETE SUBJECT — COMPLETE PREDICATE

Here's How Finding Complete Subjects and Predicates

Teens of the 1950s crammed into phone booths.

Complete subject Ask who or what is or does something.

Who crammed into phone booths? **Teens of the 1950s**

Complete predicate Ask what the subject is or does or what happens to the subject.

What did teens of the 1950s do? **crammed into phone booths**

Teens of the 1950s **crammed into phone booths.**

COMPLETE SUBJECT — COMPLETE PREDICATE

Every word in a sentence is part of a complete subject or complete predicate.

2 Why It Matters in Writing

When you add details to simple subjects and predicates, you help your readers more clearly picture what you mean.

STUDENT MODEL

DRAFT	***REVISION***
The couple won.	The weary young couple in the red outfits won a three-day dance marathon.

❸ Practice and Apply

A. CONCEPT CHECK: Complete Subjects and Predicates

Write each sentence and draw a line between the complete subject and complete predicate.

Example: Unusual contests / have drawn many participants over the years.

Rock Till You Drop?

1. Crazy tests of endurance swept the nation during the 1920s.
2. "Shipwreck" Kelly sat atop an Atlantic City flagpole for 49 days.
3. The stunt earned him the title "King of the Pole."
4. The Rocking Chair Derby was a more down-to-earth contest.
5. Contestants rocked back and forth for days.
6. Losers literally went off their rockers.
7. New York City's Noun and Verb Rodeo appealed to nonstop talkers.
8. Contestants breathlessly babbled for hours on end.
9. The toughest test of endurance was the Bunion Derby.
10. Andy Payne won the transcontinental footrace in a record 573 hours.

➜ **For a SELF-CHECK and more practice, see the EXERCISE BANK, p. 310.**

B. REVISING: Adding Details

On a separate sheet of paper, create complete subjects and predicates by adding details to the simple subjects and predicates below. Describe what's popular and newsworthy today.

Example: Teenagers are buying.
Answer: Today's teenagers are buying CD's and bell-bottom pants.

Newspapers	are reporting.
Television	is broadcasting.
Americans	are talking.
Radios	are playing.
People	are buying.

Compound Sentence Parts

1 Here's the Idea

▶ **A sentence can have more than one subject and verb.** A sentence part containing more than one of these elements is called a compound part.

A **compound subject** is made up of two or more simple subjects that share a verb. The subjects are joined by a conjunction, or connecting word, such as *and, or*, or *but*.

Alice and Leon enjoy a good adventure story.
Daring feats and thrilling chases are exciting.

A **compound verb** is made up of two or more verbs or verb phrases that are joined by a conjunction and have the same subject.

The adventure hero endures and conquers.
The hero conquers and captures the villain.

A **compound predicate** is made up of a compound verb and all the words that go with each verb.

Such stories engage the audience and fire the imagination.

CHAPTER 2

2 Why It Matters in Writing

Correctly using compound subjects and predicates can help you avoid repetition and write more concisely.

STUDENT MODEL

DRAFT

Charles Lindbergh was a real-life adventure hero. So was Amelia Earhart. Both pilots beat the odds. Both pilots successfully completed solo flights across the Atlantic Ocean.

REVISION

Charles Lindbergh and Amelia Earhart were real-life adventure heroes. Both pilots beat the odds and successfully completed solo flights across the Atlantic Ocean.

3 Practice and Apply

A. CONCEPT CHECK: Compound Sentence Parts

Write each sentence below and underline the simple subject(s) once and the verb(s) twice.

Four Continents on Foot

1. Many people walk or jog around their neighborhoods.
2. Dave Kunst took this idea and ran with it about 20 million steps farther.
3. Kunst walked 14,450 miles around the earth and set a world record.
4. Kunst and his brother began their journey on June 20, 1970.
5. A mule hauled supplies and kept them company.
6. Comedy and tragedy struck along the way.
7. In Italy, a restaurant owner greeted the brothers and escorted the mule into his cafe for a free meal.
8. In Afghanistan, Kunst and his brother were shot by bandits.
9. Kunst's brother fought for his life but died.
10. Kunst recovered and completed his odyssey on October 5, 1974.

➔ **For a SELF-CHECK and more practice, see the EXERCISE BANK, p. 311.**

B. REVISING: Constructing Compounds

Combine each pair of sentences into a single sentence with a compound subject or predicate.

Example: My parents like Minnesota. I do too.
Answer: My parents and I like Minnesota.

Greetings from Minnesota!

1 Bemidji has great statues of Paul Bunyan and Babe the Blue Ox. Brainerd does too. **2** The Brainerd Paul Bunyan is 27 feet tall. It has hidden audio speakers. **3** It sits in an alcove. It "talks" to visitors. **4** The statue made me laugh. But it terrified my little brother.

Julie Sanford
123 West Fourth Street
Chicago, IL
60660

LESSON 4 Kinds of Sentences

1 Here's the Idea

▶ **A sentence can be used to make a statement, ask a question, give a command, or show feeling.**

Kinds of Sentences

Declarative **London is a wonderful city.**

This kind of sentence expresses a statement of fact, wish, intent, or feeling. It always ends with a period.

Interrogative **Which attraction is the most popular?**
This kind of sentence asks a question and ends with a question mark.

Imperative **See for yourself! Read the guidebook.**

This kind of sentence gives a command, request, or direction, and usually ends with a period. If the command or request is strong, it may end with an exclamation point.

Exclamatory **You've got to see Madame Tussaud's wax museum!**

This kind of sentence expresses strong feeling and always ends with an exclamation point.

When an exclamatory sentence is preceded by another exclamation, either a period or an exclamation mark can be used at the end of the second sentence. **Example:** Wow! The wax figures there seem so real.

2 Why It Matters in Writing

Using the four sentence types, you can vary the tone and mood of your writing. Read the four sentences below with expression. Notice how your tone of voice changes to convey the different meaning of each sentence.

You have never visited that museum.

You have never visited that museum?

Never visit that museum.

You would love that museum!

❸ Practice and Apply

A. CONCEPT CHECK: Kinds of Sentences

Identify the following sentences as declarative, imperative, interrogative, or exclamatory. Then rewrite sentences 6–10 according to the directions in parentheses.

Example: This exhibit gives me the creeps!
Answer: exclamatory

Waxing Poetic

1. What do the Dalai Lama, Billy Idol, John McEnroe, and Nelson Mandela have in common, in addition to their being famous?
2. All of them have doubles in Madame Tussaud's wax museum.
3. The wax models are very lifelike.
4. Take an imaginary stroll through the Chamber of Horrors.
5. Is that the notorious Jack the Ripper?
6. He looks alive! (Change into a question.)
7. Would you look over there? (Change into an imperative sentence.)
8. Is that Marie Antoinette? (Change into a declarative sentence.)
9. That guillotine looks very real! (Change into a declarative sentence.)
10. Madame Tussaud narrowly escaped the guillotine during the French Revolution. (Change into an exclamation.)

➜ **For a SELF-CHECK and more practice, see the EXERCISE BANK, p. 311.**

B. WRITING: Using Sentence Variety

Writers of advertisements often use all four kinds of sentences to make their ads expressive and persuasive. Take a tip from the professionals and use all four kinds of sentences to write a tourism ad aimed at persuading vacationers to visit your town. Your ad may be serious or humorous.

Working Portfolio Take out the sentences you wrote for the **Write Away** on page 36. Revise the sentences so that all four kinds of sentences are represented.

Subjects in Unusual Positions

1 Here's the Idea

In most sentences, the subject is placed before the verb. In some sentences, however, the subject appears after the verb, while in others it is not stated at all.

Inverted Sentences

In an inverted sentence, the subject appears after the verb or between the words that make up the verb phrase. An inverted sentence can be used for variety or emphasis. What effect does the inverted order have on the following sentences?

Usual Order: An 800-pound pumpkin grew in his garden.

Inverted: In his garden grew an 800-pound pumpkin.

Usual Order: The neighbors had never seen such a squash!

Inverted: Never had the neighbors seen such a squash!

CHAPTER 2

Sentences Beginning with *Here* or *There*

When a sentence begins with *here* or *there,* the subject usually follows the verb. *Here* and *there* are almost never the subject of a sentence.

The words *here* and *there* almost always function as adverbs of place or as expletives. **Adverbs of place** modify verbs by answering the question *where?* **Expletives** do not have meaning in and of themselves. These "subject delayers" introduce and draw attention to subjects.

Here is the World Pumpkin Confederation's official Web page.

Where is the Web page? The Web page is **here.**
Here is an adverb.

There are growers of giant vegetables all over the world.

There does not tell where. It is an expletive.

Questions

▶ **In most questions, the subject appears after the verb or between the words that make up the verb phrase.**

Subject After Verb:

Was the cabbage large?

Subject Inside Verb Phrase:

Did you see it?

In many questions that begin with *whom, what,* or *how many,* the subject falls between the parts of the verb.

How many pounds did the cabbage weigh?

In some questions, however, the interrogative pronoun functions as the subject and comes before the verb.

Who won the contest?

Imperative Sentences

▶ **The subject of an imperative sentence is always *you.*** Even when not directly stated, *you* is understood to be the subject.

Request: (You) **Please eat your vegetables.**
Command: (You) **Don't complain!**

2 Why It Matters in Writing

You can vary the tone and emphasis of your sentences with inverted sentences and commands. This is especially useful in creating realistic dialogue and dialects, as in the following example.

LITERARY MODEL

"Quit that," said the woman. "Can't you see you're raising ashes?"

"What harm is ashes?"

"I'll show you what harm," she said, taking down a plate of cabbage and potato from the shelf over the fire. "There's your dinner destroyed with them."

—Mary Lavin, "Brigid"

3 Practice and Apply

A. CONCEPT CHECK: Subjects in Unusual Positions

Write the simple subject and simple predicate of each sentence below. Be sure to include all verbs that appear in verb phrases.

Example: Have you ever had a garden?
Answer: you, have had

Kings of the Cabbage Patch

1. Where can you get a good cabbage these days?
2. Come to the annual cabbage competition in Palmer, Alaska.
3. There is hot competition for the $4,000 first prize.
4. Who grew the biggest cabbage?
5. To Lesley Dinkel goes the title.
6. Among his many triumphs was a 98-pound monster.
7. Do the winners have advice for the rest of us gardeners?
8. Here is their best advice.
9. Protect your cabbages from moose.
10. How can you argue with advice like that?

→ **For a SELF-CHECK and more practice, see the EXERCISE BANK, p. 311.**

CHAPTER 2

B. REVISING: Varying Sentence Structure

Change each sentence according to the directions in parentheses.

Example: Pumpkins are native to Central America. (Make into a question.)
Answer: Are pumpkins native to Central America?

Scary Spuds

1. You should read about the history of the jack-o'-lantern. (Change into an imperative sentence.)
2. The jack-o'-lantern didn't originate in the United States. (Change into a question.)
3. This Halloween tradition comes from Ireland. (Invert sentence order.)
4. Long ago no pumpkins were available in Ireland. (Begin the sentence with *there.*)
5. The first jack-o'-lanterns were made of potatoes and turnips! (Change into a question.)

Subject Complements

1 Here's the Idea

▶ **A complement is a word or a group of words that completes the meaning of a verb.** Complements include subject complements, direct objects, indirect objects, and objective complements.

A **subject complement** follows a linking verb and describes or renames the subject. There are two kinds of subject complements: predicate adjectives and predicate nominatives. Subject complements can also have their own modifiers, as in the second example below.

Predicate adjectives describe subjects by telling *which one, what kind, how much,* or *how many.*

During the 1930s, the jitterbug became popular.
(jitterbug: SUBJECT; became: LINKING VERB; popular: PREDICATE ADJECTIVE)

In comparison, today's dances seem very tame.
(very: MODIFIER; tame: PREDICATE ADJECTIVE)

Predicate nominatives are nouns and pronouns that rename, identify, or define subjects.

The jitterbug is a dance variation.
(jitterbug: SUBJECT; is: LINKING VERB; variation: PREDICATE NOMINATIVE)

Frank Manning was an inventive jitterbug dancer.
(dancer: PREDICATE NOMINATIVE)

SENTENCE PARTS

2 Why It Matters in Writing

Subject complements, like the simple noun *man* in the model below, can themselves be modified to create a full description.

LITERARY MODEL

"Verenka's father was a very handsome, imposing, and well-preserved old man."

—Leo Tolstoy, "After the Ball"

3 Practice and Apply

A. CONCEPT CHECK: Subject Complements

Write each subject complement and identify it as a predicate adjective or a predicate nominative.

Example: Swing is big-band jazz.
Answer: jazz, predicate nominative

Swing and Slang

1. Swing music has become fashionable again.
2. One birthplace of swing was Harlem.
3. A famous swing dancer was George “Shorty” Snowden.
4. The jitterbug looks very difficult.
5. The dancers seem extraordinarily athletic.
6. Are you an alligator?
7. Alligators are fans of swing.
8. Don’t be an ickie!
9. Ickies are hopelessly unhip.
10. They feel lost on the dance floor.

→ **For a SELF-CHECK and more practice, see the EXERCISE BANK, p. 312.**

B. REVISING: Improving Subject Complements

Rewrite each sentence, replacing the vague or weak subject complement with a more precise one.

Example: After several dips and twirls, she felt weird.
Answer: After several dips and twirls, she felt dizzy.

Dangerous Dances?

1. Some dances are bad.
2. The Charleston may seem OK.
3. Still, its many kicks and twirls can become problems on a dance floor.
4. A kick in the shin is awful!
5. Bruises don’t look nice.
6. The twist may be all right for strong, young dancers.
7. It is not a good thing for people with weak backs, however.
8. After a spin on the dance floor, their backs may feel lousy.
9. The jitterbug can also be bad.
10. Dancers must be physically well.

Objects of Verbs

1 Here's the Idea

Many action verbs require complements called direct objects and indirect objects to complete their meaning.

Direct and Indirect Objects

A **direct object** is a word or group of words that names the receiver of the action of an action verb. It answers the question *what* or *whom*. Consider the following sentence:

Many people save.

Notice that the sentence is missing information. You probably wonder what many people save.

Many people save string.
DIRECT OBJECT

Other people keep twist ties from plastic bags.
DIRECT OBJECT

An **indirect object** is a word or group of words that tells to what, to whom, or for whom an action is done. In a sentence containing both a direct and an indirect object, the indirect object almost always comes before the direct object. Verbs that often take indirect objects include *bring, give, hand, lend, make, offer, send, show, teach, tell,* and *write.*

Savers give friends collecting advice.
INDIRECT OBJECT DIRECT OBJECT

What do savers give? **advice** *Advice* is the direct object.

To whom do savers give advice? **friends** *Friends* is the indirect object.

Savers will proudly show anyone their giant jars of pennies.
INDIRECT OBJECT DIRECT OBJECT

For more about action verbs, see p. 14.

The words *to* and *for* never appear before the indirect object. *To* and *for* are prepositions when they are followed by a noun or pronoun. In such cases the noun or pronoun is an object of the preposition, not an object of the verb.

SENTENCE PARTS

Objective Complements

An **objective complement** is a word or group of words that follows a direct object and renames or describes that object. Objective complements follow certain verbs and their synonyms: *appoint, call, choose, consider, elect, find, keep, make, name, think.* An objective complement may be a noun or an adjective.

Some people consider themselves savers.

DIRECT OBJECT (themselves) — OBJECTIVE COMPLEMENT (savers)

What do some people consider themselves? **savers** *Savers* is a noun.

No one could ever call the hobby wasteful.

DIRECT OBJECT (hobby) — OBJECTIVE COMPLEMENT (wasteful)

What could no one call it? **wasteful** *Wasteful* is an adjective.

Savers find trash a treasure.
Savers make tidy people crazy.

CHAPTER 2

2 Why It Matters in Writing

Objective complements convey information and add important details. They are especially useful when one is writing dialogue.

My mother took one step into my messy bedroom and joked, "I hereby rename you Pigpen!"

3 Practice and Apply

A. CONCEPT CHECK: Objects of Verbs

Each sentence below has at least one object. Write each object and identify it as a direct object, an indirect object, or an objective complement. Identify each objective complement as a noun or an adjective.

Example: Hobbies bring people pleasure.
Answer: people, indirect object; pleasure, direct object

The Man Who Would Be String King

1. You must give Francis A. Johnson some credit.
2. This Minnesotan could teach the world patience.
3. He spent 41 years on a very special project.
4. During each of those years, he truly had a ball.
5. Slowly but surely, inch by inch, Johnson wound the world's largest ball of twine.

6. At 12 feet in diameter and 17,400 pounds, Johnson's sphere offered other string savers an irresistible challenge.
7. Super string saver Frank Stoeber brought Cawker City, Kansas, a measure of fame.
8. He made an enormous ball of twine Cawker City's biggest tourist attraction.
9. Some people might consider Texan J. C. Payne an odd guy.
10. His 6-ton, 13-foot-tall twine ball has made him famous.

➜ **For a SELF-CHECK and more practice, see the EXERCISE BANK, p. 312.**

B. REVISING: Creating Objects of Verbs

Rewrite each sentence below, replacing all the objects of the verbs to create ten different sentences. Add and change modifiers as needed.

Example: Do you save things? ***Answer:*** Do you save odd items?

1. Tell us your favorite pastimes.
2. Do your hobbies include sports?
3. Other people may think your hobby unusual.
4. But your hobby may make you happy.
5. How much time do you spend on your hobby?
6. Show us the results.
7. Could you turn your hobby into a career?
8. Many hobbyists teach other people their craft.
9. You might give beginners lessons.
10. You should consider your hobby fun.

C. WRITING: Creating Sentences with Complements

Using the information below, write five sentences about Lucy the Elephant. Include direct objects, indirect objects, and objective complements.

Lucy, the world's largest elephant

Located in Margate, New Jersey

Built in 1881 by James Lafferty, a real estate developer

Historic landmark

Stands six stories tall, weighs 90 tons

25,000 tourists visit each year

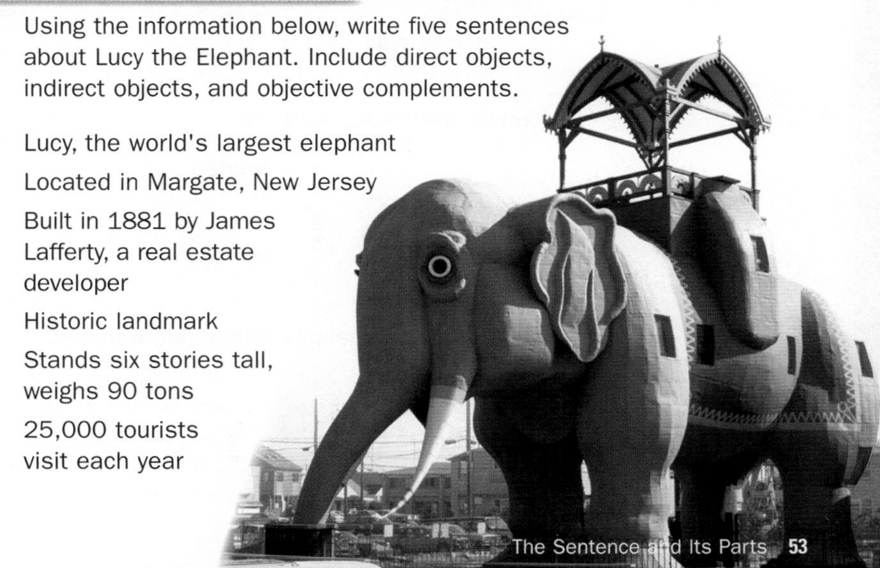

Sentence Diagramming

Watch me for diagramming tips!

Here's the Idea

Diagramming is a way of visually representing the structure of a sentence. Drawing a diagram can help you see the relationships among the words in a sentence and better understand how the words work together to form a complete thought.

Simple Subjects and Predicates

The simple subject and predicate are written on one line and separated by a vertical line that crosses the main line.

Spectators waited.

Spectators | waited

Compound Subjects and Verbs

For a compound subject or verb, split the main line. The conjunction goes on a broken line connecting the compound parts.

Spectators and contestants waited.

Compound Subject

Spectators / and / contestants | waited

Because there are two subjects, the left side of the main line is split into two parts.

Spectators waited and watched.

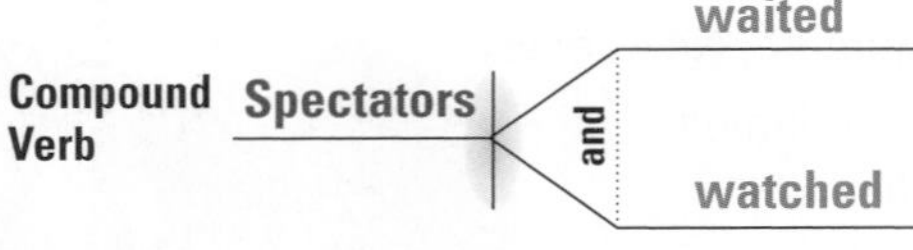

Because there are two verbs, the right side of the main line is split into two parts.

Spectators and contestants waited and watched.

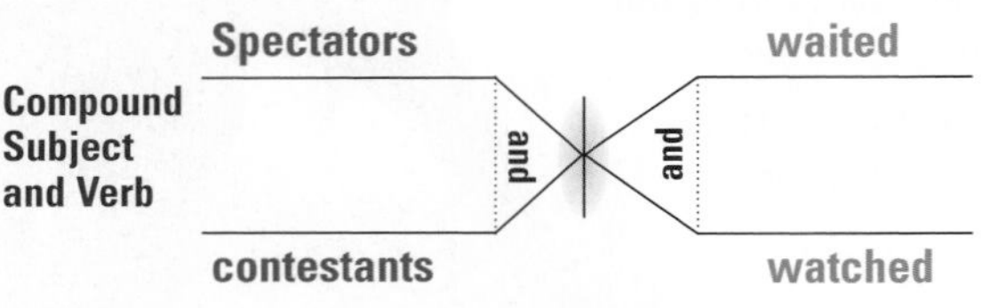

CHAPTER 2

A. CONCEPT CHECK: Subjects and Verbs

Diagram these sentences using what you have learned.

1. Reporters chuckled.
2. Reporters chuckled and cheered.
3. Spectators and reporters stood and applauded.

Adjectives and Adverbs

Because adjectives and adverbs **modify,** or tell more about, other words in a sentence, they are written on slanted lines below the words they modify.

The crazy contest ended very happily.

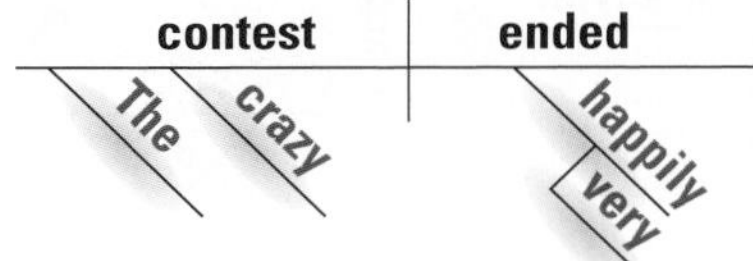

B. CONCEPT CHECK: Adjectives and Adverbs

Diagram these sentences using what you have learned.

1. The jolly judges grinned playfully.
2. A new champion finally was crowned.
3. The proud winner and her family smiled and bowed.

Subject Complements: Predicate Nominatives and Predicate Adjectives

Write a predicate nominative or a predicate adjective on the main line after the verb. Separate the subject complement from the verb with a slanted line that does not cross the main line.

May Gonzalez was the winner.

May Gonzalez | was \ winner
the

She felt wonderful.

She | felt \ wonderful

Direct Objects

A direct object follows the verb on the main line.

The winner received a paper crown.

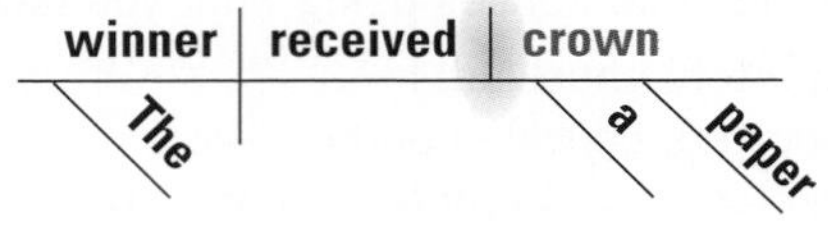

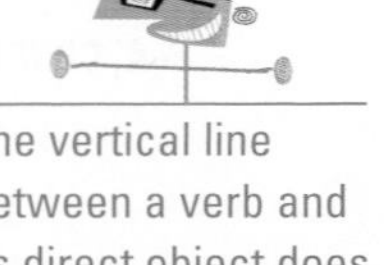

The vertical line between a verb and its direct object does not cross the main line.

Sometimes a sentence has a compound direct object. Like other compound parts, compound direct objects go on parallel lines that branch from the main line.

The winner received a paper crown and a T-shirt.

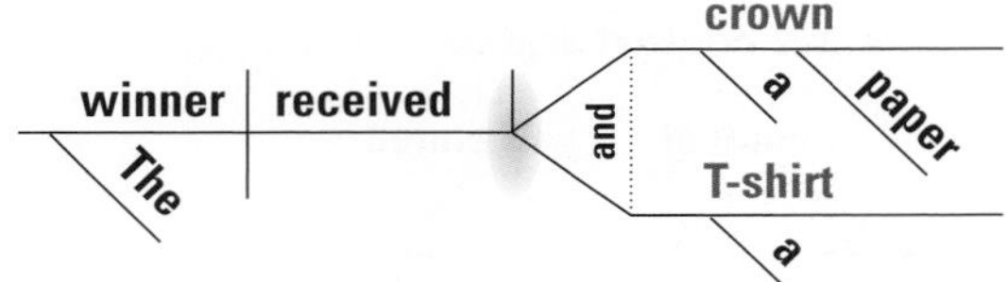

When you have a compound predicate with direct objects, split the line and show the compound parts on parallel lines.

She wore the crown and displayed the T-shirt.

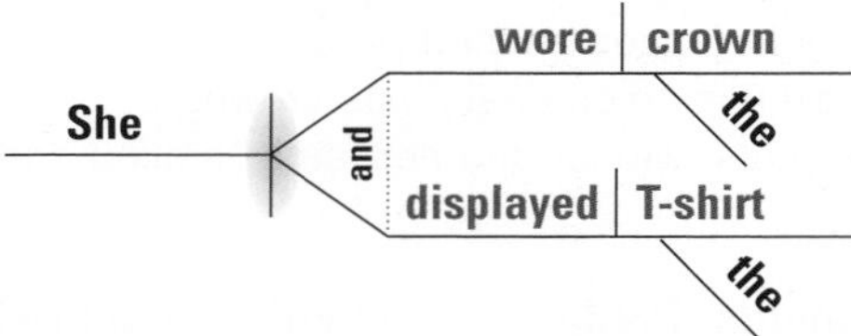

Indirect Objects

Write an indirect object below the verb, on a horizontal line connected to the verb with a slanted line.

The champion threw the crowd a kiss.

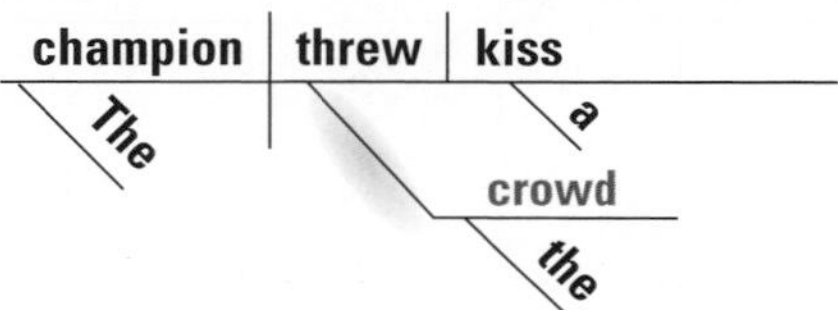

CHAPTER 2

Objective Complements

An objective complement follows a direct object on the main line. A slanted line that does not cross the main line separates the objective complement from the direct object.

The local newspaper called the contest delightful.

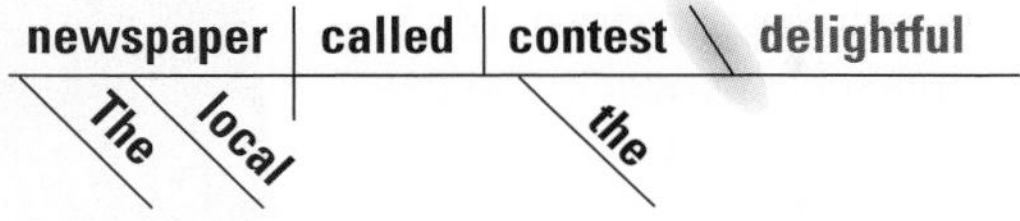

C. CONCEPT CHECK: Complements and Objects of the Verb

Diagram these sentences using what you've learned.

1. May Gonzalez was very happy.
2. The newspapers gave Gonzalez a great review.
3. Enthusiastic fans considered Gonzalez a terrific winner.

D. MIXED REVIEW: Diagramming

Diagram the following sentences.

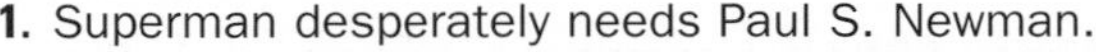

1. Superman desperately needs Paul S. Newman.
2. Sylvester and Tweety Bird do too.
3. Many cartoon characters owe Newman their lives.
4. The reason is quite simple.
5. Newman is a prolific comic-book writer.
6. He has written 4,000 stories.
7. The imaginative writer does not draw comics.
8. He creates clever plots and writes snappy dialogue.
9. Newman considers himself lucky.
10. He enjoys his job and brings other people pleasure.

Looks like George has a subject and a predicament.

Real World Grammar

Contest Application

Whether you are applying for a summer job, competing for a special award, or entering a contest, you need to present yourself in the best possible light. Using proper sentence structure and good grammar skills will distinguish you from other applicants. Here's one student's e-mail application for a special award. She asked her English teacher to comment on her first draft.

CHAPTER 2

E-mail

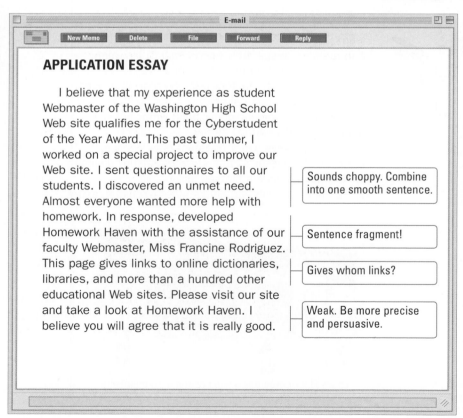

New Memo | Delete | File | Forward | Reply

APPLICATION ESSAY

I believe that my experience as student Webmaster of the Washington High School Web site qualifies me for the Cyberstudent of the Year Award. This past summer, I worked on a special project to improve our Web site. I sent questionnaires to all our students. I discovered an unmet need. Almost everyone wanted more help with homework. In response, developed Homework Haven with the assistance of our faculty Webmaster, Miss Francine Rodriguez. This page gives links to online dictionaries, libraries, and more than a hundred other educational Web sites. Please visit our site and take a look at Homework Haven. I believe you will agree that it is really good.

Sounds choppy. Combine into one smooth sentence.

Sentence fragment!

Gives whom links?

Weak. Be more precise and persuasive.

Using Grammar in Writing

Complete sentences	Communicate your ideas clearly by making sure every sentence has **both a subject and a predicate.**
Compound parts	Use **compound parts** to combine ideas and avoid repetition. Combining related ideas into one sentence makes your writing smoother and more concise.
Precise language	Use **clear, specific adjectives, pronouns, and nouns** as subject complements to express your ideas clearly and forcefully.

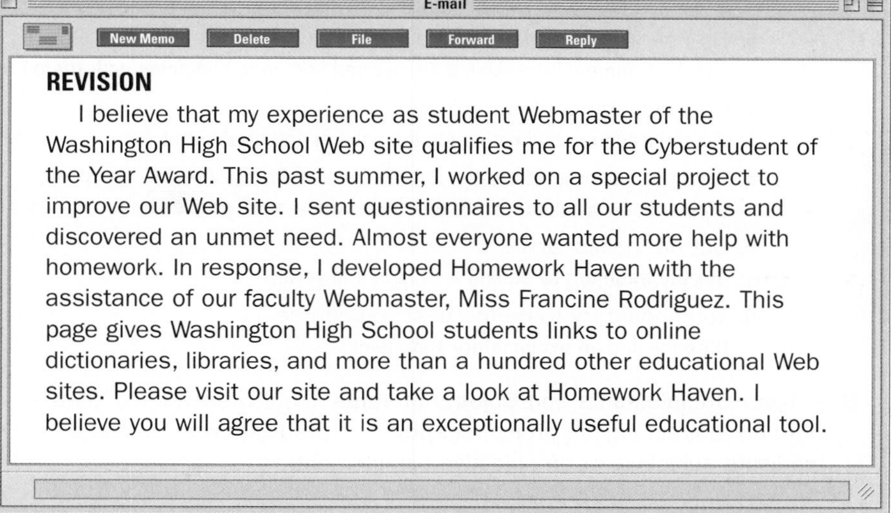

REVISION

I believe that my experience as student Webmaster of the Washington High School Web site qualifies me for the Cyberstudent of the Year Award. This past summer, I worked on a special project to improve our Web site. I sent questionnaires to all our students and discovered an unmet need. Almost everyone wanted more help with homework. In response, I developed Homework Haven with the assistance of our faculty Webmaster, Miss Francine Rodriguez. This page gives Washington High School students links to online dictionaries, libraries, and more than a hundred other educational Web sites. Please visit our site and take a look at Homework Haven. I believe you will agree that it is an exceptionally useful educational tool.

SENTENCE PARTS

PRACTICE AND APPLY: Revising

Use the three writing tips above to revise the summer-job application below.

DRAFT

I believe I am a good candidate for a job as coaching assistant. In elementary school, I participated in the park district's summer sports program. I developed an avid interest in sports. Currently play center on the high school basketball team. In junior high, was a member of the baseball team. In addition, firsthand experience working with active children. As the oldest of five kids, I often baby-sit my little brothers and sister. I would love to put my knowledge and experience to work for the park district.

Mixed Review

A. Sentences and Sentence Parts Revise each of the following sentences based on the instructions in parentheses.

1. Goals are vital.
   (What kinds of goals? Add detail to the subject.)
2. Goals give purpose and direction.
   (Give to whom? Add an indirect object.)
3. You have set goals for yourself.
   (Change into a question.)
4. Did you set achievable goals?
   (Change into a command.)
5. Your goals should be challenging. But also practical.
   (Fix the fragment by combining the predicate adjectives.)
6. No use in setting unrealistic goals.
   (Fix the fragment by making it an inverted sentence beginning with *there*.)
7. Only discourage you.
   (Fix the fragment by completing the subject and predicate.)
8. It would be nice to make *The Guinness Book of World Records*.
   (Replace the weak predicate adjective with a more precise one.)
9. But not necessary.
   (Fix the fragment by adding a subject and verb.)
10. You should try to be the best you can be.
    (Change into an exclamatory statement.)

B. Subject Complements and Objects of Verbs Identify each underlined word as a direct object, an indirect object, a predicate nominative, a predicate adjective, or an objective complement.

PROFESSIONAL MODEL

(1) When Jean Bowman graduated from high school, she was truly a senior. **(2)** In fact, she was downright old. **(3)** At 87, Bowman became the world's oldest high school graduate. **(4)** Bowman quit high school in 1926 without earning her diploma. **(5)** She became a homemaker. **(6)** She also raised three children. **(7)** Bowman did not dare tell her children her secret. **(8)** She was afraid they would consider her ignorant. **(9)** Some 70 years after dropping out of high school, Bowman entered an adult education program. **(10)** Night school gave Bowman an opportunity to finish what she started so long ago.

Mastery Test: What Did You Learn?

Choose the letter of the description or term that correctly identifies each numbered part of the passage.

Music is not only an <u>art</u> (1) but also a business. Many artists have earned <u>millions</u> (2) of dollars in the recording industry. <u>Elvis Presley and Aretha Franklin</u> (3) are the top male and female solo recording artists of all time. Presley <u>had more than 170 hit singles and 80 top-selling albums</u> (4). Franklin's magnificent voice has earned <u>her</u> (5) 14 hit singles. <u>Can you guess which rock band has sold the greatest number of records?</u> (6) This <u>honor</u> (7) goes to the Beatles. <u>The band has sold more than a billion discs and tapes!</u> (8) Today, alternative rock and rap are <u>popular</u> (9). Will people consider these types of music <u>interesting</u> (10) in the future?

1. A. describes the subject
   B. completes the meaning of the action verb
   C. tells who receives the action
   D. describes the direct object
2. A. simple subject
   B. predicate adjective
   C. direct object
   D. indirect object
3. A. compound verb
   B. compound subject
   C. simple predicate
   D. simple subject
4. A. simple subject
   B. complete subject
   C. direct object
   D. complete predicate
5. A. direct object
   B. indirect object
   C. predicate nominative
   D. objective complement
6. A. interrogative sentence
   B. imperative sentence
   C. exclamatory sentence
   D. declarative sentence
7. A. predicate nominative
   B. predicate adjective
   C. direct object
   D. simple subject
8. A. interrogative sentence
   B. imperative sentence
   C. exclamatory sentence
   D. declarative sentence
9. A. predicate nominative
   B. predicate adjective
   C. direct object
   D. simple subject
10. A. predicate adjective
    B. direct object
    C. objective complement
    D. indirect object

Student Help Desk

The Sentence at a Glance

A sentence has two parts: a subject and a predicate.

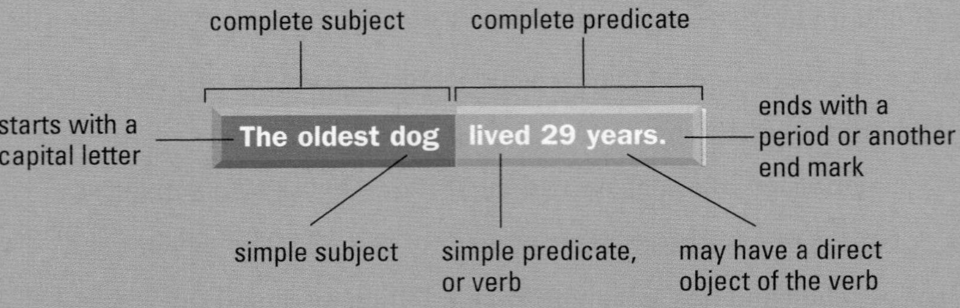

Subjects and Predicates

The Most Basic Sentence Parts

Sentence Parts	Example
Simple subject and predicate	**The bear ran.**
Compound subject and verb	**The bear and her cubs ran and climbed.**
Complete subject and predicate	**The three cubs ran past our camp.**

CHAPTER 2

Objects of Verbs

Famous Identified Flying Objects

Type	Definition	Example
Direct object	A direct object receives the action of an action verb.	The visitors photographed the smallest **car.**
Indirect object	An indirect object tells to what, to whom, or for whom the action is done.	Joe gave **me** the book.
Objective complement	An objective complement follows a direct object and renames or describes that object.	Some people make Las Vegas their **home.**

Finding the Subject in a Sentence

Subject Contorts into Many Positions

1. In an inverted sentence, find the verb and ask yourself who or what did the action in the sentence.

   Example: From the distance came the howl of a timber wolf.
   The verb is **came.** What came? Howl came. The subject is **howl.**

2. When a sentence begins with *there* or *here,* the subject usually follows the verb. To find the subject, reword the sentence with the subject at the beginning.

   Example: Here is your passport.
   Reworded: Your **passport** is here.

3. In most questions beginning with *where, when, why, how,* or *how much,* the subject falls between the parts of the verb phrase.

   Example: Where **will you go** on vacation?

4. The subject of an imperative sentence is always *you,* even when the subject is not directly stated.

   Example: **(You)** Look at these pictures.

SENTENCE PARTS

The Bottom Line

Checklist for Editing Sentences

Have I . . .

____ made all sentence fragments into complete sentences, with both a subject and a predicate?

____ used compound subjects and verbs to combine sentences with similar ideas?

____ used the right kind of sentence for the intended tone and mood?

____ varied sentence structure so the writing is interesting?

____ used inverted sentences properly?

____ placed the indirect object before the direct object?

Using Phrases

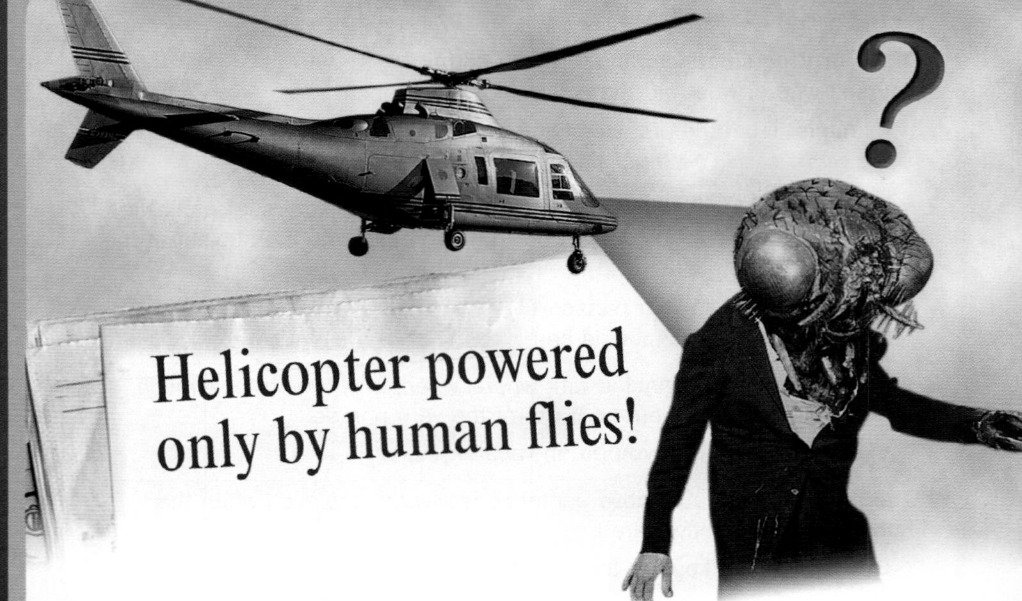
Helicopter powered
only by human flies!

Theme: Things With Wings

Human Flies?

Is there something wrong with this headline, or has genetic engineering finally caught up with Hollywood? Headlines are supposed to be condensed, but this one is mixed up—rather like the human fly himself.

One way to be more clear would be to write two sentences: *A helicopter flies. The helicopter is powered only by a human.* By using a phrase, however, you can make one sentence that uses fewer words and flows better: *Powered only by a human, a helicopter flies.* You can use phrases to improve your writing as long as—unlike the writer of the headline—you make clear what the phrase goes with.

Write Away: A Few of My Favorite Wings

What is your favorite thing with wings? A bird? A plane? A family pack from a chicken place? Answer this question in a paragraph and add it to your **Working Portfolio.**

Diagnostic Test: What Do You Know?

Choose the letter of the term that correctly identifies each numbered item.

The longtime dream <u>of human flight</u> (1) turned into reality in the early 1900s. According to Wilbur Wright, <u>one of the inventors of the first airplane</u> (2), "Flight was generally looked upon as an impossibility, and scarcely anyone believed it until he saw it <u>with his own eyes</u> (3)." The Wrights, <u>thinking</u> (4) out of the box, created their own machine <u>built</u> (5) to fly people. Now almost everyone can enjoy <u>jetting</u> (6) from place to place.

For thousands of years, people could only imagine <u>soaring gracefully through the air like birds</u> (7). To them, flying without the restraint <u>of gravity</u> (8) would have been <u>to know freedom</u> (9), but the possibility of <u>traveling more than 30,000 feet above ground</u> (10) was merely a pipe dream.

1. A. participial phrase
   B. prepositional phrase
   C. infinitive phrase
   D. appositive phrase

2. A. participial phrase
   B. prepositional phrase
   C. infinitive phrase
   D. appositive phrase

3. A. phrase modifying *it*
   B. phrase modifying *saw*
   C. phrase used as predicate nominative
   D. phrase used as direct object

4. A. present participle
   B. gerund
   C. infinitive
   D. past participle

5. A. present participle
   B. gerund
   C. infinitive
   D. past participle

6. A. present participle
   B. infinitive
   C. gerund
   D. past participle

7. A. phrase used as subject of sentence
   B. phrase used as object of preposition
   C. phrase used as direct object
   D. phrase used as predicate nominative

8. A. phrase modifying *to fly*
   B. phrase used as object of *without*
   C. phrase modifying *restraint*
   D. phrase used as subject

9. A. phrase used as subject
   B. phrase used as direct object
   C. phrase used as predicate nominative
   D. phrase used as object of preposition

10. A. gerund phrase used as subject
    B. gerund phrase used as direct object
    C. gerund phrase used as predicate nominative
    D. gerund phrase used as object of preposition

PHRASES

Prepositional Phrases

1 Here's the Idea

A **phrase** is a group of related words that does not have a subject or a predicate. It functions as a single part of speech.

▶ **A prepositional phrase consists of a preposition, its object, and any modifiers of the object.**

"On the Wings of Morning" is a poem by the talented Maya Angelou.
PREPOSITIONAL PHRASE

Prepositional phrases are used to modify, or describe, a noun or pronoun.

LITERARY MODEL

Sounds like music and sounds like flying tents filled the sky, and those were pterodactyls soaring with cavernous gray wings, gigantic bats of delirium and night fever.

—Ray Bradbury, "A Sound of Thunder"

PREPOSITIONAL PHRASES
WORDS MODIFIED

Notice that prepositional phrases can function either as adjectives or adverbs.

MODIFIES VERB   MODIFIES NOUN

The dragon flew to its secret lair inside the mountain.
ADVERB PHRASE   ADJECTIVE PHRASE

Adjective Phrases

An **adjective prepositional phrase** is a prepositional phrase that modifies a noun or a pronoun. An adjective phrase usually tells *which one* or *what kind* about the word it modifies.

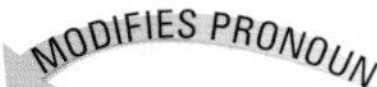

A bird in the hand is better than one in the bush.
WHICH BIRD?   WHAT KIND?

While adjectives usually come just before the words they modify, adjective phrases usually come just after.

Adverb Phrases

An **adverb prepositional phrase** is a prepositional phrase that modifies a verb, an adjective, or an adverb. Like an adverb, an adverb phrase tells *how, when, where,* or *to what extent* about the word it modifies.

MODIFIES VERB

The tricky cuckoo lays its eggs in other birds' nests.

LAYS WHERE?

MODIFIES ADJECTIVE

Even cuckoo chicks are skillful at deception.

SKILLFUL HOW?

MODIFIES ADVERB

Soon after their emergence, they begin to imitate the other chicks. WHEN?

For a list of prepositions, see p. 89.

PHRASES

2 Why It Matters in Writing

Using prepositional phrases is a good way to add specific details to your writing. Notice the kinds of details the author includes in the passage below.

LITERARY MODEL

Then one day they overheard the neighbors whispering: someone had come from Seoul with a permit from the governor-general's office to catch cranes as some kind of specimens. Then and there the two boys had dashed off to the field. That they would be found out and punished had no longer mattered; all they cared about was the fate of their crane.

—Hwang Sunwŏn, "Cranes"

ADVERB PHRASES

ADJECTIVE PHRASES

❸ Practice and Apply

A. CONCEPT CHECK: Prepositional Phrases

Write each prepositional phrase and tell whether it is an adjective phrase or an adverb phrase. Then identify the word or words the prepositional phrase modifies.

Example: Birds are the only animals with feathers.
Answer: with feathers, adjective phrase, animals

The Bird Book of Records

1. The adult bee hummingbird belongs in any bird record book.
2. Its length of approximately two inches makes it the earth's smallest bird.
3. It and all other hummingbirds can hover like helicopters.
4. They are also the only birds with backward flying ability.
5. Another bird for the record books is the ostrich.
6. At up to eight feet tall, the ostrich is the world's largest bird.
7. The flightless ostrich is also a record holder for speed.
8. Its 40-mph running speed makes it the fastest bird on land.
9. A peregrine falcon's diving speed is over 200 mph.
10. A peregrine falcon's air speed beats the ostrich's land speed by more than 160 mph.

➜ **For a SELF-CHECK and more practice, see the EXERCISE BANK, p.313.**

B. WRITING: Adding Details

Rewrite each sentence by adding a prepositional phrase that begins with the preposition shown in parentheses.

Example: We had our hummingbird feeder hanging. (under)
Answer: We had our hummingbird feeder hanging under the deck.

1. So we could see it better, we moved the hummingbird feeder. (near)
2. The first hummingbird we saw hovered. (by)
3. The second hummingbird flitted quickly. (around)
4. Soon the two hummingbirds were drinking. (from)
5. We took lots of pictures. (of)

Appositives and Appositive Phrases

1 Here's the Idea

An appositive is a noun or pronoun that identifies or renames another noun or pronoun. An **appositive phrase** is made up of an appositive plus its modifiers.

APPOSITIVE

Leonardo da Vinci, the great Renaissance painter, was also an inventor.

APPOSITIVE PHRASE

Essential and Nonessential Appositives

An **essential** (or **restrictive**) **appositive** provides information that is needed to identify the preceding noun or pronoun.

The Italian artist Leonardo da Vinci drew a flying machine with flapping wings around 1500. (ESSENTIAL APPOSITIVE)

A **nonessential** (or **nonrestrictive**) **appositive** adds extra information about a noun or pronoun whose meaning is already clear. Eliminating the appositive does not change the basic meaning. Notice that nonessential appositives are set off with commas.

Leonardo da Vinci, an Italian artist, drew a flying machine with flapping wings around 1500. (NONESSENTIAL APPOSITIVE)

You as the writer determine whether the appositive is essential to the meaning of your sentence. If it is, do not use commas.

2 Why It Matters in Writing

Appositives can draw attention to the qualities of a person, place, or thing that are important or relevant for your writing purpose.

PROFESSIONAL MODEL

In *It's a Wonderful Life,* one of the most popular movies ever made, a character named Clarence wants to get his wings. Clarence, an angel, must accomplish this goal by helping the character George Bailey realize what a wonderful life he has had.

NONESSENTIAL APPOSITIVES

ESSENTIAL APPOSITIVE

PHRASES

3 Practice and Apply

A. CONCEPT CHECK: Appositives and Appositive Phrases

Rewrite each sentence, adding the appositive or appositive phrase shown in parentheses. Include commas if necessary.

The Wright Brothers Fly

1. The Wright brothers owned a bicycle shop in Dayton, Ohio, in the late 1800s. (Wilbur and Orville)
2. Wilbur became interested in flying after reading a book about gliders. (the older brother)
3. The book was written by the German engineer. (Otto Lilienthal)
4. The Wright brothers then started building their own gliders in 1899. (engineless aircraft)
5. They tested their gliders on North Carolina's Outer Banks. (an area known for its steady winds)
6. In 1903 the brothers built their first biplane. (the *Flyer*)
7. On December 17, they flew the *Flyer.* (the world's first successful airplane)
8. This now renowned event was not officially recognized at the time. (the first airplane flight)
9. The aviator made his first official public flights while in France in 1908. (Wilbur Wright)
10. Today the *Flyer* is displayed at the National Air and Space Museum. (the Wrights' original airplane)

➜ **For a SELF-CHECK and more practice, see the EXERCISE BANK, p. 313.**

Write three sentences modeled after sentences 2, 3, and 4 above.

B. REVISING: Adding Information About Nouns

Combine each pair of sentences by incorporating the information in the second sentence as an appositive in the first sentence.

1. Old-time air shows featured stunts by performers such as Lincoln Beachey. Beachey was a famous daredevil pilot.
2. Today the world's largest air show is held in Oshkosh, Wisconsin. It is the Experimental Aircraft Association Annual International Fly-In Convention and Sport Exhibition.
3. For the yearly Fly-In, as many as 750,000 people visit Oshkosh. Oshkosh is a city of about 50,000.

Verbals: Participles

1 Here's the Idea

A **verbal** is a verb form that acts as a noun, an adjective, or an adverb. Verbals may be participles, gerunds, or infinitives.

A participle is a verb form that functions as an adjective. Like adjectives, participles modify nouns or pronouns.

MODIFIES — MODIFIES

Smiling, he ate another fried chicken wing.

PRONOUN — NOUN

Participles may be **present participles** or **past participles.**

LITERARY MODEL

> It [*Tyrannosaurus rex*] came on great oiled, resilient, striding legs.
>
> —Ray Bradbury, "A Sound of Thunder"

PAST PARTICIPLE
PRESENT PARTICIPLE
WORD MODIFIED

A **participial phrase** consists of a participle plus its modifiers and complements. The whole phrase below modifies *he.*

MODIFIER — COMPLEMENT

Foolishly wasting time, he studied the broken creature.

To learn about the present and past participle forms of verbs, see p. 130.

2 Why It Matters in Writing

By using modifiers made from action verbs, you can make your descriptions more lively and vivid.

LITERARY MODEL

> And then for some reason, Millicent thought of the heather birds. Swooping carefree over the moors, they would go singing and crying out across the great spaces of air . . . their wings flahing quick and purple in the bright sun.
>
> —Sylvia Plath, "Initiation"

PARTICIPIAL PHRASES
WORDS MODIFIED

PHRASES

3 Practice and Apply

A. CONCEPT CHECK: Participles

Write the participial phrase in each sentence, and indicate whether it contains a present participle or a past participle.

Example: Most celebrated of all the insects, butterflies are admired by many people.

Answer: Most celebrated of all the insects, past participle

The Delicate Butterfly

1. Appreciated for their color and grace, butterflies are one of nature's glories.
2. Often bursting with color, their spectacular wings are covered with thousands of tiny scales.
3. In fact, these scales are the basis for their scientific name, *Lepidoptera,* meaning "scaly wings."
4. Visiting gardens, the butterflies flit among the flowers.
5. Driven by instinct, they use the flowers as meal stops.
6. Uncoiling their proboscises, they pierce the flowers.
7. Then, sucking through these straws, they feast on nectar.
8. Pollinating at the same time, the butterflies help the flowers.
9. Picking up pollen dust on their feet, they move from flower to flower.
10. On each, they wipe their feet and thus spread the pollen needed for reproduction.

➜ **For a SELF-CHECK and more practice, see the EXERCISE BANK, p. 314.**

In the above ten sentences, identify the noun or pronoun that each participial phrase modifies.

B. REVISING: Using Participial Phrases to Combine Sentences

Use participial phrases to combine each set of sentences and achieve a livelier tone.

Example: The western pygmy blue butterfly is one of the smallest butterflies. It has a three-eighths-inch wingspan.

Answer: Having only a three-eighths-inch wingspan, the western pygmy blue is one of the smallest butterflies.

1. The Queen Alexandra's birdwing is the largest butterfly. It has an 11-inch wingspan.
2. The twin-spotted sphinx displays large eyespots on bright wings. It uses them to ward off predators.
3. The Indian leaf butterfly has a perfect camouflage. It is shaped and colored like a leaf.

Verbals: Gerunds

1 Here's the Idea

▶ **A gerund is a verb form that ends in *-ing* and functions as a noun.** A **gerund phrase** consists of a gerund plus its modifiers and complements.

GERUND
Flying an airplane while tired can be dangerous.
GERUND PHRASE

Like nouns, gerunds and gerund phrases can act as subjects, complements (direct objects, indirect objects, or predicate nominatives), or objects of prepositions.

Gerund Phrases

Function	Example
Subject	**Flying** got Icarus into trouble.
Direct object	Icarus tried **using wings made of wax.**
Indirect object	He wanted to give **flying like a bird** a chance.
Predicate nominative	His mistake was **straying too close to the sun.**
Object of preposition	The result of **doing so** was melted wings and a dip in the sea.

Don't confuse a gerund with a present participle. A gerund, as in the sentences above, can be replaced by the word *something*.

2 Why It Matters in Writing

Gerunds and gerund phrases let you turn verbs into nouns so that you can talk about actions and activities as things. Using gerunds can improve the fluency of your sentences and make them more concise.

STUDENT MODEL

DRAFT

Some people write poetry. Pegasus—the mythical horse with wings—could be ridden. The two experiences have often been compared.

REVISION

Writing poetry has often been compared to **riding Pegasus**—the mythical horse with wings.

PHRASES

❸ Practice and Apply

A. CONCEPT CHECK: Gerunds

Write the gerund or gerund phrase that appears in each sentence. Then tell whether it is a subject, a direct object, an indirect object, a predicate nominative, or an object of a preposition.

Example: Singing is more than an expression of joy for birds.
Answer: singing, subject

Bird Songs

1. Birds sing as a means of communicating with others.
2. Honking during migration, for example, helps geese guide other flock members.
3. Screeching by one bird may alert others to a predator.
4. The response to this alarm call is often dashing for cover.
5. Males announce territory claims through robust singing.
6. With elaborate songs, they often try attracting females.
7. The male winter wren's specialty is crooning its courtship song.
8. The female winter wren, in turn, communicates with her young by warbling a quiet song.
9. Vocalizing isn't the only way birds can communicate.
10. The rat-a-tat drumming of bills on trees announces the presence of woodpeckers.

➜ **For a SELF-CHECK and more practice, see the EXERCISE BANK, p. 314**

B. WRITING: Using Gerunds to Improve Sentence Fluency

Combine each pair of sentences below, turning the underlined words into a gerund phrase. Give the phrase the function indicated in parentheses.

Example: The young man <u>wore wingtips</u>. This made him feel older. (subject)
Answer: Wearing wingtips made the young man feel older.

1. The small boy <u>released the fireflies</u>. He enjoyed it. (direct object)
2. One of my favorite things to do in summer is this. <u>I grill chicken on the beach</u>. (predicate nominative)
3. I love <u>to hang by the teeth from an airplane</u>. You should give it a try. (indirect object)
4. Have you ever <u>read Poe's "The Raven"</u>? It is an awesome experience. (subject)
5. Patrice entertained her friends. She <u>played her favorite CD from the band *Wings*</u>. (object of preposition *by*)

Verbals: Infinitives

1 Here's the Idea

An infinitive is a verb form, usually beginning with the word *to*, that can act as a noun, an adjective, or an adverb. An **infinitive phrase** consists of an infinitive plus any modifiers and complements.

INFINITIVE

To find water striders, look in a freshwater pond.

INFINITIVE PHRASE

Infinitive Phrases

Function	Example
Noun (Subject)	**To skate along the surface of the water** is easy for the water strider.
Noun (Direct object)	Water striders need **to find food in the water without sinking themselves.**
Noun (Predicate nominative)	The trick is **to use surface tension for support.**
Adjective	The water strider is an interesting insect **to watch on a calm summer day.**
Adverb	**To detect insects falling into the water near them,** water striders use sense organs on their legs.

PHRASES

2 Why It Matters in Writing

By using infinitive phrases to combine sentences, you can sharpen the relationship between ideas.

STUDENT MODEL

DRAFT

Many moth species have evolved with an owl-face pattern on their wings. The pattern scares away birds.

REVISION

Many moth species have evolved with an owl-face pattern on their wings that serves **to scare away birds.**

❸ Practice and Apply

A. CONCEPT CHECK: Infinitives

Write each infinitive or infinitive phrase and indicate whether it acts as a noun, an adjective, or an adverb.

Example: Honeybees have the ability to make large quantities of honey and wax.

Answer: to make large quantities of honey and wax, adjective

Honeybees

1. A queen bee, some drones, and many worker bees are needed to form a honeybee colony.
2. The queen bee's main job is to lay eggs.
3. The drones, or male bees, exist only to mate.
4. The all-female worker bees have a lot more work to do.
5. They build the honeycomb as a place to raise young bees.
6. They also use it to store food, or honey.
7. To make their honey, bees combine their own enzymes with nectar from flowers.
8. Many animals, including bears, love to eat the honey.
9. They are eager to raid a hive.
10. To protect the hive, worker bees guard its entrance.

➜ **For a SELF-CHECK and more practice, see the EXERCISE BANK, p. 315.**

CHAPTER 3

B. WRITING: Sharpening Ideas

Combine each pair of sentences below, changing one of them into an infinitive phrase.

Example: Dragonflies have evolved four large wings. The wings help them fly swiftly.

Answer: To help them fly swiftly, dragonflies have evolved four large wings.

1. Dragonflies can fly 50 to 60 miles per hour. They escape predators.
2. A dragonfly instinctively shapes its six legs like a basket. It captures insects in the basket.
3. A dragonfly nymph must molt, or shed its skin, 10 or more times. Through molting the nymph becomes an adult.

Mixed Review

A. Verbals Write each underlined portion of the passage below and identify the kind of verbal or verbal phrase it is.

LITERARY MODEL

As the clouds gathered outside, **(1)** unnoticed, the ringmaster cracked his whip, shouted his introduction, and pointed to the ceiling of the tent, where the **(2)** Flying Avalons were perched. They loved **(3)** to drop gracefully from nowhere, like two **(4)** sparkling birds, and blow kisses as they threw off their **(5)** plumed helmets and high-collared capes. . . . In the final vignette of their act, they actually would kiss in midair, pausing, **(6)** almost hovering as they swooped past one another. . . .

Anna was pregnant at the time, seven months and **(7)** hardly showing, her stomach muscles were that strong. It seems incredible that she would work high above the ground when any fall could be so dangerous, but the explanation—I know from **(8)** watching her go blind—is that my mother lives comfortably in extreme elements.

Harry launched himself and swung, once, twice, in huge **(9)** calibrated beats across space. He hung from his knees and on the third swing stretched wide his arms, held his hands out **(10)** to receive his pregnant wife as she dove from her shining bar.

—Louise Erdrich, "The Leap"

Specify the function of each underlined verbal or verbal phrase in its sentence in the passage above.

B. Rewrite Sentences, Using Verbals Combine each pair of sentences below, changing one of them into a verbal phrase.

1. Wasps are insects with wings. They are related to bees and ants.
2. Female wasps use their stingers for protection. With the stingers, they defend their nests against predators.
3. People often mistake yellow jackets for bees. This is a common error with sometimes painful results.

In your **Working Portfolio,** find the paragraph you wrote for the **Write Away** on page 64. Using verbal phrases, combine some of your sentences to eliminate unnecessary words.

PHRASES

Placement of Phrases

1 Here's the Idea

When a phrase functions as a modifier in a sentence, you need to make clear what the phrase modifies in order to avoid confusing the reader.

A **misplaced modifier** is a word or phrase that is placed so far away from the word it modifies that the meaning of the sentence is unclear or incorrect.

Draft: The **ranger** explained how to find ducks **in her office.** (WHY WERE THERE DUCKS IN HER OFFICE?)

Revision: **In her office,** the **ranger** explained how to find ducks.

A **dangling modifier** results when the word being modified is missing from the sentence.

Draft: **Coming home with the groceries,** our parrot said, "Hello!" (THE PARROT SHOPS?)

Revision: **Coming home with the groceries, we** heard our parrot say, "Hello!"

CHAPTER 3

Here's How **Fixing a Misplaced or Dangling Modifier**

1. Find the word the phrase modifies and move the phrase as close to that word as possible.
2. If the word the phrase should modify is missing from the sentence, add the word.

2 Why It Matters in Writing

Misplaced and dangling modifiers result in writing that is confusing and sometimes unintentionally humorous.

STUDENT MODEL

DRAFT

Peacocks are the favorite birds of many people, **with their colorful tails. Prancing around in search of a mate,** most observers are charmed.

REVISION

With their colorful tails, peacocks are the favorite birds of many people. **Prancing around in search of a mate, peacocks** charm most observers.

3 Practice and Apply

A. CONCEPT CHECK: Placement of Phrases

Rewrite each sentence below that has a misplaced or dangling modifier. If a sentence has neither, write *Correct.*

Example: Flying in a car-plane, the cornfields looked tiny.
Answer: Flying in a car-plane, my grandfather thought the cornfields looked tiny.

The Flying Car

1. Combining a car and an airplane into one vehicle for many inventors was a long-time dream.
2. Called "flying flivvers," Ford and other automobile manufacturers produced prototypes of flying cars.
3. These car-planes were a novelty for pilots including models with removable wings.
4. Using a flying car, trips could be made by air or the highway.
5. Long ago, one model, the Aerocar, was featured on a TV show.
6. Although produced from 1946 to 1967, the Aerocar company sold only five cars.
7. Less sturdy and less spacious than regular cars, comfortable ground transportation was not provided.
8. The car-planes had a problem with safety, handling worse than conventional airplanes.
9. Priced sky-high, flying cars were not only unsafe, but also expensive.
10. Flying cars never really caught on with the American public, making more sense in theory than in practice.

➜ **For a SELF-CHECK and more practice, see the EXERCISE BANK, p. 315.**

B. REVISING: Fixing Misplaced and Dangling Modifiers

Fix any dangling or misplaced modifiers in the following paragraph.

STUDENT MODEL

In their heyday from the late 1930s to the early 1940s, people flew from Europe to the United States in "flying boats." The flying boats had large staterooms and served full-course meals offering many of the same luxuries as ocean liners.

PHRASES

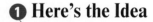

Sentence Diagramming: Phrases

1 Here's the Idea

Diagramming phrases can help you understand how phrases function in a sentence and enable you to use them more effectively in your writing.

Watch me for diagramming tips!

Prepositional Phrases

- Write the preposition on a slanted line below the word the prepositional phrase modifies.
- Write the object of the preposition on a horizontal line attached to the slanted line and parallel to the main line.
- Write words that modify the object of the preposition on slanted lines below the object.

Adjective Phrase

The nightingale sang a song of true love.

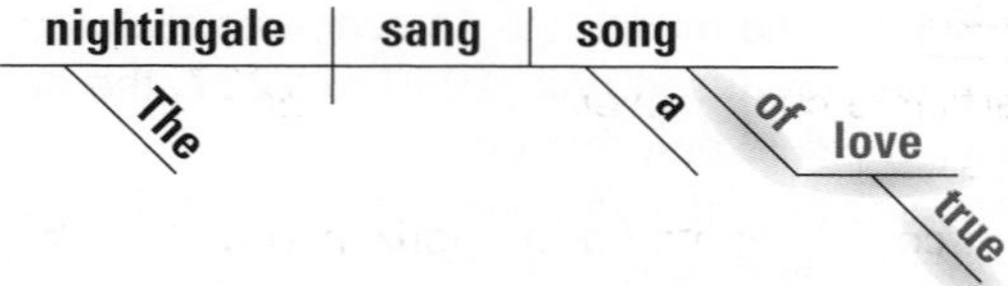

This adjective phrase modifies a noun used as a direct object. Adjective phrases can also modify pronouns.

Adverb Phrase

The eagle perched on a cliff by the sea.

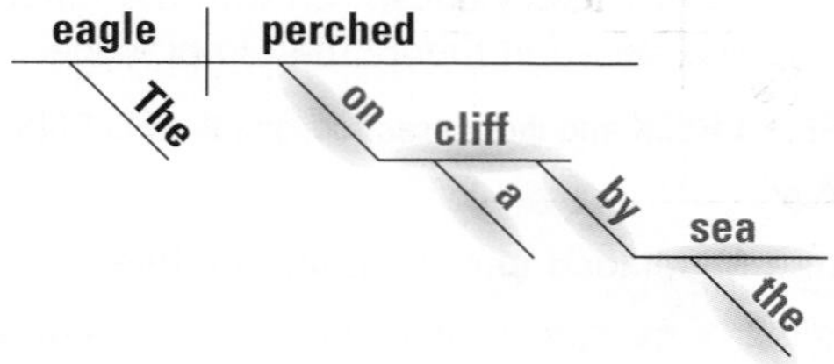

The first adverb phrase modifies a verb. The second phrase modifies the object in the first phrase.

A. CONCEPT CHECK: Prepositional Phrases

Diagram these sentences using what you have learned.

1. The farmer built the birdhouse of his dreams.
2. A falcon flew over my house.

Appositives and Appositive Phrases

Write the appositive in parentheses after the word it identifies or renames. Attach words that modify the appositive to it in the usual way.

The dipper, an aquatic bird of North America, can walk underwater.

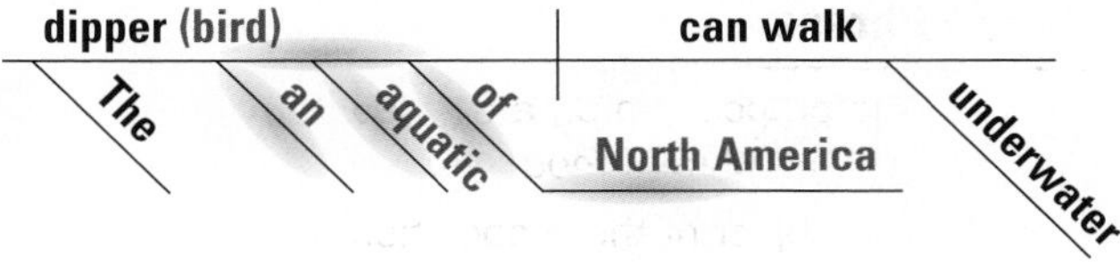

B. CONCEPT CHECK: Appositives and Appositive Phrases

Diagram these sentences using what you have learned.

1. The ostrich, a large bird from Africa, can run fast.
2. The kiwi, a bird from New Zealand, cannot fly.

PHRASES

Participial Phrases

- The participle curves over an angled line below the word it modifies.
- Diagram complements on the horizontal part of the angled line in the usual way.
- Write modifiers on slanted lines below the words they modify.

Suddenly leaving the flock, the goose disappeared.

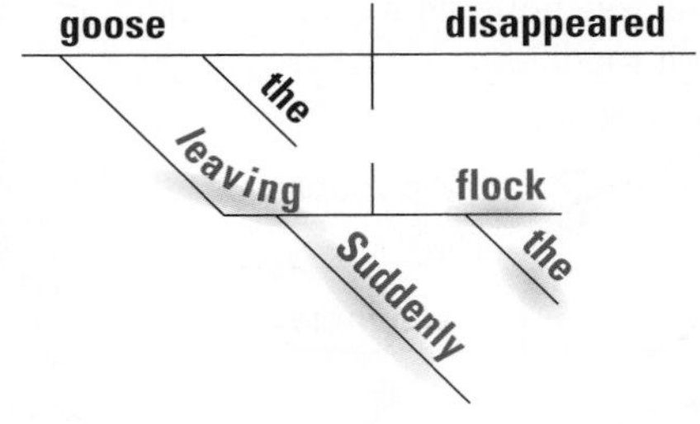

This is a present participial phrase. Past participial phrases are diagrammed in the same way. Notice how the participle is slightly curved.

Gerund Phrases

- The gerund curves over a line that looks like a step.
- With a vertical forked line, connect the step to the part of the diagram that corresponds to the role of the gerund phrase in the sentence.
- Diagram complements and modifiers in the usual way.

Flying a plane successfully usually requires experience.

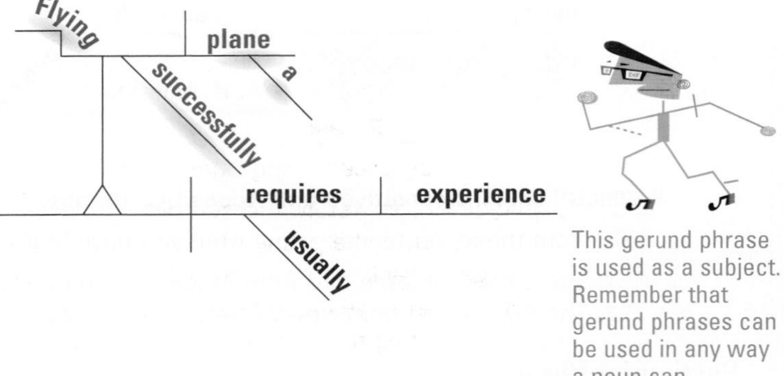

This gerund phrase is used as a subject. Remember that gerund phrases can be used in any way a noun can.

Infinitive Phrases

- Write the infinitive on an angled line, with the word *to* on the slanted part and the verb on the horizontal part.
- When the infinitive or infinitive phrase functions as a noun, use a vertical forked line to connect the infinitive to the part of the diagram that corresponds to its role in the sentence.
- When the phrase functions as a modifier, place the angled line below the word it modifies.

Infinitive Phrase as Noun

I want to see a spotted sandpiper soon.

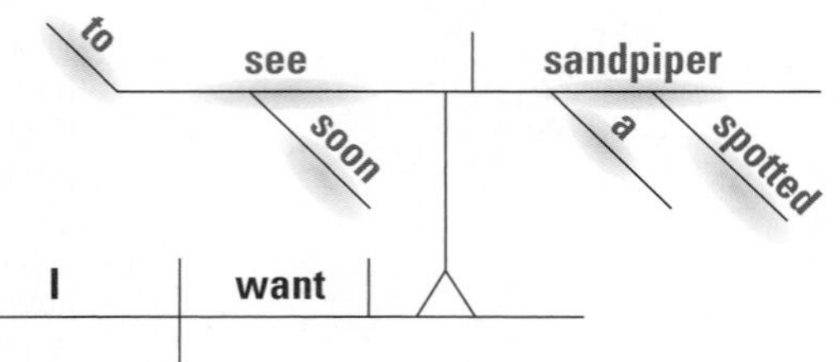

This infinitive phrase is a direct object. An infinitive phrase acting as a noun can also be a subject or a predicate nominative.

Infinitive Phrase as Modifier

It is time to launch my hang glider.

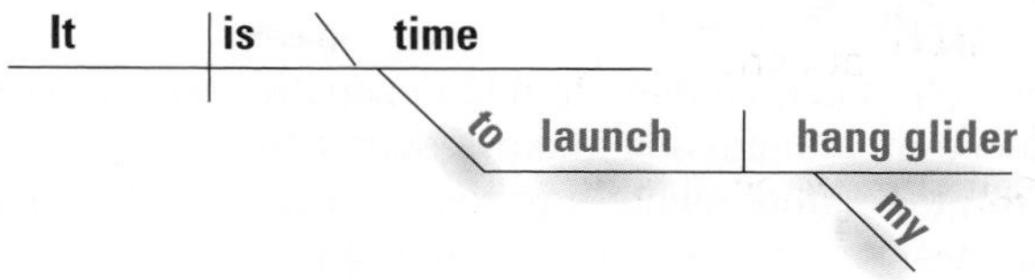

This infinitive phrase is an adjective modifying *time.* An infinitive phrase acting as a modifier can also be an adverb.

C. CONCEPT CHECK: Verbal Phrases

Diagram these sentences using what you have learned.

1. Camouflaged completely, the ptarmigan can hide easily.
2. Squawking loudly, the geese took off.
3. Hummingbirds enjoy drinking nectar from flowers.
4. We hope to see a yellow-shafted flicker today.
5. To find interesting things with wings is easy.

PHRASES

D. MIXED REVIEW: Diagramming

Diagram the following sentences. Look for all types of phrases.

1. The penguin, a flightless bird, can swim underwater.
2. Swimming swiftly requires strength.
3. Penguins breed in a rookery.
4. Incubated carefully, a penguin egg will hatch normally.
5. To see an emperor penguin someday would be a thrill.
6. Scientists have worked for years to understand penguins.
7. Penguins live in Chicago's Lincoln Park Zoo.
8. Swimming in cold water, they beat the summer heat.
9. People enjoy watching penguins through underwater windows.
10. Visitors come for miles to see birds in tuxedos.

Grammar in Literature

Enriching Description

Writers often use phrases to add descriptive details, streamline sentence structures, and improve sentence fluency. In the following excerpt, the author paints a picture of a young girl's impressions as she watches a white heron. What stands out in this passage is the use of phrases to develop a mood and reveal feelings.

Springtime (1885), Lionel Percy Smythe. Private collection. Photo by Christopher Newall.

A White Heron

—Sarah Orne Jewett

The child gives a long sigh a minute later when a company of shouting catbirds comes also to the tree, and vexed by their fluttering and lawlessness, the solemn heron goes away. She knows his secret now, the wild, light, slender bird that floats and wavers, and goes back like an arrow presently to his home in the green world beneath. Then Sylvia, well satisfied, makes her perilous way down again, not daring to look far below the branch she stands on, ready to cry sometimes because her fingers ache and her lamed feet slip. Wondering over and over again what the stranger would say to her, and what he would think when she told him how to find his way straight to the heron's nest.

Participial phrases contrast the noisy catbirds with the solemn heron.

Prepositional phrases express the beauty of the heron and his home.

Well-developed **participial phrases** give specific indications of Sylvia's mixed emotions.

Using Phrases to Improve Description

Using phrases, writers can combine sentences to make their writing more fluid and concise. Each type of phrase can also help writers add specific kinds of detail.

Prepositional phrases	Use to express relationships of location, direction, time, or manner
Appositive phrases	Use to focus on the qualities of a person, place, or thing that are most important for your writing purpose
Participial phrases	Use to make your descriptions more lively and energetic by adding action words as modifiers
Gerund phrases	Use to talk about actions and activities as things
Infinitive phrases	Use to sharpen the relationship between ideas and make your writing more concise

PHRASES

PRACTICE AND APPLY: Combining Sentences

Combine each pair of sentences, turning the second one into the kind of phrase indicated in parentheses.

1. Herons preen the plumage of their prospective mates. They do this as part of their courtship ritual. (prepositional)
2. Herons feed in flocks when the food supply is limited. Herons are birds that usually prefer to be solitary. (appositive)
3. Herons learn where the good fishing spots are. They watch other fish-eaters from afar. (participial)
4. This is the normal behavior pattern for male and female herons. They build their nest as a joint project. (gerund)
5. Males and females also split responsibility for sitting on the eggs. This enables both of them to eat. (infinitive)

When you are done, compare your answers with a partner's.

Choose a draft from your **Working Portfolio** and revise it by combining sentences, using at least three kinds of phrases.

Mixed Review

A. Phrases Read the selection. Then, for each underlined group of words, identify the kind of phrase it is and how it functions in its sentence.

PROFESSIONAL MODEL

(1) Putting on a display to attract and impress a potential mate is a common behavior pattern among the males of many bird species. **(2)** Adding action to their natural gifts of brilliant plumage and melodious song, they sometimes also strut, dance, and occasionally offer **(3)** carefully selected gifts of fruit, feathers, or flowers. But the bowerbird's strategy is **(4)** to do something entirely different. He is not interested in **(5)** building a permanent nest, but wants only **(6)** to create a temporary "bower."

"Come **(7)** into my parlor," the male bowerbird seems to beckon to females that stop **(8)** to admire the mating courtyard he has constructed. "Look at my beautiful creation, **(9)** a perfect love nest, and behold all the decorations I've gathered: bright feathers, colorful straws, bottle caps, leaves, and shells." He might add that, aside from humans, no other creature in the world rivals his willingness **(10)** to go to so much trouble simply to please a mate.

B. Misplaced and Dangling Modifiers Read the following paragraph for misplaced or dangling modifiers. Then, rewrite the paragraph to correct the errors.

Of the East Indies and southeastern Asia, the common name for the so-called flying lizard is flying dragon. Using outstretched folds of skin, the flying dragon does not actually fly but glides. Its "wings" fold close to its body when resting. The males attract females by displaying their colorful "wings" during the mating season.

CHAPTER 3

Mastery Test: What Did You Learn?

Choose the letter of the term that correctly identifies each numbered part of this passage.

> Sleeping with one eye open and one-half of the brain awake (1) is an unusual ability of birds (2). This phenomenon, unihemispheric slow-wave sleep (3), allows a bird to watch for predators as it sleeps (4).
>
> Recently, researchers at Indiana State University (5) investigated this phenomenon in the laboratory (6). They showed that birds are actually able to increase their unihemispheric sleeping time (7) when there is a greater risk of predators. By studying ducks (8), they learned that birds vulnerable to predators spend more than twice the amount of time dozing in unihemispheric sleep (9) than those not in danger. Birds using unihemispheric sleep (10) can literally "keep an eye out" for their enemies.

1. A. gerund phrase
   B. infinitive phrase
   C. appositive phrase
   D. participial phrase

2. A. participial phrase
   B. gerund phrase
   C. prepositional phrase
   D. infinitive phrase

3. A. infinitive phrase
   B. appositive phrase
   C. gerund phrase
   D. prepositional phrase

4. A. adjective prepositional phrase
   B. adverb prepositional phrase
   C. essential appositive phrase
   D. infinitive phrase

5. A. adjective prepositional phrase
   B. adverb infinitive phrase
   C. adverb prepositional phrase
   D. adjective infinitive phrase

6. A. adverb infinitive phrase
   B. adjective prepositional phrase
   C. adjective infinitive phrase
   D. adverb prepositional phrase

7. A. adjective infinitive phrase
   B. adjective prepositional phrase
   C. adverb infinitive phrase
   D. adverb prepositional phrase

8. A. gerund phrase acting as subject
   B. gerund phrase acting as predicate nominative
   C. gerund phrase acting as direct object
   D. gerund phrase acting as object of a preposition

9. A. participial phrase modifying *they*
   B. gerund phrase acting as object of a preposition
   C. participial phrase modifying *time*
   D. gerund phrase acting as direct object

10. A. gerund phrase
    B. appositive phrase
    C. past participial phrase
    D. present participial phrase

Student Help Desk

Phrases at a Glance

Kind of Phrase	Functions as	Example
Prepositional phrase	Adjective	The plane **on the left** is mine.
	Adverb	Ras flew **over the mountain.**
Appositive phrase	Noun	Mr. Foy, **the pilot,** is here.
Participial phrase	Adjective	Bats **wearing hats** look funny.
Gerund phrase	Noun	**Flying a helicopter** is exciting.
Infinitive phrase	Noun	Sue loves **to fly her ultralight.**
	Adjective	Crashing is something **to avoid.**
	Adverb	Ari flies **to relax.**

Clarifying What Is Modified

Up in the Air

Misplaced Modifiers

I was looking for the keys to the car **in the kitchen.**
(WHY IS THE CAR IN THE KITCHEN? THE WORD BEING MODIFIED IS *LOOKING.*)

I was looking **in the kitchen** for the keys to the car.

Dangling Modifiers

While talking on the telephone, my flying dragon ate my cereal.
(WHO WAS TALKING ON THE TELEPHONE? *I* WAS. THIS WORD IS NOT IN THE SENTENCE.)

While I was talking on the telephone, my flying dragon ate my cereal.

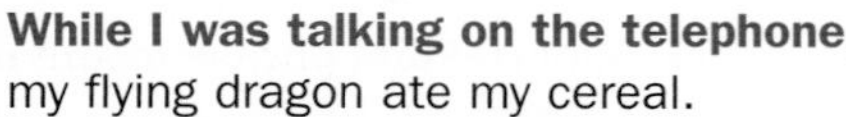

Prepositions

Getting Prepositional Phrases Off the Ground

about	as	down	off	toward
above	at	for	on	under
across	before	from	onto	underneath
after	behind	in	out	until
against	below	inside	over	up
along	beside	into	past	upon
among	between	near	through	with
around	by	of	to	without

Shoe by MacNelly

Dangling Participles

PHRASES

The Bottom Line

Checklist for Phrases

Have I . . .

____ used phrases to add details and to elaborate on my ideas?

____ used phrases to combine sentences and use fewer words?

____ used phrases to improve sentence fluency?

____ moved misplaced modifiers to make what they refer to clear?

____ added needed words to sentences with dangling modifiers?

Chapter 4

Clauses and Sentence Structure

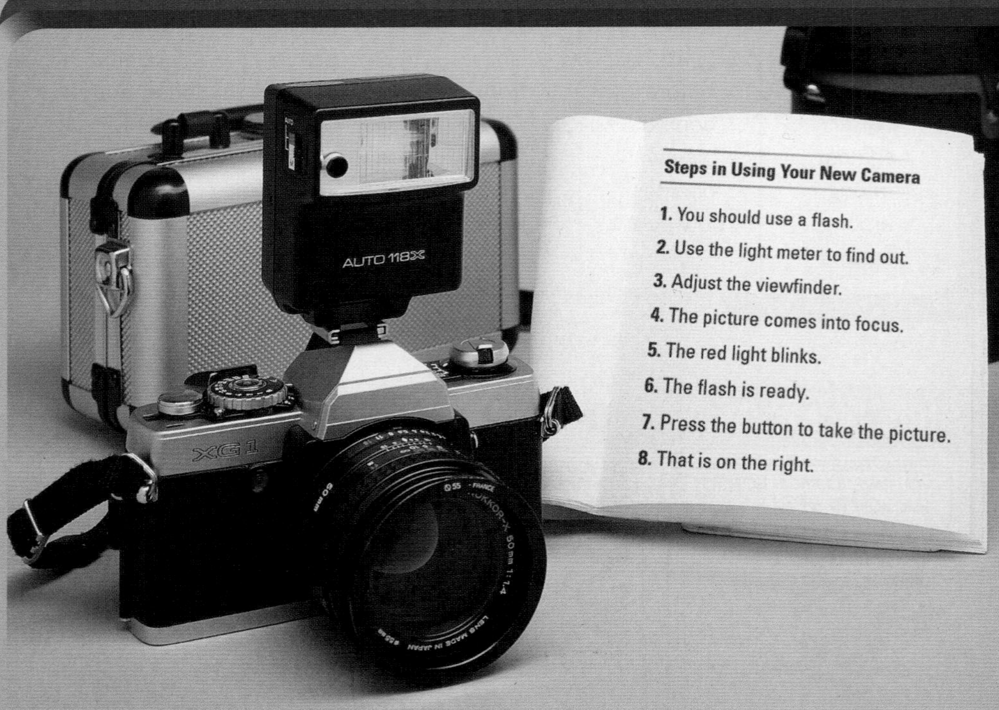

Steps in Using Your New Camera
1. You should use a flash.
2. Use the light meter to find out.
3. Adjust the viewfinder.
4. The picture comes into focus.
5. The red light blinks.
6. The flash is ready.
7. Press the button to take the picture.
8. That is on the right.
AUTO 118X
XG1

Theme: Inventions

What Am I Supposed to Do?

Have you ever tried to figure out how to do something from poorly written instructions? To improve the instructions in the illustration above, you could combine sentences to show the relationships between ideas: "Use the light meter to find out whether you should use the flash. Turn the lens until the picture comes into focus. When the red light blinks, the flash is ready. Press the button that is on the right to take the picture."

In this chapter, you will learn how to use clauses to construct sentences that show relationships between ideas clearly.

Write Away: How It Works

Write a paragraph explaining how one of your favorite inventions works. Put the explanation in your **Working Portfolio.**

Diagnostic Test: What Do You Know?

Choose the letter that correctly identifies each numbered part of this passage.

We take zippers for granted (1), but think about how much easier our lives have become since zippers were invented slightly more than 100 years ago (2). The first zipper was patented by Whitcomb L. Judson, an American inventor, in 1893. (3) Judson's zipper was called a clasp locker, and it had a series of hooks and eyes (4) that fastened together with a slider. Today's zipper also has a slider, but it fastens together rows of snugly fitting teeth. (5) These rows remain fastened until the slider is pulled back, unlocking the teeth (6). The toothed zipper that we use today (7) was invented by Gideon Sundback in 1913. The word *zipper* was not used until 1922, when a company marketed galoshes that were called Zippers (8). They were given that name because their sliding fasteners could close so quickly. (9) Judson and Sundback rarely get the credit they deserve for what they contributed to modern life (10).

1. A. independent clause
   B. subordinate clause
   C. simple sentence
   D. compound sentence

2. A. independent clause
   B. subordinate clause
   C. simple sentence
   D. compound sentence

3. A. simple sentence
   B. compound sentence
   C. complex sentence
   D. compound-complex sentence

4. A. independent clause
   B. adjective clause
   C. adverb clause
   D. noun clause

5. A. simple sentence
   B. compound sentence
   C. complex sentence
   D. compound-complex sentence

6. A. independent clause
   B. adjective clause
   C. adverb clause
   D. noun clause

7. A. adjective clause
   B. adverb clause
   C. noun clause
   D. independent clause

8. A. essential adjective clause
   B. nonessential adjective clause
   C. noun clause
   D. independent clause

9. A. simple sentence
   B. compound sentence
   C. complex sentence
   D. compound-complex sentence

10. A. noun clause as subject
    B. noun clause as direct object
    C. noun clause as indirect object
    D. noun clause as object of a preposition

Kinds of Clauses

1 Here's the Idea

▶ **A clause is a group of words that contains a subject and a verb.**

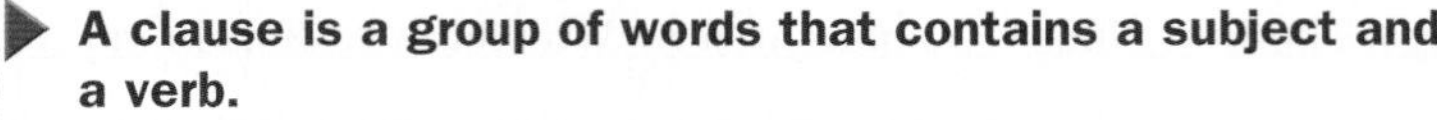

Professor Hardy is a brilliant inventor.
SUBJECT VERB

Independent Clauses

An **independent** (or **main**) **clause** expresses a complete thought and can stand alone as a sentence.

Professor Hardy is a brilliant inventor.
INDEPENDENT CLAUSE

Independent clauses can be connected by words like *and* and *but* to make sentences that express related ideas.

She is an inventor and her husband is a patent attorney.
INDEPENDENT CLAUSE INDEPENDENT CLAUSE

CHAPTER 4

Subordinate Clauses

A **subordinate** (or **dependent**) **clause** contains a subject and a verb but does not express a complete thought and cannot stand alone as a sentence. Subordinate clauses are introduced by such words as *because, that, when,* and *which* (see following pages).

Because she is imaginative
SUBORDINATE CLAUSE

By itself, a subordinate clause is a sentence fragment. For a complete thought to be expressed, a subordinate clause must be part of a sentence that contains an independent clause.

Because she is imaginative, her inventions are unusual.
SUBORDINATE CLAUSE INDEPENDENT CLAUSE

She creates gadgets that no one has ever thought of before.
INDEPENDENT CLAUSE SUBORDINATE CLAUSE

Do not confuse a subordinate clause with a verbal phrase, which does not have a subject and a verb:

She creates gadgets, inventing mostly household tools.

For more on verbals, see pp. 71–76.

You can add important details to your writing through the use of subordinate clauses. In the cartoon below, Snoopy tries to improve on his usual beginning for a story—"It was a dark and stormy night"—by adding a subordinate clause. How well do you think he succeeds?

Peanuts by Charles Schulz

CLAUSES

❷ Why It Matters in Writing

Recognizing independent and subordinate clauses will help you avoid one of the most common kinds of sentence fragments: a subordinate clause accidentally written as a sentence.

STUDENT MODEL

DRAFT

The synthetic fiber nylon generated great excitement. When it was introduced in 1939. Women soon came to prefer nylon stockings. Because they were much more durable than silk stockings. FRAGMENTS

REVISION

When it was introduced in 1939, the synthetic fiber nylon generated great excitement. Women soon came to prefer nylon stockings because they were much more durable than silk stockings.

3 Practice and Apply

A. CONCEPT CHECK: Kinds of Clauses

Write the subordinate clause in each sentence below. If there is no subordinate clause, write *None.*

Good Car, Bad Car

1. Some useful inventions have caused serious problems.
2. A good example is the automobile, which became popular in the early 1900s.
3. The automobile is now one of our most important means of transportation, but it also causes much of our air pollution.
4. Some people who worry about our environment believe in restricting the use of cars.
5. They think that people should not be able to drive cars in certain places.
6. Others want to solve the problem by creating new inventions.
7. When we have better engines and fuels, they think, the problem will disappear.
8. Human beings, who are inventors by nature, will continue to create new inventions.
9. We should anticipate the effects that inventions can have.
10. If we do, perhaps future generations will not be endangered.

➔ **For a SELF-CHECK and more practice, see the EXERCISE BANK, p. 316.**

Write original sentences that imitate the clause structure of the first five sentences in exercise A.

B. REVISING: Eliminating Fragments

Rewrite the paragraph below, combining the fragments with complete sentences.

STUDENT MODEL

It's a Good Thing

The emission control system is one invention. That has reduced air pollution from automobile exhausts. The system helps to eliminate harmful gases. Which can escape into the air and affect its quality. In many states, cars are inspected. If a car does not pass a series of tests that measure its emissions. It must be repaired and retested.

Adjective and Adverb Clauses

1 Here's the Idea

Subordinate clauses can be adjective, adverb, or noun clauses.

Adjective Clauses

▶ **An adjective clause is a subordinate clause that is used as an adjective to modify a noun or a pronoun.**

MODIFIES NOUN

Willy Higinbotham is the scientist who invented the first computer game.
ADJECTIVE CLAUSE

MODIFIES PRONOUN

It was he who developed computer tennis.
ADJECTIVE CLAUSE

An adjective clause is introduced by a **relative pronoun** or by a **relative adverb.** These words are called relative because they relate adjective clauses to the words they modify.

Words Used to Introduce Adjective Clauses	
Relative pronouns	that, who, whom, whose, which
Relative adverbs	where, when, why

Have you seen the computer that Higinbotham used?

Have you seen the desk where Higinbotham sat?

Essential and Nonessential Adjective Clauses

An **essential** (or **restrictive**) adjective clause provides information that is necessary to identify the preceding noun or pronoun.

Tourists can visit the laboratory that employed Higinbotham.

A **nonessential** (or **nonrestrictive**) adjective clause adds additional information about a noun or pronoun whose meaning is already clear. Notice that nonessential clauses are set off with commas.

Brookhaven National Laboratory, which employed Higinbotham, is in Upton, New York.

That or *which?* Use *that* to introduce essential clauses. Use *which* to introduce nonessential clauses.

CLAUSES

Adverb Clauses

An adverb clause is a subordinate clause that modifies a verb, an adjective, or an adverb.

MODIFIES VERB

Charles Babbage paved the way for the computer when he devised his "analytical engine."

MODIFIES ADJECTIVE

Babbage's invention was important because it proved machines' ability to perform mathematical operations.

Computers can solve complicated math problems faster than people can.

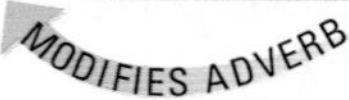

Words Used to Introduce Adverb Clauses	
Subordinating conjunctions	when, because, than, where, after, before, although

For a more complete list of subordinating conjunctions, see p. 27.

CHAPTER 4

2 Why It Matters in Writing

Adjective and adverb clauses can supply details necessary to explain, support, and connect your ideas.

STUDENT MODEL

DRAFT

The first microwave ovens were too big for homes. These ovens weighed 750 pounds and stood five and a half feet tall. Moreover, they had to be attached to a source of water. These huge ovens cost more than most people could afford.

REVISION

When the first microwave ovens were introduced in 1953, they were too big for homes. These ovens weighed 750 pounds and stood five and a half feet tall. Moreover, they had to be attached to a source of water **because they overheated very easily.** These huge ovens, **which cost $3,000,** were too expensive for most people.

Provides a specific time frame

Explains why they needed water

Supports the claim that the ovens were too expensive

❸ Practice and Apply

A. CONCEPT CHECK: Adjective and Adverb Clauses

Write the adjective or adverb clauses in the following sentences. After each clause, write the word or words that it modifies.

The Big Jump

1. Long before the Wright brothers flew the first airplane, the French inventor J. P. Blanchard was testing parachutes.
2. Sébastien Lenormand, who was a French physicist, made the first successful parachute jump from a tower in 1783.
3. With parachutes, early aviators could descend from balloons that stayed in the air.
4. Since the airplane was invented, parachutes have been used for emergency jumps from aircraft.
5. They can also deliver cargo, such as food and medicine, to places where land travel is difficult.
6. Parachutes work because air resistance slows them down.
7. They have large surfaces that trap a lot of air.
8. Because parachutists descend fairly rapidly, they sometimes injure themselves upon landing.
9. This is particularly true when jumpers land on rough ground.
10. Although parachuting is risky, many people love it.

➜ **For a SELF-CHECK and more practice, see the EXERCISE BANK, p. 316.**

B. REVISING: Adding Details

Combine each pair of sentences by changing one into an adjective or adverb clause. Use appropriate introductory words.

Example: Balloons are hard to steer. *Balloons do not have rudders.*
Answer: Balloons, which do not have rudders, are hard to steer.

Would You Like to Fly?

1. Jacques and Joseph Montgolfier invented the hot-air balloon. Jacques and Joseph were brothers.
2. The balloon was filled with hot air produced by burning wool and straw. The balloon was made of linen.
3. One of their balloons floated for more than five miles over the city of Paris. The balloon landed safely.
4. The airship developed from the hot-air balloon. The airship was kept aloft by hot air or gas.
5. The airship was easier to handle. The airship had propellers.

LESSON 3

Noun Clauses

1 Here's the Idea

▶ **A noun clause is a subordinate clause used as a noun.**

Like a noun, a noun clause can function in a sentence as a subject, a complement (direct object, indirect object, or predicate nominative), or an object of a preposition.

What you accomplish is up to you.
SUBJECT

You know that you hold the key.
DIRECT OBJECT

Give whatever is most worthy your best effort.
INDIRECT OBJECT

Then you will be who you were meant to be.
PREDICATE NOMINATIVE

Think about how you can reach your goals.
OBJECT OF A PREPOSITION

If you can substitute the word *someone* or *something* for a clause in a sentence, the clause is a noun clause.

A noun clause may be introduced by a **subordinating conjunction** or by a **pronoun.** A pronoun that introduces a noun clause does not have an antecedent in the sentence.

Words Used to Introduce Noun Clauses	
Subordinating conjunctions	that, how, when, where, whether, why
Pronouns	what, whatever, who, whom, whoever, whomever, which, whichever

That an inventor's life is hard is obvious.

What inventors must do to succeed is astounding.

The introductory word in a noun clause is sometimes omitted:

The owner's manual states (that) the time machine is guaranteed to work.

❷ Why It Matters in Writing

Noun clauses give you a way of referring to things that can't be named in one word but can be identified by what they're doing.

PROFESSIONAL MODEL

Whoever bought the professor's inventions soon regretted the mistake. The machines did whatever they felt like doing instead of what they were supposed to do.

SUBJECT
DIRECT OBJECT
OBJECT OF PREPOSITION

❸ Practice and Apply

CLAUSES

A. CONCEPT CHECK: Noun Clauses

Write the noun clause in each sentence. Then indicate whether the clause functions as a subject, a direct object, an indirect object, a predicate nominative, or an object of a preposition.

Making a Spectacle

1. We do not know who invented the first eyeglasses, but glasses are mentioned in books written in the 1200s.
2. However, early spectacles probably offered whoever wore them little help.
3. In the 1700s, lenses were ground according to what was known about the science of light.
4. What kinds of lenses people need depends on the defects in their eyes.
5. A concave lens is what a nearsighted eye needs.
6. Whoever has a farsighted eye needs a convex lens.
7. Some people's lens needs depend on whether they are looking at close objects or distant ones.
8. This is why Ben Franklin invented the bifocal lens.
9. Bifocal lenses provide people with whichever kind of correction they need at a particular time.
10. Only an eye doctor can tell a person what kinds of lenses he or she needs.

➜ **For a SELF-CHECK and more practice, see the EXERCISE BANK, p. 317.**

B. WRITING: Using Noun Clauses

Use each of the noun clauses below in a complete sentence to make a paragraph describing the theft of a hovercraft. Give the noun clause the function indicated in parentheses.

What I Need Is Help!

1. whoever took my hovercraft (subject)
2. what that person was thinking (direct object of *know*)
3. whoever saw what happened (indirect object of *give*)
4. which way the culprit went (direct object of *saw*)
5. where my hovercraft is now (object of preposition *to*)
6. what I would like to happen (predicate nominative)
7. that this is frustrating (subject)
8. how to get my hovercraft back (object of preposition *of*)
9. whoever finds it (direct object of *reward*)
10. how I plan to deal with the situation (predicate nominative)

CHAPTER 4

C. WRITING: Explaining What It Does

Write a paragraph describing how someone might use the robotic underwater camera pictured at the right to explore the ocean floor or to investigate a sunken wreck. Use at least three noun clauses.

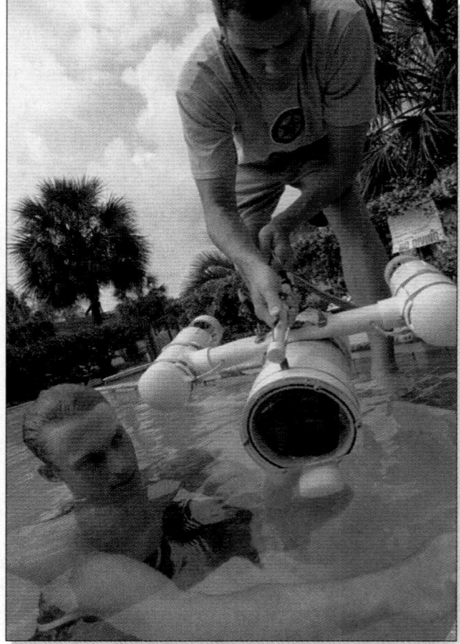

A robotic underwater camera designed and built as a part of a mechanical engineering class at the University of Florida.

LESSON 4 Sentence Structure

1 Here's the Idea

A sentence's structure is determined by the number and kind of clauses it contains.

▶ **The structure of a sentence may be simple, compound, complex, or compound-complex.**

Simple Sentences

A **simple sentence** consists of one independent clause and no subordinate clauses.

Two friends invented the first trivia game.

A simple sentence may have a compound subject or verb.

Chris Haney and Scott Abbott created and marketed it.
COMPOUND SUBJECT — COMPOUND VERB

For more on compound sentence parts, see pp. 42–43.

Compound Sentences

In a **compound sentence** two or more independent clauses are joined together.

INDEPENDENT CLAUSE
[Bette Nesmith typed on an electric typewriter,] and [she often made mistakes.]
INDEPENDENT CLAUSE

Independent clauses can be joined by a comma and a coordinating conjunction, a semicolon, or a semicolon with a conjunctive adverb and a comma.

She could have erased them, but that took a lot of time.

Nesmith did not erase her errors; she covered them with a mixture of water and white paint.

Nesmith was not happy with the name "paper correction fluid"; consequently, she gave the mixture a catchy brand name.

For more on conjunctions and conjunctive adverbs, see pp. 26–27.

Avoid using commas to join independent clauses that should be separate sentences. For more on "comma splices," see page 120.

CLAUSES

Complex Sentences

A **complex sentence** contains one independent clause and one or more subordinate clauses.

SUBORDINATE CLAUSE

If cockleburs had not clung to his jacket, George de Mestral might never have invented Velcro. INDEPENDENT CLAUSE

INDEPENDENT CLAUSE

He was curious to know the reason why they clung so tightly.

SUBORDINATE CLAUSE

Compound-Complex Sentences

A **compound-complex sentence** contains two or more independent clauses and one or more subordinate clauses.

SUBORDINATE CLAUSE INDEPENDENT CLAUSE

When de Mestral studied the burs, he saw tiny hooks on their surfaces becoming entangled in loops of fiber, and this observation inspired him to invent the hook-and-loop fastener.

INDEPENDENT CLAUSE

SUBORDINATE CLAUSE INDEPENDENT CLAUSE

While another might have been annoyed, he was intrigued, and he thought of a use to which the phenomenon could be put.

INDEPENDENT CLAUSE SUBORDINATE CLAUSE

2 Why It Matters in Writing

By using compound sentences to connect main ideas and complex sentences to add subordinate ideas, you can express complicated thoughts clearly and achieve sentence variety.

STUDENT MODEL

Kurt Vonnegut's story "Harrison Bergeron" is about a futuristic society in which people are forced to be equal. In this society, no one is allowed to be bright, and no one is allowed to be talented. These qualities are forbidden because they threaten the equality policy of those who are in power. However, one person—Harrison Bergeron—demands that his uniqueness be acknowledged.

SUBORDINATE IDEAS

CONNECTED MAIN IDEAS

❸ Practice and Apply

A. CONCEPT CHECK: Sentence Structure

Identify each sentence as simple, compound, complex, or compound-complex.

Bubble Gum

1. Some inventions are created by accident.
2. Walter E. Diemer worked for a chewing-gum company.
3. He was an accountant, but he wanted to improve the company's gum.
4. He did experiments because he wanted chewier gum.
5. He didn't succeed, but he did come up with something that became a successful product.
6. He produced a mixture that could be blown into bubbles.
7. This mixture was the first bubble gum.
8. Diemer had pink food coloring, which he added to the gum.
9. The gum was fun to chew, and the color made it attractive.
10. If Walter Diemer had not experimented, he would not have discovered bubble gum, and we might not have it today.

➜ **For a SELF-CHECK and more practice, see the EXERCISE BANK, p. 318.**

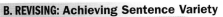

CHALLENGE Combine sentences 6 and 7 into a compound-complex sentence.

B. REVISING: Achieving Sentence Variety

Rewrite this paragraph by following the directions below it.

Chewing Through the Ages

(1) Chewing gum has a long history. **(2)** The ancient Greeks chewed hardened sap. **(3)** It came from the mastic tree. **(4)** Over 1,000 years ago the Maya of Mexico chewed chicle. **(5)** Native Americans later taught European settlers to chew gum. **(6)** During the 1850s people chewed paraffin wax. **(7)** It wasn't as good as gum. **(8)** It crumbled or stuck to the teeth. **(9)** Modern chewing gum was originally made with sugar. **(10)** In the mid-1900s companies began making sugarless gum.

1. Combine sentences 2 and 3 to form a complex sentence.
2. Combine 4 and 5 to form a compound sentence.
3. Combine 6, 7, and 8 to form a compound-complex sentence.
4. Combine 9 and 10 to form a compound sentence.

In your **Working Portfolio,** find the paragraph you wrote for the **Write Away** on page 90. Use clauses to combine sentences and vary the sentence structure of your paragraph.

Sentence Diagramming

Here's the Idea

Diagramming can help you understand sentence structures by showing how the clauses in sentences are related.

Watch me for diagramming tips!

Simple Sentences

Simple sentences are diagrammed on one horizontal line, with a vertical line separating subject and predicate. The horizontal line may be split on either side to show a compound subject or a compound verb.

Orville Wright and Wilbur Wright tossed a coin.

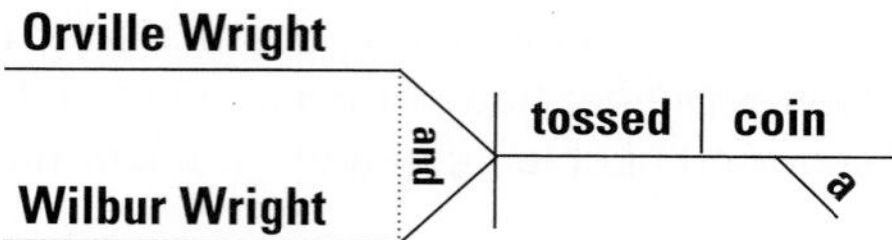

Remember that sentences with compound subjects and verbs are still simple sentences. To refresh your memory about diagramming simple sentences, see pages 54–57.

CHAPTER 4

Compound Sentences

- Diagram the independent clauses on parallel horizontal lines.
- Connect the verbs in the two clauses by a broken line with a step.

Orville won and Wilbur lost.

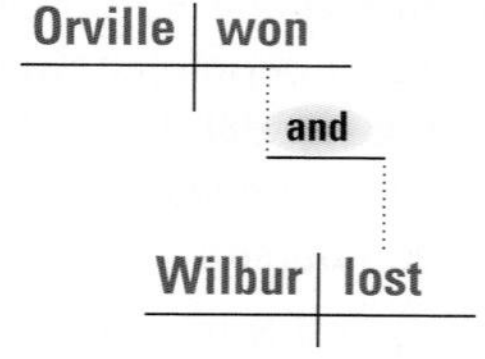

The conjunction goes on the step.

A. CONCEPT CHECK: Compound Sentences

Diagram these sentences, using what you have learned.

1. Orville piloted the plane, and Wilbur stayed on the ground.
2. Orville flew first, but Wilbur flew longer.

Complex Sentences

Adjective and Adverb Clauses

- Diagram the subordinate clause on its own horizontal line below the main line, as if it were a sentence.
- Use a dotted line to connect the word introducing the clause to the word it modifies.

Adjective Clause Introduced by a Relative Pronoun

The brothers, who did not like school, never graduated.

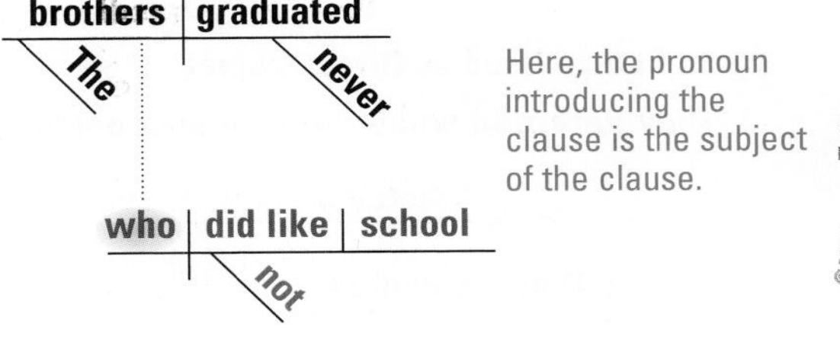

Here, the pronoun introducing the clause is the subject of the clause.

Adjective Clause Introduced by a Relative Adverb

The schools where they were enrolled frustrated them.

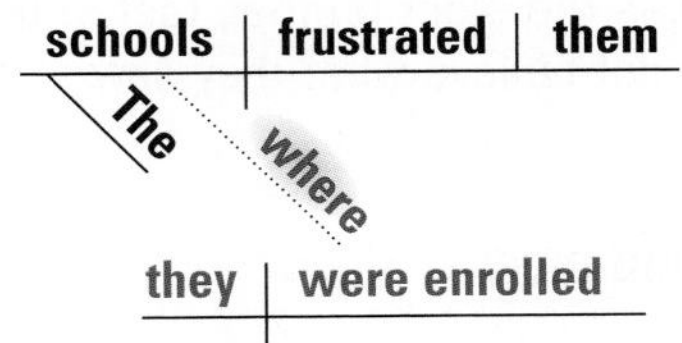

The adverb introducing the clause goes on the broken line.

Adverb Clause

After Orville started a printing business, they launched a newspaper.

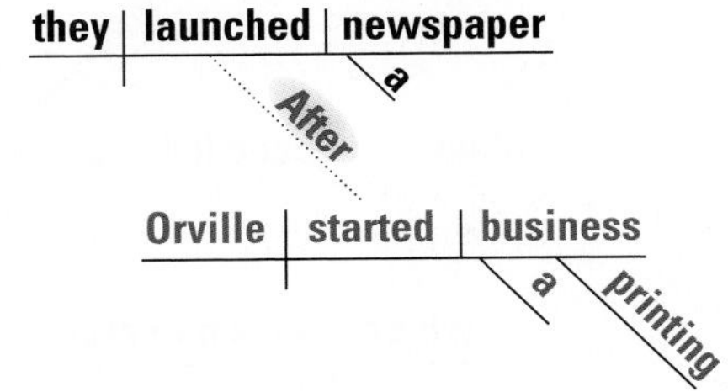

The conjunction goes on the dotted line, which connects the verbs in the two clauses.

Noun Clauses Diagram the subordinate clause on a separate line that is attached to the main line with a forked line. Place the forked line in the diagram according to the role of the noun clause in the sentence. Diagram the word introducing the noun clause according to its function in the clause.

Noun Clause Used as Subject

What they designed was a glider.

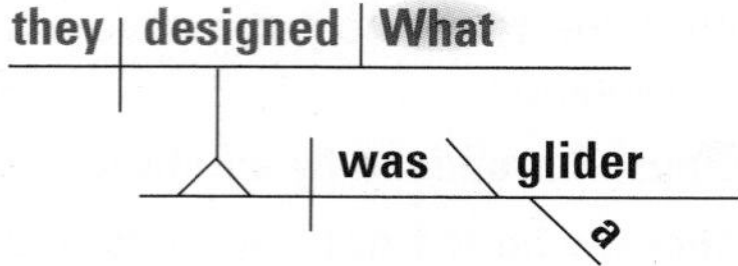

Here, the pronoun introducing the clause functions as a direct object in the clause.

Noun Clause Used as Direct Object

They patented whatever was successful.

Here, the pronoun introducing the clause functions as the clause's subject.

B. CONCEPT CHECK: Complex Sentences

Diagram these sentences, using what you have learned.

1. Wilbur, who was the older brother, tested the glider.
2. People could not believe what they saw.

Compound-Complex Sentences

Diagram the independent clauses first. Attach each subordinate clause to the word it modifies.

They designed next a motorized airplane, and the plane, which was powered by gasoline, succeeded.

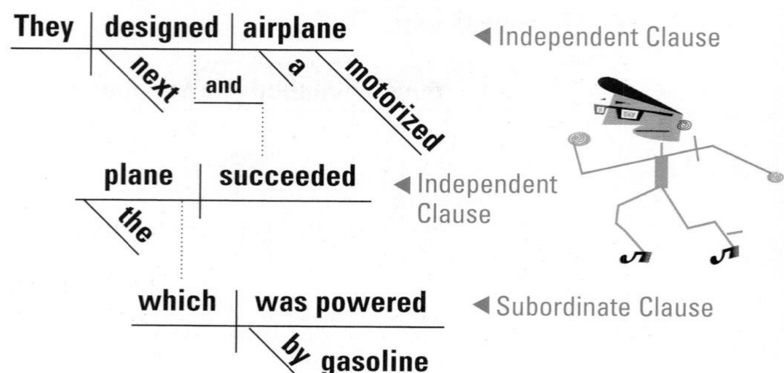

They conducted their first successful flight at Kitty Hawk, and residents are proud of what their town contributed to the history of flight.

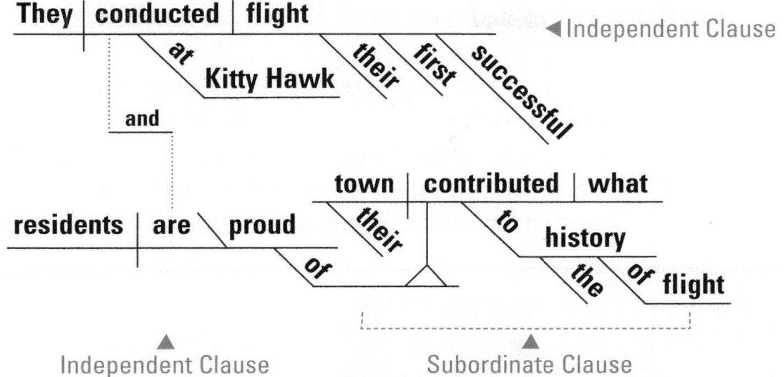

C. CONCEPT CHECK: Compound-Complex Sentences

Diagram these sentences, using what you have learned.

1. Orville flew a plane that crashed, and he was injured.
2. Orville, who was injured, recovered, but his passenger died.

CLAUSES

D. MIXED REVIEW: Diagramming

Diagram the following sentences. Look for all types of clauses.

1. The brothers earned money but had problems.
2. Wilbur died and Orville worked alone.
3. Every airplane that flies uses their ideas.
4. After Orville retired, he won many awards.
5. Whoever flies can thank the Wrights.
6. After they invented the airplane, travel became easier and the world became smaller.
7. Their first plane is on view, and it impresses whoever sees it.

Frank and Ernest by Thaves

Grammar in Literature

Sentence Structure and Dramatic Writing

In writing the passage below, Ray Bradbury had a tough job. He wanted to describe a scene with no people but much human drama—a "smart" house whose owners have died in a nuclear holocaust. Using a variety of sentence structures, Bradbury created a mood of hysteria, desperation, and finally resignation.

Yellow Vase (1990), Roy Lichtenstein. Copyright © 1990 Estate of Roy Lichtenstein/Gemini G.E.I.

There Will Come Soft Rains

Ray Bradbury

At ten o'clock the house began to die.

The wind blew. A falling tree bough crashed through the kitchen window. Cleaning solvent, bottled, shattered over the stove. The room was ablaze in an instant!

"Fire!" screamed a voice. The house lights flashed, water pumps shot water from the ceilings. But the solvent spread on the linoleum, licking, eating, under the kitchen door, while the voices took it up in chorus: "Fire, fire, fire!"

The house tried to save itself. Doors sprang tightly shut, but the windows were broken by the heat and the wind blew and sucked upon the fire.

The house gave ground as the fire in ten billion angry sparks moved with flaming ease from room to room and then up the stairs. While scurrying water rats squeaked from the walls, pistoled their water, and ran for more. And the wall sprays let down showers of mechanical rain.

But too late. Somewhere, sighing, a pump shrugged to a stop. The quenching rain ceased. The reserve water supply which had filled baths and washed dishes for many quiet days was gone.

Short **simple sentences** list chance events leading to the disaster.

A **complex sentence** shows the house reacting to the spread of the fire.

A **compound sentence** ties an action of the house to opposing actions of heat and wind.

An **adverb clause** shows the power and speed of the fire.

A return to short **simple sentences** slows the pace.

Revising to Vary Sentence Structure

Good writers do not plan their sentence structures in advance. As they compose and revise, they use structures that feel right for particular purposes—structures that have the right tones and rhythms. Every sentence structure is based on one of three ways of arranging clauses.

Letting an independent clause stand alone	Focuses attention on a single idea. In a series, can create a choppy rhythm.
Combining independent clauses	Connects ideas of equal importance. Can create a smooth and balanced flow.
Adding subordinate clauses	Adds a layer of supporting ideas. Can help create momentum and complexity.

CLAUSES

PRACTICE AND APPLY: Revising Sentence Structure

The paragraph below consists entirely of simple sentences. To improve its clarity and style, try rewriting it, varying the sentence structures. Follow the directions below, or think of your own way of revising the paragraph.

(1) The principal flipped a switch. **(2)** The "smart" classroom began to operate. **(3)** The students looked around for the teacher. **(4)** The teacher was not there. **(5)** A friendly face appeared in a screen. **(6)** The screen was mounted on the wall. **(7)** The desks automatically gave the students an electric jolt. **(8)** They didn't pay attention. **(9)** Some students talked. **(10)** They were ejected from their seats into the hallway.

1. Combine sentences 1 and 2 to form a compound sentence.
2. Combine 3 and 4 to form a compound sentence.
3. Combine 5 and 6 by making sentence 6 an adjective clause.
4. Combine 7 and 8 by making 8 an adverb clause.
5. Combine 9 and 10 by making 9 a noun clause (using *whoever*).

After you have revised the paragraph, read both versions aloud with a partner and discuss how you think your changes have improved it.

Choose a draft from your **Working Portfolio** and revise it by combining sentences in at least three of the ways suggested above.

Mixed Review

Clauses and Sentence Structure Read the passage. Then write the answers to the questions that follow.

LITERARY MODEL

(1) For a refugee who had never seen a motorized vehicle or indoor plumbing until he was 9, this was an unimaginable honor. **(2)** When the Worcester paper ran a picture of me standing next to President Kennedy, my father rushed out to buy a new suit in order to be properly dressed to receive the congratulations of the Worcester Greeks. **(3)** He clipped out the photograph, had it laminated in plastic and carried it in his breast pocket for the rest of his life to show everyone he met. **(4)** I found the much-worn photo in his pocket on the day he died 20 years later.

(5) In our isolated Greek village, my mother had bribed a cousin to teach her to read, for girls were not supposed to attend school beyond a certain age. **(6)** She had always dreamed of her children receiving an education. **(7)** She couldn't be there when I graduated from Boston University, but the person who came with my father and shared our joy was my former teacher, Marjorie Hurd. **(8)** We celebrated not only my bachelor's degree but also the scholarships that paid my way to Columbia's Graduate School of Journalism. **(9)** There, I met the woman who would eventually become my wife. **(10)** At our wedding and at the baptisms of our three children, Marjorie Hurd was always there, dancing alongside the Greeks.

—Nicholas Gage, "The Teacher Who Changed My Life"

1. What kind of clause is the first subordinate clause in sentence 1?
2. What kind of clause is the second subordinate clause in sentence 1?
3. What words are modified by the clauses referred to in questions 1 and 2?
4. What kind of subordinate clause is in sentence 2?
5. What is the independent clause in sentence 2?
6. Is sentence 2 complex or compound-complex?
7. Is sentence 3 simple, compound, or complex?
8. What is the adjective clause with *that* left out in sentence 4?
9. Is sentence 5 simple, compound, or complex?
10. Is sentence 6 simple, compound, or complex?
11. Is sentence 7 compound, complex, or compound-complex?
12. Is sentence 8 simple, compound, or complex?
13. What is the subordinate clause in sentence 9?
14. Is sentence 10 simple, compound, or complex?
15. How many essential adjective clauses are there in the last four sentences?

CHAPTER 4

Mastery Test: What Did You Learn?

Choose the letter that correctly identifies each numbered part of the passage.

<u>Inventions differ from discoveries</u> (1), <u>although the two are closely related</u> (2). A discovery occurs <u>when something in nature is first observed or recognized</u> (3). An invention is the creation of something <u>that never existed before</u> (4). <u>For example, humans discovered fire, but they invented the match to start a fire.</u> (5)

Before the 1900s <u>whatever was invented</u> (6) was made mainly by people <u>who worked alone</u> (7). <u>Many were artisans or mechanics, and they had little education.</u> (8) <u>Today, most inventors are engineers and scientists who work for large companies, and their inventions belong to the companies.</u> (9) We can thank inventors for <u>what they have done to improve our lives</u> (10).

1. A. simple sentence
   B. independent clause
   C. subordinate clause
   D. compound sentence

2. A. simple sentence
   B. independent clause
   C. subordinate clause
   D. compound sentence

3. A. essential adjective clause
   B. nonessential adjective clause
   C. adverb clause
   D. noun clause

4. A. essential adjective clause
   B. nonessential adjective clause
   C. adverb clause
   D. noun clause

5. A. simple sentence
   B. compound sentence
   C. complex sentence
   D. compound-complex sentence

6. A. noun clause as subject
   B. noun clause as direct object
   C. noun clause as indirect object
   D. noun clause as object of a preposition

7. A. nonessential adjective clause
   B. essential adjective clause
   C. adverb clause
   D. noun clause

8. A. simple sentence
   B. compound sentence
   C. complex sentence
   D. compound-complex sentence

9. A. compound-complex sentence with two subordinate clauses
   B. complex sentence with two subordinate clauses
   C. compound sentence with two independent clauses
   D. compound-complex sentence with two independent clauses and a subordinate clause

10. A. noun clause as subject
    B. noun clause as direct object
    C. noun clause as indirect object
    D. noun clause as object of a preposition

Student Help Desk

Sentence Structure at a Glance

A clause is a group of words that contains a subject and a verb. A clause may be either independent or subordinate. An independent clause may be a simple sentence, or it may be combined with one or more other clauses.

independent clause = **simple sentence**

independent clause + **independent clause** = **compound sentence**

independent clause + **subordinate clause** = **complex sentence**

independent clause + **independent clause** + **subordinate clause** = **compound-complex sentence**

Punctuating Clauses

Hinges and Bolts

Use a Comma	Example
• when joining independent clauses with a coordinating conjunction	I may be young, but I have great ambitions.
• after a subordinate clause that begins a sentence	After I discover a cure for the common cold, I'll receive the Nobel Prize.
• to set off a nonessential adjective clause	My acceptance speech, which will last for hours, will be brilliant.
Use a Semicolon	
• to join independent clauses without a conjunction	It won't be a good speech; it will be a great speech.
Use a Semicolon and a Comma	
• to join independent clauses with a conjunctive adverb	Everyone will adore me; moreover, I will deserve it.

Sentence Structure Pieces and Parts

Kind of Sentence	Structure	Example
Simple sentence	One independent clause	The pilot waves her hat.
Compound sentence	Two or more independent clauses	The pilot waves her hat and the crowd cheers.
Complex sentence	One independent clause and at least one subordinate clause	As she disappears over a hill, the crowd grows quiet.
Compound-complex sentence	Two or more independent clauses and at least one subordinate clause	After an hour passes, the plane reappears, and the crowd rushes to greet it.

CLAUSES

Subordinate Clauses Supporting Structures

Kind of Clause	Function	Example
Adjective clause	Modifies a noun or pronoun	The airplane, **which ran entirely on human power,** took off.
Adverb clause	Modifies a verb, adjective, or adverb	It stayed in the air **as long as the pilot worked its pedals.**
Noun clause	Acts as a subject, complement, or object of a preposition	**Whether she would crash** was the main thing on her mind.

The Bottom Line

Checklist for Clauses and Sentence Structure

Have I . . .

____ made sure that every sentence contains at least one independent clause?

____ put supporting ideas into subordinate clauses?

____ combined some simple sentences to show relationships between ideas?

____ varied sentence structure?

Writing Complete Sentences

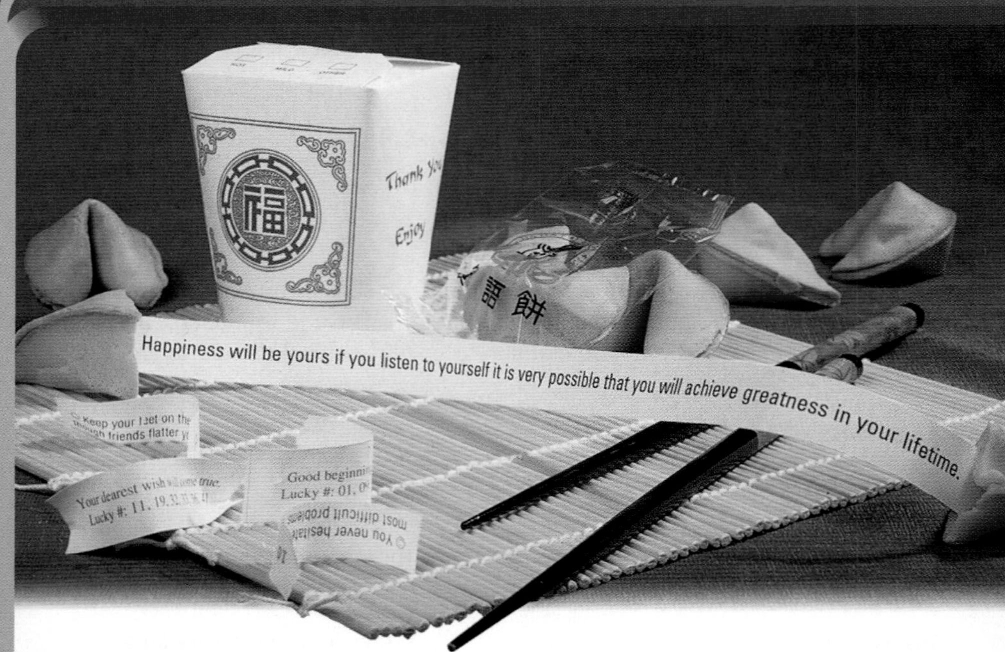

Thank You
Enjoy
Happiness will be yours if you listen to yourself it is very possible that you will achieve greatness in your lifetime.

Theme: Teenagers and Jobs

On the Job

Congratulations! You've just landed a job as a fortune editor at a fortune-cookie factory. Your main responsibility is to make sure that each fortune makes sense and is a complete sentence. As an editor, how would you change the fortune shown above so that it makes sense and fits in the cookie?

If the sentences in your paragraphs are missing punctuation or if they include punctuation in the wrong places, your ideas will run together or be cut short. Be sure to present your ideas in complete sentences so that your readers will understand them.

Write Away: Dream Job

What job would be just perfect for you? Write a paragraph about your dream job. Don't worry if it isn't realistic. Save your paragraph in your **Working Portfolio.**

Diagnostic Test: What Do You Know?

Choose the best way to rewrite each underlined word group.

By getting a summer job. You can earn money to spend or save. (1) You can also gain valuable work experience and even have fun. Although a job may sound boring. (2) It might even give you ideas about future careers.

You may be asking yourself, Where should I begin looking for a job? Make lists of your talents, skills, and interests. Before you begin your search. (3) A list will help you identify the kinds of jobs you might enjoy. To learn about available jobs, skim the want ads. (4) Also look for Help Wanted signs in shops and businesses. A veterinarian may need an assistant, a café may need a counterperson. (5) You might even apply for work at places that haven't advertised for help if they interest you.

1. A. By getting a summer job, you can earn money. To spend or save.
   B. By getting a summer job, and you can earn money to spend or save.
   C. By getting a summer job, you can earn money to spend or save.
   D. Correct as is

2. A. Although a job may sound boring but may turn out to be interesting.
   B. Although a job may sound boring, it could turn out to be interesting and challenging.
   C. Although a job may sound boring, however it may not be.
   D. Correct as is

3. A. Making lists of your talents, skills, and interests before you begin your search.
   B. Make lists of your talents, skills, and interests before begin to search.
   C. Make lists of your talents, skills, and interests before you begin your search.
   D. Correct as is

4. A. To learn about available jobs. Skim the want ads.
   B. To learn about available jobs; skim the want ads.
   C. Skim the want ads. To learn about available jobs.
   D. Correct as is

5. A. A veterinarian may need an assistant, or a café may need a counterperson.
   B. A veterinarian may need an assistant a café may need a counterperson.
   C. A veterinarian may need an assistant, a café may need a counterperson or a short-order cook.
   D. Correct as is

SENTENCES

Sentence Fragments

Here's the Idea

A sentence fragment is a part of a sentence that is punctuated as if it were a complete sentence.

To figure out whether a word group is a fragment, ask the following questions. If the answer to any of the questions is no, the word group is a sentence fragment.

- Does the word group have a subject?
- Does it have a verb?
- Does it express a complete thought?

The first word group below is a fragment because it doesn't have a subject or express a complete thought.

Fragment: Hired a student to work in the office.

Sentence: The principal hired a student to work in the office.

CHAPTER 5

Subordinate Clauses as Fragments

A subordinate (dependent) clause contains a subject and a verb. By itself, however, a subordinate clause is a fragment because it does not express a complete thought.

More and more students have found technology-related jobs. Although traditional after-school jobs are still popular.

SUBORDINATE–CLAUSE FRAGMENT

Here's How Fixing Subordinate-Clause Fragments

Here are two ways to fix a subordinate-clause fragment.

- Combine the subordinate clause with the preceding or following sentence.

More and more students have found technology-related jobs, although traditional after-school jobs are still popular.

- Write the missing part of the sentence.

Although traditional after-school jobs are still popular, *computers have created new job opportunities for teens.*

Sometimes you can correct a subordinate-clause fragment by simply deleting the subordinating conjunction.

~~When~~ **we interviewed a group of students about their jobs.**

Phrases as Fragments

A phrase is a group of words that functions as a part of speech, such as an adjective or a noun. A phrase by itself is a sentence fragment because it does not have a subject or a verb and does not express a complete thought. The paragraph below shows three kinds of phrase fragments.

STUDENT MODEL

Some students enjoy working for others. However, there are plenty of opportunities for students. To create their own jobs. Maybe you are an outgoing person. With good computer skills. You could teach less-experienced people how to use computers or the Internet. If you like kids, you might want to be a baby sitter. Get experience first by volunteering. At a daycare center. Having worked with children.

INFINITIVE PHRASE

PREPOSITIONAL PHRASES

PARTICIPIAL PHRASE

SENTENCES

You can correct a phrase fragment by combining it with the sentence before or after it or by writing the missing subject or verb.

HELP WANTED

Fixing Phrase Fragments

Type of Phrase	Correction
Infinitive phrase	However, there are plenty of opportunities for students, ~~T~~to create their own jobs.
Prepositional phrase	Maybe you are an outgoing person, ~~W~~with good computer skills. Get experience first by volunteering, ~~A~~at a daycare center.
Participial phrase	Having worked with children, *you will have an advantage over less-experienced sitters.*

Other Kinds of Fragments

Compound Predicate

Sometimes a fragment occurs when a writer inserts end punctuation between the parts of a compound predicate. Fix this fragment by combining it with the sentence before it.

Fragment: Nicole works at the cash register. **And waits tables.**

Sentence: Nicole works at the cash register **and waits tables.**

Items in a Series

A series of words or phrases cannot stand alone as a sentence. Combine the series with the sentence to which it belongs.

Fragment: Martin has three main responsibilities at the restaurant. **Clearing tables, setting tables, and filling water glasses.**

Sentence: Martin has three main responsibilities at the restaurant: **clearing tables, setting tables, and filling water glasses.**

Because sentence fragments occur naturally in conversation, writers use fragments to make dialogue more realistic.

LITERARY MODEL

"I may have a job, Ma," she said.

"That's nice," Mrs. Wilson said. **"Baby-sitting?"**

"On the stage," Elise said.

—John Cheever, "The Opportunity"

2 Why It Matters in Writing

You may write fragments when you take notes. If you use your notes to write a formal letter or a report, however, you should turn the fragments into complete sentences.

job notes
photographer's assistant
must have office experience
knowledge of equipment

. . . I am applying for the job of photographer's assistant. I was an office assistant at my mother's travel agency last summer, and I have experience using photo equipment . . .

❸ Practice and Apply

A. CONCEPT CHECK: Sentence Fragments

Rewrite the following paragraphs, eliminating the fragments. You may combine the fragments with complete sentences or add words to them.

The Organizers

Last summer, Lisa, Ruben, and Eva decided. To start their own business. Helping others get organized. Eva wrote advertising copy. And designed a flyer on her computer.

If you can't find your soccer cleats or haven't seen the top of your desk in weeks. Call the Organizers. We'll help you finish those chores you've been putting off. Cleaning crammed closets, shelving CDs in alphabetical order, and sorting through boxes of junk.

With help from Ruben and Eva. Lisa posted the flyers throughout the neighborhood. The three friends were surprised. By the enthusiastic response to their ad. Having seen the flyer on a telephone pole. One neighbor hired the Organizers to arrange family photos in albums. Because they did such a good job. Using their abilities and interests. They helped people, earned money, and had a lot of fun.

➜ **For a SELF-CHECK and more practice, see the EXERCISE BANK, p. 318.**

SENTENCES

B. WRITING: Adding Missing Parts

Correct each fragment by adding words to make it a complete sentence.

At Work in a Pool

1. Because she has always loved swimming.
2. In the pool.
3. Before Lisa could be a lifeguard.
4. To make sure all the swimmers are safe.
5. The dog paddle, the backstroke, and the crawl.

LESSON 2 Run-On Sentences

1 Here's the Idea

▶ **A run-on sentence is two or more sentences written as though they were one sentence.**

A run-on is created when sentences are run together with no punctuation between them, or run together with only a comma between them (called a **comma splice**). The easiest way to fix a run-on is to separate the sentences with a period and a capital letter.

A gopher runs errands for others, gophers should be energetic.

Here's How Fixing Run-Ons

Here are four more techniques you can use to fix a run-on.

- Add a comma and a conjunction.

  Many professionals are too busy to do errands themselves they need someone who can help them.

- If the two sentences are closely related, add a semicolon.

  Some gophers are required to have a driver's license most gophers ride bicycles.

- Add a semicolon, a conjunctive adverb, and a comma if needed.

  Gophers may be paid for the gasoline they use they should negotiate the payment before accepting each job.

- Make one of the clauses subordinate by adding a subordinating conjunction.

  Bike-riding gophers ride fast, they can become dangerous to pedestrians.

When checking for run-ons, don't look only for long sentences. Run-ons can be short.

That's my bike, it has a flat tire.

2 Why It Matters in Writing

Run-ons are confusing and frustrating. Readers can't tell where one idea ends and the next one begins.

Louisa ran errands for her boss all day now she is exhausted.

❸ Practice and Apply

A. CONCEPT CHECK: Run-On Sentences

Write *R* for each run-on or *S* for each correctly written sentence. Then correct the run-ons using the techniques in this lesson.

Teenage Techies

1. Most students use computers on a daily basis now many students are using their computer skills to earn money.
2. Entrepreneurs are people who start their own businesses, using the Internet, some teenagers are doing exactly this.
3. A 16-year-old in Washington created a Web site for reviews of computer hardware. His site is called *The View.*
4. Another teenager started a business designing Web pages his first customer was an author of novels for preteens.
5. A teen in Ohio created a Web page to sell the beaded jewelry that she makes, many teens have used the Web to find customers for their products.
6. Unlike most adults, many teenagers have been using computers all their lives they have an advantage when it comes to dreaming up computer-related businesses.
7. Twenty years ago, teens might have set up lemonade stands to make money, today they can use computers.
8. Teenagers are also earning money by teaching older people how to use computers.
9. Young children are eager to learn computer skills, many parents do not have the time or knowledge to teach them.
10. For some teens, this situation is a golden opportunity.

➜ **For a SELF-CHECK and more practice, see the EXERCISE BANK, p. 319.**

B. REVISING: Checking Sentences

Revise this paragraph, correcting run-ons.

Business Basics

If you set up your own business, you need to know how much to charge your customers. You don't want to overcharge you don't want to work for just pennies either. The first thing to do is to find out how much professionals are paid for the same job, you are not yet a professional, you should charge somewhat less than professionals do. After you get a little working experience, you can decide whether your price is right.

Real World Grammar

Summer Internship Letter

July 2002
DataPhile
The Magazine of Multimedia Technology
Cover Story:
Finding Your Way
10 tips for using search engines effectively

When applying for a summer job or internship, you may need to write a letter describing your abilities. You might begin by jotting down notes, in the form of fragments, about what you want to say. As you draft, be careful not to carry the fragments into your letter or create run-ons by combining too many ideas into single sentences. Remember, your letter will make your first impression on the person in charge of hiring. Here is the draft of a letter one student sent with her application. She asked a friend to review the draft.

Dear Ms. Epstein:

I am writing in regard to the editorial internship program at DataPhile magazine. I would like to be an intern at DataPhile. Because I am interested in a career that combines writing and technology. I believe that the internship will give me a preview of what such a career might be like. A head start in training and experience.

I am a responsible, well-organized person as well as a hard worker, I learn quickly and have strong communication skills. I have done well in all my courses, especially in English and computers. Enclosed are two teacher recommendations, as requested. I hope you will consider my application. Thank you. For your time. I look forward to hearing from you.

Sentence fragments. Combine with preceding sentences.

Run-on sentence. Separate sentences.

Fix fragment.

Using Grammar in Writing	
Avoid sentence fragments and run-on sentences.	After you draft a letter, reread it at least twice. Look for and correct sentence fragments during your first pass. Then do the same for run-on sentences during your second pass.

REVISED LETTER

225 Garland Avenue
Seattle, WA 98197
March 18, 2002

Ms. Gloria Epstein, Editor
DataPhile
1704 Crane Road
Seattle, WA 98199

Dear Ms. Epstein:

I am writing in regard to the editorial internship program at *DataPhile* magazine. I would like to be an intern at *DataPhile* because I am interested in a career that combines writing and technology. I believe that the internship will give me a preview of what such a career might be like and a head start in training and experience.

I am a responsible, well-organized person as well as a hard worker. I learn quickly and have strong communication skills. I have done well in all my courses, especially in English and computers. Enclosed are two teacher recommendations, as requested. I hope you will consider my application. Thank you for your time. I look forward to hearing from you.

Sincerely,

Julia Rowe

Julia Rowe

SENTENCES

PRACTICE AND APPLY: Fixing Fragments and Run-ons

A friend is applying for a position as a camp counselor. Read this section of your friend's application letter and correct any run-ons or fragments you find.

I believe I am an ideal candidate for a counselor-in-training position. At Camp Cedar Lake. First, I like working with young children. And get along well with them. Second, I have interests and talents in drama, music, and dance, I enjoy sharing them with children. I would welcome the opportunity. To work with young campers at Cedar Lake.

Mixed Review

A. Fragments and Run-Ons Identify each numbered item as a complete sentence, a fragment, or a run-on. Then revise each incorrect item.

(1) Perhaps you and your friends make beaded bracelets maybe you build wooden toys. **(2)** If you have a craft hobby. You may be able to turn it into a money-making project. You can display your crafts. **(3)** And sell them at craft fairs. **(4)** To find out about the times and locations of fairs. Contact your local craft store. This store should have information. **(5)** About how to rent a sales table at a fair. **(6)** If you doubt there is a market for craftwork, just visit one of these fairs. You'll find crowds browsing and buying all sorts of items. **(7)** Homemade candles, hand-stitched quilted pillows, beaded jewelry, carved animals, and silk-flower arrangements, to name a few. **(8)** Fairs are not the only places to sell your crafts some craft stores and gift shops may agree to sell them for you. **(9)** By visiting stores and showing the owners samples. You may interest them in your work. **(10)** Setting up an agreement to sell your work can be the beginning of a lasting business relationship.

B. Editing and Revising Read the article below. Identify and correct any fragments or run-on sentences.

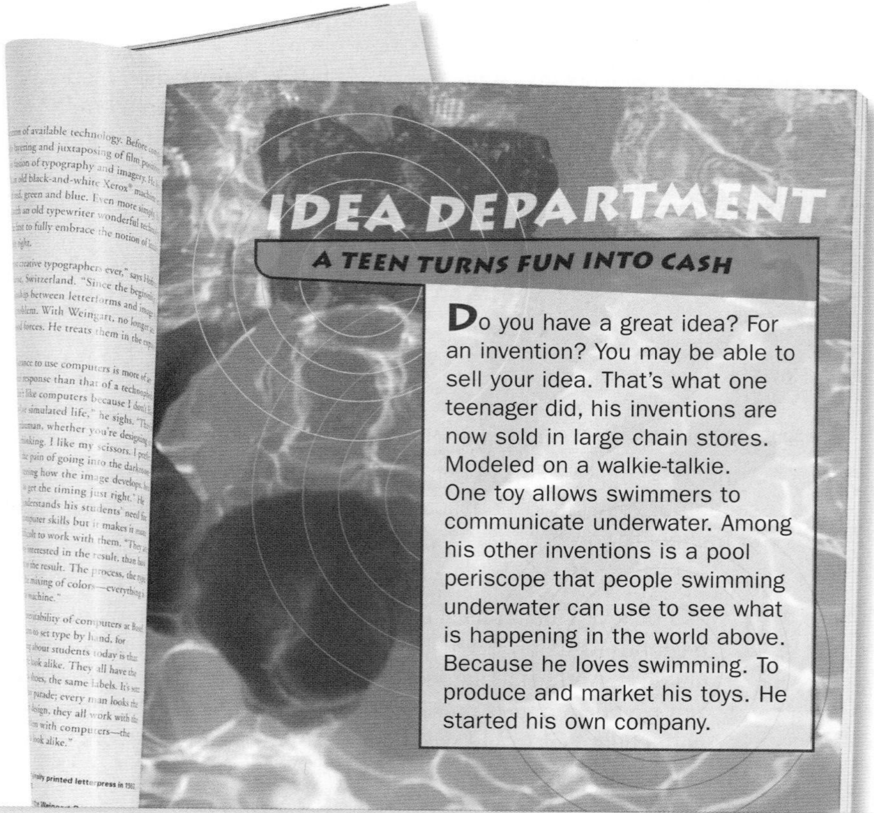

IDEA DEPARTMENT

A TEEN TURNS FUN INTO CASH

Do you have a great idea? For an invention? You may be able to sell your idea. That's what one teenager did, his inventions are now sold in large chain stores. Modeled on a walkie-talkie. One toy allows swimmers to communicate underwater. Among his other inventions is a pool periscope that people swimming underwater can use to see what is happening in the world above. Because he loves swimming. To produce and market his toys. He started his own company.

Mastery Test: What Did You Learn?

Choose the best way to rewrite each underlined word group.

After eating a meal in a restaurant. Most people leave a tip. (1) Although this custom is common. (2) In fact, even the origin of the word *tip* is a mystery. Tips are usually paid to service workers, such as waiters, waitresses, taxi drivers, and hairdressers. A tip is often about 20 percent of the cost. Of the service. (3)

Over time, the meaning of tipping has changed. In the past a tip was a reward for good service. (4) Now it is an expected payment. Nobody knows exactly why tips are given, it seems strange that we continue to follow this custom. (5) Some social scientists are trying to understand this.

1. A. After eating a meal in a restaurant, and most people leave a tip.
   B. After eating a meal in a restaurant, most people leave a tip.
   C. After eating a meal. In a restaurant, most people leave a tip.
   D. Correct as is

2. A. Although this custom is common. Its origins are unknown.
   B. Although this custom is common, however its origins are unknown.
   C. Although this custom is common, its origins are unknown.
   D. Correct as is

3. A. A tip is often about 20 percent of the cost of the service.
   B. A tip is often about 20 percent of the cost, of the service.
   C. A tip is often about 20 percent. Of the cost of the service.
   D. Correct as is

4. A. In the past a tip was a reward. For good service.
   B. In the past. A tip was a reward for good service.
   C. In the past a tip was a reward and for good service.
   D. Correct as is

5. A. Nobody knows exactly why tips are given it seems strange that we continue to follow this custom.
   B. Nobody knows exactly why tips are given, seems strange that we continue to follow this custom.
   C. Nobody knows exactly why tips are given, so it seems strange that we continue to follow this custom.
   D. Correct as is

Student Help Desk

Fragments and Run-Ons at a Glance

- A **sentence fragment** is a part of a sentence that is punctuated as if it were a complete sentence.
- A **run-on sentence** is two or more sentences written as though they were one sentence.

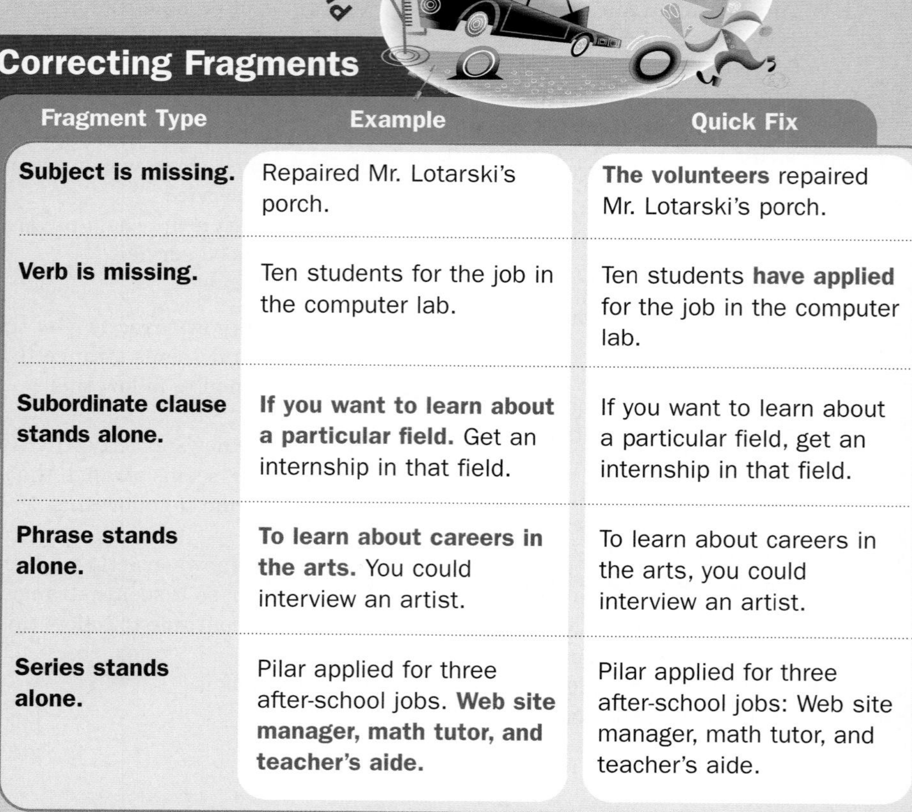

Correcting Fragments

Fragment Type	Example	Quick Fix
Subject is missing.	Repaired Mr. Lotarski's porch.	**The volunteers** repaired Mr. Lotarski's porch.
Verb is missing.	Ten students for the job in the computer lab.	Ten students **have applied** for the job in the computer lab.
Subordinate clause stands alone.	**If you want to learn about a particular field.** Get an internship in that field.	If you want to learn about a particular field, get an internship in that field.
Phrase stands alone.	**To learn about careers in the arts.** You could interview an artist.	To learn about careers in the arts, you could interview an artist.
Series stands alone.	Pilar applied for three after-school jobs. **Web site manager, math tutor, and teacher's aide.**	Pilar applied for three after-school jobs: Web site manager, math tutor, and teacher's aide.

Put an end to run-on sentences, these sentences will confuse readers.

Correcting Run-Ons

Technique	Run-on	Quick Fix
Add a period and a capital letter.	Yoshiko designed the school Web site, she is very creative.	Yoshiko designed the school Web site**. S**he is very creative.
Add a comma and a conjunction.	Several teenagers have started their own computer businesses they are making a profit.	Several teenagers have started their own computer businesses**, and** they are making a profit.
Add a semicolon.	Some students work after school others work on the weekends.	Some students work after school**;** others work on the weekends.
Add a semicolon and a conjunctive adverb.	Alan was not certain he wanted to work in a video store, he applied for the job.	Alan was not certain he wanted to work in a video store**; nevertheless,** he applied for the job.

SENTENCES

The Bottom Line

Checklist for Complete Sentences

Have I . . .

____ included a subject in each sentence?

____ included a verb in each sentence?

____ expressed a complete thought in each sentence?

____ corrected any run-ons?

____ corrected any fragments?

Using Verbs

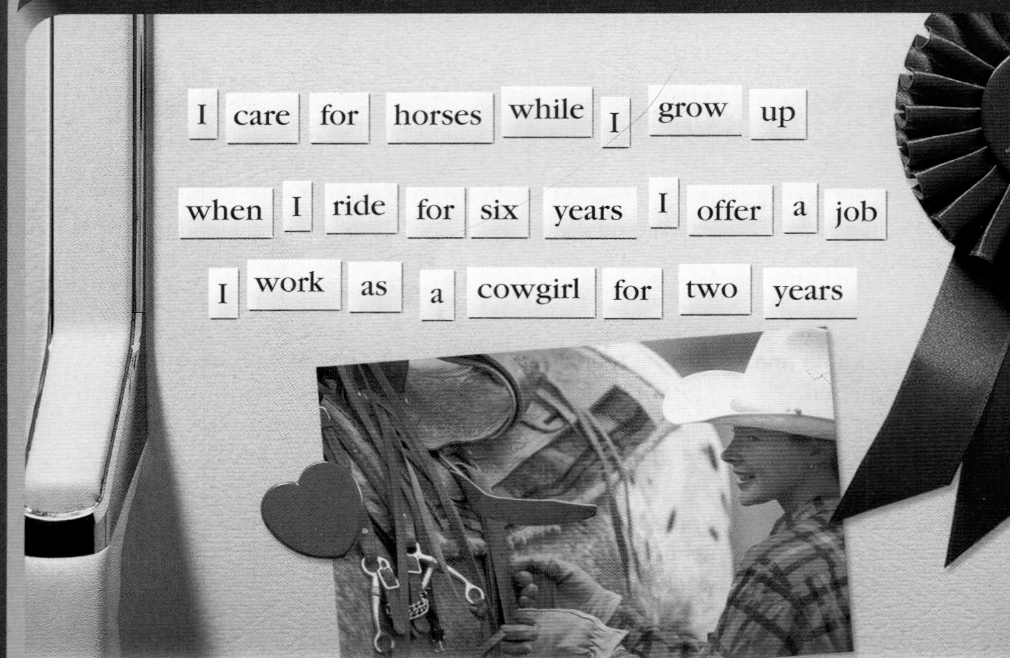

I care for horses while I grow up
when I ride for six years I offer a job
I work as a cowgirl for two years

Theme: Writers' Lives

What Happened When?

What if you had a set of magnet words with plenty of verbs but no way to show verb forms? It would be hard to say when events happened or even to whom. Compare the version below to the one in the illustration above.

*I **cared** for horses while I **was growing** up. When I **had been riding** for six years, I **was offered** a job. I **have worked** as a cowgirl for two years.*

In this chapter, you will learn to use verb forms in your writing to describe action precisely. Then it's up to you to come up with some good verbs!

Write Away: Let's Talk About You

In a paragraph, tell a few important or interesting facts about your life. Be sure to include information about your past, your present, and your future. Put the paragraph in your **Working Portfolio.**

Diagnostic Test: What Do You Know?

Choose the best way to rewrite each underlined word or group of words.

Christy Brown's life almost stop (1) before it ever got started. Because he was borned (2) with cerebral palsy, he was almost completely paralyzed. Until he had been (3) five years old, many people thought he would never be able to communicate at all; but Christy's mother has (4) faith that he would. Christy's life did change (5) the day he picked up a piece of chalk with the toes of his left foot. His mother drew the letter *A* in chalk on the floor and was asking (6) him to copy it. He tried, but the letter could not be copied by him (7). After his mother said, "Try again, Chris," he has made up (8) his mind to succeed; and with great effort, he did. Now Brown has written (9) four novels, a collection of poetry, and the script for *My Left Foot,* a movie based on a book he wrote about his life. If it was (10) not for Brown's determination, he would not have the rewarding life he leads today.

1. A. was stopping
   B. had stopped
   C. stopped
   D. Correct as is

2. A. born
   B. had been born
   C. has born
   D. Correct as is

3. A. was
   B. will be
   C. is
   D. Correct as is

4. A. has had
   B. was having
   C. had
   D. Correct as is

5. A. had changed
   B. have changed
   C. will change
   D. Correct as is

6. A. was asked
   B. asked
   C. did ask
   D. Correct as is

7. A. the letter was not able to be copied
   B. he were not able to copy the letter
   C. he could not copy the letter
   D. Correct as is

8. A. made up
   B. was making up
   C. makes up
   D. Correct as is

9. A. has wrote
   B. had written
   C. was writing
   D. Correct as is

10. A. is
    B. were
    C. had
    D. Correct as is

VERBS

The Principal Parts of a Verb

1 Here's the Idea

Verbs take different forms to show time of action and other kinds of information. In the passage below, the use of different verb forms makes it clear when everything occurs.

PROFESSIONAL MODEL

People probably **know** Maya Angelou best as a poet and as the author of a best-selling autobiography series. But she also **has written** plays and screenplays, **composed** music, and **performed** on stage and screen. Most recently, she **directed** a feature film, *Down in the Delta*. Currently, she **is teaching** at Wake Forest University in North Carolina.

PRESENT ACTION

PAST ACTION

▶ **Every verb has four basic forms called principal parts: the present, the present participle, the past, and the past participle.** The principal parts are used to make all of a verb's tenses and other forms.

The Four Principal Parts of a Verb

Present	Present Participle	Past	Past Participle
talk	(is) talking	talked	(has) talked
sing	(is) singing	sang	(has) sung

Regular Verbs

The past and past participle of a **regular verb,** like *talk,* are formed by adding *-ed* or *-d* to the present. Most verbs are regular.

talk (present) + ed = talked (past and past participle)

hope (present) + d = hoped (past and past participle)

For some verbs, consonants are doubled in forms other than the present: *ho**p**, ho**pp**ing, ho**pp**ed.* For others, an e is dropped in the present participle: *hop**e**, hoping.* For more on these spelling rules, see page 341.

CHAPTER 6

Irregular Verbs

The past and past participle of an **irregular verb,** like *sing,* are formed in some way other than by adding *-ed* or *-d* to the present.

Most irregular verbs can be classified into five groups. Learning these groups will help you to remember the verbs.

Common Irregular Verbs

	Present	Past	Past Participle
Group 1 The forms of the present, the past, and the past participle are the same.	burst	burst	(have) burst
	cost	cost	(have) cost
	cut	cut	(have) cut
	hit	hit	(have) hit
	hurt	hurt	(have) hurt
	let	let	(have) let
	put	put	(have) put
	set	set	(have) set
	shut	shut	(have) shut
Group 2 The forms of the past and the past participle are the same.	bring	brought	(have) brought
	catch	caught	(have) caught
	find	found	(have) found
	get	got	(have) got *or* gotten
	lay	laid	(have) laid
	lead	led	(have) led
	lend	lent	(have) lent
	lose	lost	(have) lost
	say	said	(have) said
	send	sent	(have) sent
	shine	shone *or* shined	(have) shone *or* shined
	sit	sat	(have) sat
	swing	swung	(have) swung
	teach	taught	(have) taught
Group 3 The vowel changes from *i* to *a* to *u.*	begin	began	(have) begun
	drink	drank	(have) drunk
	ring	rang	(have) rung
	shrink	shrank	(have) shrunk
	sink	sank	(have) sunk
	spring	sprang *or* sprung	(have) sprung
	swim	swam	(have) swum

VERBS

Common Irregular Verbs

	Present	Past	Past Participle
Group 4 The past participle is formed by adding *-n* or *-en* to the **past.**	beat	beat	(have) beaten
	bite	bit	(have) bitten *or* bit
	break	broke	(have) broken
	lie	lay	(have) lain
	speak	spoke	(have) spoken
	steal	stole	(have) stolen
	tear	tore	(have) torn
	wear	wore	(have) worn
Group 5 The past participle is formed from the **present**—frequently by adding *-n, -en,* or *-ne.*	become	became	(have) become
	blow	blew	(have) blown
	do	did	(have) done
	draw	drew	(have) drawn
	drive	drove	(have) driven
	eat	ate	(have) eaten
	give	gave	(have) given
	go	went	(have) gone
	grow	grew	(have) grown
	know	knew	(have) known
	rise	rose	(have) risen
	run	ran	(have) run
	see	saw	(have) seen
	take	took	(have) taken
	throw	threw	(have) thrown
	write	wrote	(have) written

❷ Why It Matters in Writing

Incorrect verb forms confuse your reader and make a bad impression in situations in which standard English is expected.

STUDENT MODEL

I would like to apply for the part-time job as cashier that I ~~seen~~ saw advertised in your window. Your ad ~~catch~~ caught my eye because last year I ~~have~~ worked for the whole summer at a pet store just like yours. The owner ~~say~~ said I ~~shown~~ showed responsibility and a good attitude in my work.

❸ Practice and Apply

A. CONCEPT CHECK: The Principal Parts of a Verb

Write the correct past or past participle of each verb that is shown in parentheses.

Career Beginnings

1. Gwendolyn Brooks (become) a published poet at age 14.
2. But not all writers (begin) their writing careers so early.
3. Before he became a well-known humorist, Mark Twain had (search) for gold as a prospector in California.
4. The poet and historian Carl Sandburg (drive) a milkwagon when he was young.
5. As a baseball captain in college, Sandburg (lead) his team to victory.
6. Isaac Asimov had (teach) biochemistry at Boston University's medical school before he turned to writing full time.
7. Maya Angelou (take) a job as a streetcar driver in San Francisco.
8. The novelist Amy Tan (assemble) pizzas in a restaurant.
9. O. Henry allegedly had (steal) money from the bank he worked in.
10. Even though O. Henry fled the country to escape capture, he was (catch) when he returned to Texas to see his dying wife.

➜ **For a SELF-CHECK and more practice, see the EXERCISE BANK, p. 320.**

B. WRITING: Reporting News

List the principal parts of the following pairs of irregular verbs and then use any of the word pairs to write a paragraph describing an interesting news event.

1. sink–swim
2. bring–take
3. give–get
4. drink–eat
5. lend–lose
6. speak–write

In your **Working Portfolio,** find the paragraph you wrote for the **Write Away** on page 128. Change three verbs; then make sure you have used the correct principal parts.

VERBS

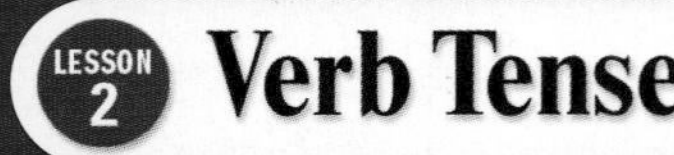

LESSON 2 Verb Tense

1 Here's the Idea

A tense is a verb form that shows the time of an action or condition.

English verbs have six tenses. These tenses are used to indicate whether an action or condition is in the past, the present, or the future, and to indicate how events are related in time. A verb's tenses are formed from its principal parts.

Simple Tenses

	Singular	Plural
Present + *s* or *es* in third-person singular	I sneeze you sneeze he/she/it sneezes	we sneeze you sneeze they sneeze
Past	I sneezed you sneezed he/she/it sneezed	we sneezed you sneezed they sneezed
Future *will (shall)* + present	I will (shall) sneeze you will sneeze he/she/it will sneeze	we will (shall) sneeze you will sneeze they will sneeze

Perfect Tenses

	Singular	Plural
Present Perfect *have* or *has* + past participle	I have sneezed you have sneezed he/she/it has sneezed	we have sneezed you have sneezed they have sneezed
Past Perfect *had* + past participle	I had sneezed you had sneezed he/she/it had sneezed	we had sneezed you had sneezed they had sneezed
Future Perfect *will (shall) have* + past participle	I will (shall) have sneezed you will have sneezed he/she/it will have sneezed	we will (shall) have sneezed you will have sneezed they will have sneezed

All of the perfect tenses are made from the past participle.

CHAPTER 6

The Far Side by Gary Larson

Zahn
"IT DOESN'T GET ANY BETTER THAN THIS, RALPH!"

To understand the following examples of how the tenses are used, refer to the cartoon above.

VERBS

Using the Simple Tenses

The **present tense** shows that an action or condition

- is occurring in the present:

The fishermen are unaware of any danger.

- occurs regularly:

They usually fish in another river.

- is constantly or generally true:

Unknown waters can be dangerous.

The **past tense** shows that an action or condition occurred in the past:

The friends fished calmly all morning.

The **future tense** shows that an action or condition will occur in the future:

The calm soon will be broken.

Using the Perfect Tenses

The **present perfect** shows that an action or condition

- was completed at one or more indefinite times in the past:

The buddies have fished together often.

This time they have gone to a new fishing spot.

- began in the past and continues in the present:

They have been fishing since dawn.

The **past perfect** shows that an action or condition in the past preceded another past action or condition:

They had looked over several maps before choosing this river.

The **future perfect** shows that an action or condition in the future will precede another future action or condition:

Before the day ends, they will have experienced quite an adventure.

CHAPTER 6

The "historical present tense" is sometimes used to make a story more vivid:

Then pandemonium breaks out.

The present is also often used in referring to events in literature:

In her essay, the author discusses the imagery in *Julius Caesar.*

2 Why It Matters in Writing

Choosing the correct verb tense allows you to be clear about when events occur in time.

STUDENT MODEL

The most significant experience in my life so far has been my trip to an old growth forest in Washington State. I had reluctantly gone on vacation with my parents, not realizing how much I would enjoy it. We visited a forest that is about 10,000 years old. I will never forget the dark silence and the damp, green smell of ancient cedars, pines, and spruces. The setting was like that of a Brothers Grimm fairy tale!

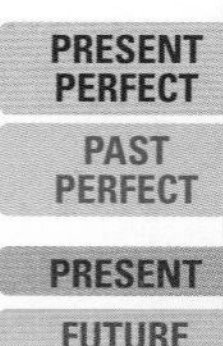

PAST

❸ Practice and Apply

A. CONCEPT CHECK: Verb Tense

Choose the better tense of the verb in parentheses.

Small-Town Boy Makes Good

1. Even now, four centuries after his death, William Shakespeare (ranks, has ranked) as the greatest writer in English.
2. Over the years, many critics (argued, have argued) that his greatness comes in part from the ordinariness of his life.
3. Perhaps only someone who (has immersed, had immersed) himself completely in the joys and sorrows of normal life could have written with such humanity.
4. Shakespeare (grew, has grown) up in a middle-class family in the small town of Stratford-on-Avon.
5. By the time he was 28, he (became, had become) a popular actor and playwright in London.
6. When the London theaters were closed because of the plague, Shakespeare (writes, wrote) poetry instead of plays.
7. He (has produced, produced) about two plays a year.
8. Not much (is, was) known today about his private life.
9. Although scholars continue to search, it's not likely that they (will find, have found) anything new about Shakespeare.
10. By the 400th anniversary of Shakespeare's death in 2016, many more theatergoers (have become, will have become) admirers of Shakespeare.

➜ **For a SELF-CHECK and more practice, see the EXERCISE BANK, p. 320.**

B. REVISING: Correcting Verb Tense

Revise the following paragraph by correcting the verb tenses.

STUDENT MODEL

The original Globe Theatre, built in 1599, **(1)** <u>will accommodate</u> 3,000 people. This first Globe **(2)** <u>burn</u> down in 1613. By then, performances of some of Shakespeare's greatest plays **(3)** <u>take</u> place on the Globe's stage. Today, visitors **(4)** <u>have enjoyed</u> performances at the new Globe, which opened in 1997. If you visit, you **(5)** <u>will have found</u> that it holds 1,500 people, far fewer than in Shakespeare's day.

Change the verbs in a draft from your **Working Portfolio** to another tense.

VERBS

Progressive and Emphatic Forms

1 Here's the Idea

▶ **The progressive form of a verb expresses an event in progress.**

She was reading a book when the lights went out.

Each of the six tenses has a progressive form, made by using a tense of the verb *be* with the present participle.

The Six Progressive Forms	
Present Progressive	We **are dancing.**
Past Progressive	We **were dancing.**
Future Progressive	We **will be dancing.**
Present Perfect Progressive	We **have been dancing.**
Past Perfect Progressive	We **had been dancing.**
Future Perfect Progressive	We **will have been dancing.**

The present progressive is often used with an adverb of time to indicate future action: **Rosa is leaving next week.**

▶ **The emphatic form gives special force to a verb.** The emphatic form is used only in the present and past tenses. It is commonly used to correct or contradict.

I did finish my homework. I do try to be neat. It does matter.

2 Why It Matters in Writing

The progressive and emphatic forms allow you to stress verbs in particular ways. Notice their effect in this mother's warning.

LITERARY MODEL

Then she began, patiently, to describe to the girl the difficulties of the theater. Thousands of experienced, beautiful, and talented actresses were out of work. Even those who did work, didn't work often. . . . When Mrs. Wilson had finished, Elise said nothing.

"Well, what are you thinking, dear?"

—John Cheever, "The Opportunity"

PAST EMPHATIC

PRESENT PROGRESSIVE

CHAPTER 6

❸ Practice and Apply

A. CONCEPT CHECK: Progressive and Emphatic Forms

Write a progressive or emphatic form of the verb in parentheses, using the correct tense.

Success with Stories

1. American writer John Cheever had some emotional problems, but he (manage) to create many remarkable short stories and novels.
2. While he (attend) prep school, he got expelled for smoking.
3. Although he was not concerned about his formal education, he (care) about becoming a writer.
4. By 1930, he (begin) to publish short stories.
5. Despite his problems, Cheever (succeed) as a writer.
6. His stories include characters who (try) to express individuality in a society that demands conformity.
7. Even though society (tolerate) individuality to a greater extent now, Cheever's writing remains very popular with readers.
8. Booksellers (sell) his books well into the new millennium.
9. Although she began writing at a later age than her father, Cheever's daughter Susan (become) a published writer as well.
10. By the end of 2010, she (write) books for about 30 years.

➜ **For a SELF-CHECK and more practice, see the EXERCISE BANK, p. 321.**

B. EDITING: Different Verb Forms

Substitute progressive or emphatic forms for the underlined verbs.

STUDENT MODEL

Although John Cheever's life may have seemed ordinary, it **(1)** <u>features</u> some interesting ironies. True, he **(2)** <u>got</u> expelled from prep school. However, he wrote about the experience in his first published short story, titled, appropriately enough, "Expelled." Cheever never **(3)** <u>attended</u> college. During the 1950s and the 1970s, however, he **(4)** <u>taught</u> at several prestigious schools, such as Barnard College and the University of Iowa. While teaching writing to convicts at Sing Sing prison in the 1970s, Cheever **(5)** <u>wrote</u> stories about middle-class suburbanites.

VERBS

Mixed Review

A. Verb Tenses and Forms Choose the better verb tense or form.

1. Many critics today (praise, praised) Pablo Neruda as the greatest Latin American poet of the 20th century.
2. Born Neftalí Ricardo Reyes Basoalto in Chile in 1904, he (was writing, has written) poetry by the age of ten.
3. He first published his poems under his pen name, Pablo Neruda, because his father (was not approving, did not approve) of his poetry.
4. By 1946, he (adopts, had adopted) his pen name as his legal name.
5. By the time he was 20, Neruda (has become, had become) famous.
6. Because he couldn't make a living from his poetry, he (went, has gone) to work as a diplomat, living in such countries as Burma, Indonesia, Spain, France, Argentina, and Mexico.
7. Back home in the 1940s, Neruda (served, will have served) in the Chilean senate for two years.
8. He was forced to flee the country, however, after he (did publish, had published) a letter that was critical of another politician.
9. The political climate (is changing, did change) in the 1950s, however, so Neruda returned to Chile and lived a prosperous and productive life as a world-famous poet.
10. In 1971, although he was terminally ill from cancer, Neruda (traveled, had been traveling) to Stockholm to accept the Nobel Prize.

CHAPTER 6

B. Progressive and Emphatic Verb Forms Identify the tense of each underlined verb. Where appropriate, also identify the verb as progressive or emphatic.

LITERARY MODEL

And, lastly, I **(1)** do not think that I **(2)** will forget days spent, a few summers ago, at a beautiful lodge built right into the rocky cliffs of a bay on the Maine coast. We **(3)** met a woman there who **(4)** had lived a purposeful and courageous life and who **(5)** was then dying of cancer. She **(6)** had, characteristically, just written a book and **(7)** taken up painting. She **(8)** had also been of radical viewpoint all her life; one of those people who energetically **(9)** believe that the world *can* be changed for the better and **(10)** spend their lives trying to do just that. And that **(11)** was the way she **(12)** thought of cancer; she absolutely **(13)** refused to award it the stature of tragedy. . . .

—Lorraine Hansberry, "On Summer"

The Voice of a Verb

1 Here's the Idea

The voice of an action verb indicates whether the subject **performs** or **receives** the action. Voice affects the meaning and tone of the sentence.

Active Voice

When a verb's subject *performs* the action expressed by the verb, the verb is in the active voice.

Rita Dove writes poetry. She has been writing since childhood.

Most of the sentences you write will be in the active voice. The active verb forms are the ones shown earlier in this chapter.

Passive Voice

When a verb's subject *receives* the action expressed by the verb, the verb is in the passive voice.

In 1993, Dove was named poet laureate.

The passive voice is often used when the person or thing performing the action is indefinite or unknown.

The announcement was made in all the major media.

To form the passive in a particular tense, use the appropriate tense of the verb *be* with the past participle of the main verb.

Many people write poetry. Poetry is written by many people.

(write: PRESENT; is: PRESENT; written: PAST PARTICIPLE)

VERBS

2 Why It Matters in Writing

The active voice is used more frequently, but sometimes the passive voice will express the exact meaning you need. In the passage below, think about why the author chose the passive.

LITERARY MODEL

God give you a good day, grandfather. This is how I was taught as a child to greet my grandfather, or any grown person.

—Rudolfo A. Anaya, "A Celebration of Grandfathers"

Passive voice here focuses attention on the person receiving the teaching.

3 Practice and Apply

A. CONCEPT CHECK: The Voice of a Verb

Write each verb in parentheses using the correct tense and the correct voice—active or passive.

A Child at Manzanar

1. Jeanne Wakatsuki Houston (live) in Los Angeles; she was seven years old when war broke out between Japan and the United States in December 1941.
2. Because of the war, some Americans (develop) anti-Japanese feelings.
3. Executive Order 9066 (sign) by President Roosevelt.
4. The order (authorize) the removal of all persons of Japanese descent from coastal areas.
5. During 1942, more than 110,000 Japanese Americans living along the West Coast (remove) from their homes.
6. They (send) inland to internment camps.
7. The young Jeanne Wakatsuki (transport) along with members of her family to the internment camp called Manzanar.
8. Earlier, her father (imprison) at a camp in North Dakota.
9. Manzanar (build) in a dry, isolated area in south central California.
10. Each of the camp's wooden barracks (accommodate) about 36 people.

➜ **For a SELF-CHECK and more practice, see the EXERCISE BANK, p. 321.**

B. REVISING: Being Direct

Revise the following paragraph, changing passive verb forms to active ones where appropriate.

(1) What happened in Manzanar was not even discussed by Jeanne Wakatsuki Houston for 25 years after she was released. **(2)** Her whole life had been affected by the years she spent there. **(3)** But a book about the experience that was written by her and her husband, James D. Houston, helped her deal with the trauma. **(4)** The book was published in 1973. **(5)** It has been hailed by critics and readers alike as a much needed personal account of one of the darker chapters in U.S. history.

Shifts in Tense, Form, and Voice

1 Here's the Idea

Switch tenses, introduce progressive and emphatic forms, and change active into passive voice only as needed for clarity or style. Improper or unnecessary shifts will make your writing awkward and confusing.

Shifts in Tense and Form

▶ **Combine different verb tenses and forms to show how events are related in time or to emphasize them differently.**

He arrived just as he had promised he would.
(arrived: PAST; had promised: PAST PERFECT)

When the bus came, I had been waiting for two hours.
(came: PAST; had been waiting: PAST PERFECT PROGRESSIVE)

She hated lasagna as a child, but now she thinks it divine.
(hated: PAST; thinks: PRESENT)

I have read your essay, and I love it!
(have read: PRESENT PERFECT; love: PRESENT)

I have had enough, and I will take no more.
(have had: PRESENT PERFECT; will take: FUTURE)

▶ **Stick with one tense when describing actions related to a single period or event or when writing about a series of events.**

STUDENT MODEL

DRAFT

Sammy **clobbered** the ball, and it **sails** over the center-field bleachers. Sammy **drove** in three runs in that game, and the next day he **has knocked** in three more.

(one event; two events in a series)

REVISION

Sammy **clobbered** the ball, and it **sailed** over the center-field bleachers. Sammy **drove** in three runs in that game, and the next day he **knocked** in three more.

Most of the time, you will use the same tense for both parts of a compound verb or predicate, or in a compound sentence:

Sammy hits the ball and runs. He scores a run, and his team wins.

VERBS

Shifts in Voice

When you change a verb from active to passive, the object of the verb becomes the subject of the sentence. This change alters the focus of the sentence.

Active: Rita Dove won the 1987 Pulitzer Prize in poetry.
SUBJECT — OBJECT

Passive: The 1987 Pulitzer Prize in poetry was won by Rita Dove.
SUBJECT

You can also change the emphasis of the sentence by changing the verb as well as using the passive voice.

Active: Rita Dove won a Pulitzer Prize in 1987.
EMPHASIZES ACTIVE ROLE

Passive: Rita Dove was awarded a Pulitzer Prize in 1987.
EMPHASIZES PASSIVE ROLE

CHAPTER 6

▶ **Don't use the passive voice unnecessarily or as a way to avoid indicating who is responsible for an action.**

STUDENT MODEL

DRAFT	***REVISION***
Mistakes **were made.** The assignment **was** not **completed.**	I **made** mistakes. I **did** not **complete** the assignment.
Awkward—performer of action unclear	Simple and direct—performer of action clear

❷ Why It Matters in Writing

Shifting voice allows the author of the passage below to keep attention focused on himself regardless of whether he is performing or receiving the action.

LITERARY MODEL

By the time I met Marjorie Hurd four years later, I had learned English, had been placed in a normal, graded class and had even been chosen for the college preparatory track. . . .

—Nicholas Gage, "The Teacher Who Changed My Life"

ACTIVE
PASSIVE

❸ Practice and Apply

A. CONCEPT CHECK: Shifts in Tense, Form, and Voice

Each of the following sentences contains an incorrect or an awkward use of verb tense, form, or voice. Revise each sentence to correct the problem.

A Voice of Her Own

1. Sandra Cisneros grew up for the most part in Chicago, but her father occasionally moves the family to Mexico.
2. As a child, Cisneros watched idealized families on television and wishes they were her own.
3. Because she felt lonely as a child, books were read by Cisneros for comfort.
4. One of her favorite children's books is *The Little House,* because it told of a family in a small but stable home.
5. Although some poetry had been written by Cisneros in high school, she did not start writing seriously until college.
6. By the time Cisneros published her first book, she already spent time teaching high-school dropouts in a Latino neighborhood.
7. Cisneros did not find her own voice for some time; at first she imitates favorite male poets such as Theodore Roethke.
8. Now she recognizes her own female voice and emphasized the importance of her ethnic background.
9. Her unique experience was embraced by Cisneros, and she found her literary voice.
10. Cisneros's loyal readers look forward to her books, which combined elements of fiction and poetry.

➜ **For a SELF-CHECK and more practice, see the EXERCISE BANK, p. 322.**

B. WRITING: Using Verb Tense and Voice Correctly

Use the following time line to write a short biographical sketch about Sandra Cisneros. Use at least three different verb forms.

1954	1976	1978	1984	1985	1995
Born in Chicago	B.A. English Loyola University	M.F.A. Iowa Writers Workshop	*The House on Mango Street*	Before Columbus American Book Award	MacArthur Foundation Fellowship

VERBS

The Mood of a Verb

1 Here's the Idea

▶ **The mood of a verb conveys the status of the action or condition it expresses.** Verbs have three moods: indicative, subjunctive, and imperative.

Indicative Use the **indicative mood** to make statements or ask questions. The indicative is the most commonly used mood; all of the verb forms taught earlier in this chapter are indicative.

Subjunctive Use the **subjunctive mood** to express a wish or state a condition that is contrary to fact.

Comparison of Indicative and Subjunctive

Indicative	Subjunctive
Mr. Green **is** my teacher.	I wish Ms. Li **were** my teacher. (wish)
Fran **has** money; I'll ask her for some.	If Ted **had** money, I would ask him for some. (contrary to fact)

Notice that the subjunctive forms in the chart above are identical to past plural forms.

You can also use the subjunctive, in more formal communication, to express a command or request after the word *that.* In this case, the form of the verb is identical to its base form.

She insisted that I sit still and tell the story.

Imperative Use the **imperative mood** to make a request or give a command. This mood has only one tense, the present. Notice that the subject, *you,* is omitted.

Remember to call your sister. Please do it soon.

2 Why It Matters in Writing

The subjunctive mood allows you to write about things as they might be or might have been rather than simply as they are or were.

LITERARY MODEL

His heart thudded more than if he had been lying behind a bush in the forest waiting for Bilgan the Giant. . . .

—Heinrich Böll, "The Balek Scales"

SUBJUNCTIVE

CHAPTER 6

❸ Practice and Apply

A. CONCEPT CHECK: The Mood of a Verb

Identify each underlined verb or verb phrase in the following quotations as indicative, imperative, or subjunctive.

LITERARY MODELS

The Words to Say It

1. Love is not all: it is not meat nor drink
Nor slumber nor a roof against the rain;
—Edna St. Vincent Millay, "Sonnet 30"
2. "Put your mother on the phone," I said. "Put *your* mother on the phone," she said, "and I'll ask her how it feels to have a crazy son." "Crazy, huh? . . . Have you already forgotten our plans to have children?" "Well, start without me. I'm definitely not having them if they're yours." —Bill Cosby, *Love and Marriage*
3. I admired the watch at length, and tried it in various of my pockets, and said that, had I known, I would have worn a vest. —David Mamet, "The Watch"
4. I close my eyes, and side by side I see the Charley of my boyhood and the Charley of this afternoon, as clearly as if I were looking at a split TV screen.
—Eugenia Collier, "Sweet Potato Pie"

➜ **For a SELF-CHECK and more practice, see the EXERCISE BANK, p. 323.**

B. REVISING: Changing Moods

Rewrite the following sentences as indicated.

1. When I am famous, I will sign autographs for my fans. (Change from indicative to subjunctive.)
2. You shouldn't count on fame in your future. (Change from indicative to imperative.)
3. If I went to Hollywood, I would become a star. (Change from subjunctive to indicative.)
4. If I were you, I'd be more realistic. (Change from subjunctive to imperative.)
5. I want you to give me a chance. (Change from indicative to imperative.)

Grammar in Literature

Verbs and Lively Writing

In the passage below, noted writer Maya Angelou shares her memories of working as a streetcar driver in San Francisco. By choosing interesting action verbs and using the active voice, Angelou successfully conveys to readers her elation at getting the job, the excitement of the job itself, and the feelings of freedom and independence she derived from it.

from I Know Why the Caged Bird Sings

—Maya Angelou

Mother gave me the money to have my blue serge suit tailored, and I learned to fill out work cards, operate the money changer and punch transfers. The time crowded together and at an End of Days I was swinging on the back of the rackety trolley, smiling sweetly and persuading my charges to "step forward in the car, please."

For one whole semester the streetcars and I shimmied up and scooted down the sheer hills of San Francisco. I lost some of my need for the Black ghetto's shielding-sponge quality, as I clanged and cleared my way down Market Street, with its honky-tonk homes for homeless sailors, past the quiet retreat of Golden Gate Park and along closed undwelled-in-looking dwellings of the Sunset District.

VIVID ACTION VERB
Conveys the swift passage of time

PROGRESSIVE FORMS
Stress the flow of ongoing action

PRECISE VERBS
Bring the scene to life with sensory detail

When good writers revise their sentences, they try to replace overused or vague verbs with ones that are fresh and precise, and they use the active voice whenever possible.

Using Verbs Effectively	
Fresh verbs	Attract the reader's interest with unusual, vivid description. **Example:** Mahmoud *deposited* himself at his desk. (instead of *sat*)
Precise verbs	Provide exact, specific information that is easy to picture. **Example:** The dog *trotted* down the sidewalk. (instead of *walked*)
Active voice	Sounds more direct and forceful than the passive voice. **Example:** The opposing guard knocked the ball from Ceretha's hand. (instead of *The ball was knocked from Ceretha's hand.*)

VERBS

PRACTICE AND APPLY: Using Verbs Effectively

The following paragraph needs revision because the writer has chosen several verbs that are dull and imprecise and has used the passive voice inappropriately. Revise the paragraph to make it more lively by replacing the underlined verbs and verb phrases.

> My most unusual, although not my favorite, summer job was working as a swimming waitress at a seafood restaurant on Cape Cod in Massachusetts. There were three of us; and our job was to entertain the diners by doing a sort of water ballet in a huge tank, then come out soaking wet and with dripping hair to hurriedly don uniforms and give soggy fish and chips to the customers. If our performances were enjoyed by them, they didn't choose to show it by bestowing lavish tips.

After you have revised the paragraph, discuss with a partner how you think you have made it more effective.

Choose a piece of writing from your **Working Portfolio** and change some verbs to make the piece more interesting and lively.

Mixed Review

A. Verb Tense, Form, and Voice Read each sentence and write the correct tense, form, and voice of the verb in parentheses.

1. Emily Dickinson's poetry was virtually unknown during her lifetime, although she (write) 1,775 poems by the time she died in 1886.
2. The extent of her genius only became fully known in 1955 when a complete edition of her poems (publish).
3. Dickinson's long anonymity was caused partly by her own shyness, but it also (perpetuate) by the bad judgment of some literary men.
4. By the time a newspaper editor did publish five of her poems, her confidence in the reading public (shake).
5. One literary friend of Dickinson's, Thomas Wentworth Higginson, advised her not to publish her poems because they (be) so unusual.
6. By the time Dickinson was 32 years old, she (decide) not to have any more of her poems published.
7. Even though she had given up trying to publish, she never (give) up writing.
8. While she lived the rest of her life secluded from the world, Dickinson (write) steadily and quietly.
9. After her death, those closest to her were amazed to find so many poems; the poems (tie) in neat packets and hidden in her room.
10. Critics today classify Dickinson as a founder of modern American poetry, and she (stand) among the great American poets.

CHAPTER 6

B. Verb Tense in Different Forms, Voices, and Moods Replace each numbered verb with a verb or a verb phrase whose tense, voice, and mood better express the paragraph's meaning.

STUDENT MODEL

For generations, readers **(1) be** fascinated by Edgar Allan Poe's tales of horror and mystery. If you **(2) get** acquainted with Poe's work, you would see why. Read the opening paragraphs of any story. Soon, you **(3) draw** inside the mind of the main character as if it **(4) be** your own.

In many ways, Poe **(5) lead** a life as mysterious and tragic as one depicted in his stories. Orphaned at age three, he **(6) raise** by foster parents John and Frances Allan. John Allan refused to support Poe's literary ambitions, even though he **(7) provide** Poe with a first-class education earlier in his life. Ultimately Allan **(8) die** without leaving Poe a penny. If Poe **(9) receive** an inheritance from Allan, his life might not have been so desperate and poverty stricken. Poe never succeeded in earning a living from his writing, even though he **(10) become** famous in his lifetime.

Mastery Test: What Did You Learn?

Choose the best way to rewrite each underlined word or group of words.

Aside from college and the years he teached (1) in West Africa, Joseph Bruchac has lived all his life in a small town in the Adirondacks. Bruchac is presently lives (2) two lives. In one, he is (3) a writer, a businessman, a father, and a husband; in the other, he is the best-known Native American storyteller alive today. For his many highly acclaimed story collections, Bruchac had drawn (4) heavily on his heritage. Moreover, he doesn't just write his stories; they are also performed by him (5). In doing so, he does carry on (6) a tradition that begun (7) hundreds of years ago. Bruchac is believing (8) that his first job as a writer and storyteller is to entertain and his second is to teach. He taught (9) college students and has also worked to help start writing workshops in prisons. Instead of wishing that his life was (10) different, he believes that "if you follow a sort of natural flow, the results are usually much better."

1. A. had taught
   B. taught
   C. will teach
   D. Correct as is

2. A. having lived
   B. being alive
   C. living
   D. Correct as is

3. A. was
   B. were
   C. had been
   D. Correct as is

4. A. has drawn
   B. will draw
   C. was drawing
   D. Correct as is

5. A. he also performs them
   B. he is also performing them
   C. he also performed them
   D. Correct as is

6. A. carried on
   B. carries on
   C. did carry on
   D. Correct as is

7. A. has begun
   B. had begun
   C. began
   D. Correct as is

8. A. has believed
   B. believed
   C. believes
   D. Correct as is

9. A. has taught
   B. had taught
   C. will have taught
   D. Correct as is

10. A. has been
    B. were
    C. is
    D. Correct as is

VERBS

Student Help Desk

Verbs at a Glance

TENSE

	Active VOICE	Passive VOICE
Present	I help.	I am helped.
Past	I helped.	I was helped.
Future	I will help.	I will be helped.
Present Perfect	I have helped.	I have been helped.
Past Perfect	I had helped.	I had been helped.
Future Perfect	I will have helped.	I will have been helped.

MOOD

Indicative

Imperative
Help!

Subjunctive
If you had helped, the job would be done by now.

CHAPTER 6

Troublesome Verb Pairs

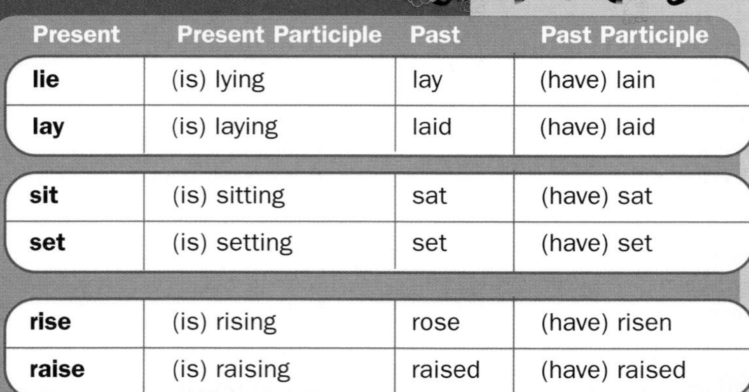

Present	Present Participle	Past	Past Participle
lie	(is) lying	lay	(have) lain
lay	(is) laying	laid	(have) laid
sit	(is) sitting	sat	(have) sat
set	(is) setting	set	(have) set
rise	(is) rising	rose	(have) risen
raise	(is) raising	raised	(have) raised

Do not take a direct object

Lie: I lie in my bed.
I lay there yesterday.
Sit: I sit on my chair.
Rise: I rise early.

Do take a direct object

Lay: I lay my book on my bed.
I laid it there yesterday.
Set: I set my book on my chair.
Raise: I raise my weary eyelids.

Verbs Tenses and Forms

Tense but Not Nervous

Past	
Past	I **wrote** a lot of stories as a child.
Past Progressive	I **was** always **dreaming** about something.
Past Perfect	By the age of seven, I **had written** ten stories.

Present	
Present	I still **enjoy** the experience of writing.
Present Perfect	Writing **has given** me a way to express my dreams.
Present Progressive	Ideas **are** always **popping** into my head.

Future	
Future	One day I **will write** the complete story of my life.
Future Progressive	Probably, I **will be writing** a long time.
Future Perfect	Then I **will have done** something amazing.

Rhymes with Orange

Improve Your Life with Verbs

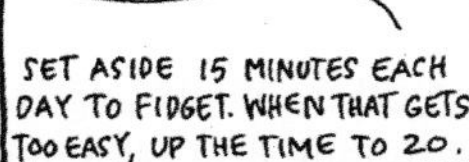

The Bottom Line

Checklist for Using Verbs

Have I . . .

____ checked forms of irregular verbs?

____ checked to make sure I've used the tenses I need?

____ checked for unnecessary shifts in tenses and other forms?

____ checked for correct use of the passive voice?

VERBS

Chapter 7

Subject-Verb Agreement

Theme: The Movies

What's Up?

In the movies, Superman flies. Dinosaurs spring to life, and starships speed through distant galaxies. How does this happen? Only through special effects.

One kind of special effect is created by combining two separate sequences. The actor playing Superman is first filmed in front of a special screen. The image of the screen is later replaced with the desired background. For the effect to work, the two images must blend together perfectly. In a similar way, a writer must seamlessly match the subject and verb in every sentence.

Write Away: Sentence Loops

Have one person in a small group write the beginning of a sentence on a piece of paper and then pass the paper to another person, who writes the end of that sentence and starts another one. Keep going until each person has had a turn, with the first person finishing the last sentence. Have one group member read the story aloud and save it in his or her **Working Portfolio.**

Diagnostic Test: What Do You Know?

Choose the letter of the best revision for each underlined section.

Many think of Stephen King as a writer of horror fiction and expects (1) his films to be typical horror films. Rob Reiner has directed two films based on King's books and have said (2) that King's fiction is intelligent and realistic. King's story "The Body," about four young boys, is the basis of Reiner's film *Stand by Me.* The group look for a dead body and confront (3) a gang of thugs. There is (4) scary moments and fighting in the film, but no gory horror-movie effects. *Misery,* King's novel about a writer and a fan, have also been made into a scary movie that has become (5) popular. Neither *Stand by Me* nor *Misery* is a typical horror film.

1. A. thinks of Stephen King as a writer of horror fiction and expects
   B. think of Stephen King as a writer of horror fiction and expect
   C. thinks of Stephen King as a writer of horror fiction and expect
   D. Correct as is

2. A. has directed two films based on King's books and has said
   B. have directed two films based on King's books and have said
   C. have directed two films based on King's books and has said
   D. Correct as is

3. A. looks for a dead body and confront
   B. look for a dead body and confronts
   C. looks for a dead body and confronts
   D. Correct as is

4. A. be
   B. are
   C. am
   D. Correct as is

5. A. has also been made into a scary movie that has become
   B. have also been made into a scary movie that have become
   C. has also been made into a scary movie that have become
   D. Correct as is

SUBJECT-VERB

Agreement in Number

1 Here's the Idea

▶ **Verbs must agree with their subjects in number.** *Number* refers to whether a word is singular or plural.

Matching Verbs with Subjects

Singular subjects take singular verbs. Plural subjects take plural verbs.

AGREE

A ferocious fistfight looks real in a film.

AGREE

The fighters look as if they were really being punched.

A stunt person knows many tricks to avoid being hurt.

Stunt people know they must make a scene appear real.

If a noun ends in *s*, it is usually plural. However, a verb that ends in *s* is usually singular.

CHAPTER 7

Agreement with Helping Verbs

In a verb phrase, it is the first helping verb that must agree with the subject.

Some movie stars have been trained to do stunts safely.

Often an untrained star has been replaced by a stunt double.

2 Why It Matters in Writing

When you revise, you might change a subject from singular to plural or vice versa. Watch for errors here. If you change the number of a subject, be sure to change the verb too.

STUDENT MODEL

DRAFT	***REVISION***
Stunt people perform action scenes safely and make a film exciting.	**A stunt person** performs action scenes safely and makes a film exciting.

❸ Practice and Apply

A. CONCEPT CHECK: Agreement in Number

For each sentence, write the verb form that agrees with the subject.

Pow! Bam! Crash!

1. A stunt person (undergoes, undergo) training for dangerous scenes.
2. Untrained stunt performers (has, have) had broken bones.
3. Camera angles (helps, help) make a fight seem real.
4. On the set the sheriff (has, have) met an outlaw in an alley.
5. In reality, no punches actually (lands, land) on the actors.
6. The camera (stands, stand) behind one of the actors.
7. The fighter (throws, throw) punches from side to side.
8. The receivers of punches (has, have) learned to throw their head back.
9. Each stunt person also (staggers, stagger) around as if being knocked about.
10. Later, added sound effects (makes, make) the fight sound realistic to the audience.

➔ **For a SELF-CHECK and more practice, see the EXERCISE BANK, p. 323.**

CHALLENGE

Rewrite each sentence above, changing the number of the subject.

B. PROOFREADING: Making Subjects and Verbs Agree

Find and correct ten agreement errors in these paragraphs.

Fakes Make It Look Real

Audiences has seen many dangerous scenes on the screen. But movie props provides safety for the actors. When a character fall through a glass window, it seem that he or she should be cut to pieces. Actually, the "glass" is made of plastic. The plastic sheet shatter into many pieces without sharp edges. This fake glass is called candy glass. Why? In the old days it were made of hardened sugar syrup.

While one actor plunges through a window, other characters breaks tables over one another's heads. Ouch! Luckily, the tables is constructed of balsa wood. This lightweight material do not cause injury to the actors. Isn't it interesting that it take fake materials to make movies look real!

SUBJECT-VERB

Phrases Between Subject and Verb

1 Here's the Idea

When a phrase comes between the subject and verb, the number of the subject is not changed. Focus on the subject when deciding whether the verb should be singular or plural.

Prepositional Phrase

The success of Hollywood films is based on the grosses.
SINGULAR SUBJECT — SINGULAR VERB

Filmgoers at the box office give a financial thumbs up to a film.
PLURAL SUBJECT — PLURAL VERB

Appositive Phrase

***Jurassic Park,* a high-grossing film, has made many millions.**
SINGULAR SUBJECT — SINGULAR VERB

Sequels—*The Lost World* and others—generally make less.
PLURAL SUBJECT — PLURAL VERB

Participial Phrase

Sometimes a movie loved by millions receives a poor review.

Movie lovers, playing critic, turn the movie around.

CHAPTER 7

2 Why It Matters in Writing

Writers often insert phrases between subjects and verbs in order to put relevant information where it belongs. They must keep track of each subject so that they can make the verb agree.

STUDENT MODEL

In the popular movie *Jurassic Park,* a rich man creates a theme park filled with dinosaurs. A **professor** from Arizona, an expert in dinosaur remains, **visits** the park. Unfortunately, the **dinosaurs,** huge and uncontrollable animals, **get** loose and **kill** some humans. The park must be destroyed.

The subject *professor* takes the singular verb *visits.*

The plural subject *dinosaurs* takes the plural verbs *get* and *kill.*

3 Practice and Apply

A. CONCEPT CHECK: Phrases Between Subjects and Verbs

For each sentence, write the verb form that agrees with the subject.

Dinosaurs Up Close

1. *Jurassic Park*, a film about a unique theme park, (combines, combine) real science with imaginative theories.
2. In the movie, DNA fragments from a dinosaur (is, are) found in a prehistoric mosquito.
3. Amber, fossilized resin from trees, (has, have) preserved the mosquito and the DNA.
4. The DNA segments, placed in an ostrich egg, eventually (produces, produce) a dinosaur.
5. Soon the theme park, on a supposedly secure island, (contains, contain) several vicious dinosaurs.
6. Bob Bakker, one of today's leading dinosaur specialists, (says, say) the movie's premise is an impossibility.
7. A mosquito with dinosaur DNA (is, are) an impossibility, since the insect would have digested the DNA before being preserved.
8. DNA from prehistoric times (is, are) likely to be contaminated with other organisms' DNA.
9. Chemicals inside a mother animal (is, are) needed to create a baby of the same species.
10. Most plant foods needed by a herbivorous dinosaur (has, have) died out.

➜ **For a SELF-CHECK and more practice, see the EXERCISE BANK, p. 324.**

SUBJECT-VERB

B. PROOFREADING: Making Subjects and Verbs Agree

Find and correct five agreement errors in this paragraph.

Bringing Dinosaurs to Life

Stan Winston, one of Hollywood's special-effects designers, have brought dinosaurs to life. The *Jurassic Park* creations by his studio seems amazingly realistic. Over a two-year period, small models of a *Tyrannosaurus rex* was transformed into a 9,000-pound, 20-foot sculpture. One model, hooked electronically to the sculpture's joints, were moved about. The movements of the model was reproduced exactly by the life-size "beast."

LESSON 3 Compound Subjects

1 Here's the Idea

▶ **A compound subject contains two or more simple subjects. Compound subjects can take either singular or plural verbs.**

Parts Joined by *And*

A compound subject whose parts are joined by *and* requires a plural verb.

Pictures and movement come together in animated films.

Some compounds act as a single unit and take singular verbs.

An animator's bread and butter is cartoons.

Parts Joined by *Or* or *Nor*

When the parts of a compound subject are joined by *or* or *nor,* the verb should agree with the part closest to it.

SINGULAR OR PLURAL + SINGULAR → SINGULAR VERB

Neither animation cels nor celluloid film was used for that movie.

SINGULAR OR PLURAL + PLURAL → PLURAL VERB

Neither celluloid film nor animation cels were used for that movie.

2 Why It Matters in Writing

In terms of meaning, it often doesn't matter which part of a compound subject comes first. A writer may use whichever order sounds better.

Either the projector or the reels are damaged.

Either the reels or the projector is damaged.

HOT TIP

If a compound subject sounds odd, you can revise the sentence to replace it.

ODD: **Neither the reels nor the projector was replaced.**

BETTER: **No one has replaced the projector or the reels.**

CHAPTER 7

❸ Practice and Apply

A. CONCEPT CHECK: Compound Subjects

For each sentence, write the verb form that agrees with the subject.

Characters in Motion

1. Mickey Mouse and Roger Rabbit (is, are) both products of film animation.
2. In cel animation, an animator and artists called in-betweeners (works, work) together to create a series of drawings.
3. "Extremes" and in-between drawings (makes, make) up an animated scene.
4. Either traditional methods or computer techniques (is, are) used for coloring frames.
5. Neither light pens nor the electronic drawing pad (has, have) been around longer than computers.
6. Animated cartoon figures and human actors (appears, appear) together in *Who Framed Roger Rabbit.*
7. Humans and "toons" (inhabits, inhabit) the same world.
8. Cel animation and computer animation (is, are) not the only animation techniques.
9. Sand-cel animation and finger-painting animation (is, are) two more film animation methods.
10. Hefty box office receipts and high television cartoon ratings (shows, show) the continuing popularity of animation.

➜ **For a SELF-CHECK and more practice, see the EXERCISE BANK, p. 324.**

Rewrite sentences 2, 4, and 5 with the parts of the subjects reversed.

B. WRITING: Interpreting a Cartoon

Describe what's happening in this cartoon, using two sentences that have compound subjects.

By Jack Ziegler

"Action! And this time believe!"

SUBJECT-VERB

Indefinite-Pronoun Subjects

1 Here's the Idea

When used as subjects, some indefinite pronouns are always singular, some are always plural, and some can be either singular or plural, depending on how they're used.

Indefinite Pronouns	
Singular	another, anybody, anyone, anything, each, either, everybody, everyone, everything, much, neither, nobody, no one, nothing, one, somebody, someone, something
Plural	both, few, many, several
Singular or plural	all, any, more, most, none, some

Singular indefinite pronouns take singular verbs.

Everyone has a favorite film star.

Nobody is without opinions on films.

Plural indefinite pronouns take plural verbs.

Many of the films are nominated for Oscars. Few win, however.

Some indefinite pronouns take singular verbs when they refer to one person or thing. They take plural verbs when they refer to two or more people or things.

REFERS TO

Most of the Oscar show is broadcast from Hollywood.
SINGULAR

REFERS TO

Most of the winners appear at the Oscars.
PLURAL

2 Why It Matters in Writing

Writers use indefinite pronouns frequently, especially in making generalizations.

LITERARY MODEL

> **Everyone** knows the location of any number from 1 to 12 on the clock dial and easily can use such a reference to find an object.
>
> —Isaac Asimov, "Dial Versus Digital"

CHAPTER 7

3 Practice and Apply

A. CONCEPT CHECK: Indefinite-Pronoun Subjects

For each sentence, write the verb form that agrees with the subject.

A Night of Excitement

1. Many (watches, watch) the Academy Awards show annually.
2. Few (knows, know), however, that the Oscar statuette is named for a Hollywood librarian's uncle.
3. All of the program (is, are) broadcast live on television.
4. Some of the ceremony (consists, consist) of performances.
5. Several of America's most popular actors (has, have) won more than one Oscar.
6. A few, however, (has, have) never won.
7. Nobody ever (agrees, agree) with all the awards.
8. Most of the nominees (prepares, prepare) speeches.
9. Still, many (talks, talk) too long when accepting their awards.
10. Everyone (is, are) not as brief as Barbra Streisand, who said, "Hello, gorgeous!"

➜ **For a SELF-CHECK and more practice, see the EXERCISE BANK, p. 325.**

SUBJECT-VERB

B. PROOFREADING: Checking Indefinite-Pronoun Agreement

Correct each verb that does not agree with its subject. If a sentence is correct, write *Correct.*

A Range of Talent

(1) Denzel Washington has never realized his ambitions of becoming a doctor or a journalist. **(2)** However, both of these has been played by him on screen. **(3)** Many recalls Washington as a doctor on TV's *St. Elsewhere* and as a reporter in *The Pelican Brief.* **(4)** Some of Washington's best roles has been in historical films. **(5)** Everyone probably remember him as a brave soldier in *Glory.* **(6)** Few have expressed surprise at his Oscar for that role. **(7)** Another of his roles are the title character, an African-American activist, in *Malcolm X.* **(8)** All of the critics has praised Washington's portrayal of the South African activist Steve Biko in *Cry Freedom.* **(9)** Each of these roles have shown Washington's intense dramatic side. **(10)** But none of his fans doubts his talent for light romantic parts, as in *The Preacher's Wife.*

LESSON 5

Other Problem Subjects

1 Here's the Idea

Sometimes the number of a subject can be hard to determine. To decide whether a subject takes a singular or a plural verb, you sometimes need to decide whether the subject refers to a unit or to individuals.

Collective Nouns

A collective noun takes a singular verb if the members of the group act together. A collective noun takes a plural verb if the members of the group act as individuals.

In *Major League*, an inferior team (unit) **strives to improve.**
SINGULAR VERB

The team (individuals) **have different ideas about how to improve.**
PLURAL VERB

CHAPTER 7

Nouns Plural in Form

Some nouns ending in *-s* or *-ics* appear to be plural but are singular in meaning. Use singular verbs with these subjects.

civics	mumps	physics
mathematics	news	politics

In *The Candidate*, politics is the major theme.
SINGULAR VERB

Some words ending in *-ics*, such as *ethics*, can be singular or plural, depending on the context.

Ethics does not play much of a role in the movie.
SINGULAR VERB

The candidate's ethics are questionable.
PLURAL VERB

Titles and Numerical Amounts

▶ **Titles of works of art, literature, film, or music are singular. Words and phrases that refer to weights, measures, numbers, and lengths of time are usually treated as singular.**

Titles and Amounts		
Titles	***Cats*** **is** a long-running musical.	***The Mists of Avalon*** **tells** about the women of King Arthur's time.
Amounts	**Eight dollars seems** too much to pay for a movie.	**Five cups is** the amount in the largest soft drink.
Time	**Two hours is** the running time of this film.	**Five days is** the limit for borrowing library videos.

Fractions, such as *three-quarters* and *seven-eighths,* can be considered singular or plural, depending on the context.

REFERS TO

Three-quarters of the audience was asleep.

SINGULAR

REFERS TO

Two-thirds of the viewers were eager to see another movie.

PLURAL

2 Why It Matters in Writing

In writing about certain topics, you may need to use tricky subjects, such as titles or nouns that sound plural but are not. If you are uncertain whether to use plural or singular verbs, try substituting another word or phrase for each problem subject.

Raiders of the Lost Ark **is a very popular movie.**

(The adventure film) is a very popular movie.

Twenty million dollars was budgeted for the film.

(A large amount of money) was budgeted for the film.

SUBJECT-VERB

3 Practice and Apply

A. CONCEPT CHECK: Other Problem Subjects

For each sentence, write the verb form that agrees with the subject.

Enduring Classics

1. The big news in Hollywood (is, are) the popularity of films based on classic literature.
2. Jane Austen's novel *Sense and Sensibility* (has, have) been made into a popular movie.
3. In that film, an English family (moves, move) to a new home.
4. A pair of sisters (falls, fall) in love with two very different men.
5. Politics (plays, play) no central role in Austen's novels.
6. In *Emma,* a group of people in an English village (deals, deal) with issues of love and marriage.
7. For many movie fans, two hours in a 19th-century English village (is, are) an engaging experience.
8. The literary audience (has, have) always appreciated films based on Shakespeare's plays.
9. *Romeo and Juliet* (has, have) been the basis of several films.
10. A fine cast (portrays, portray) scenes from Shakespeare's life and works in *Shakespeare in Love.*

➜ **For a SELF-CHECK and more practice, see the EXERCISE BANK, p. 325.**

CHAPTER 7

B. EDITING AND PROOFREADING: Correcting Agreement Errors

Rewrite any sentence that contains an error in subject-verb agreement. Write *Correct* if there is no error.

Mad for Musicals

1. Nine-tenths of us has probably enjoyed a musical film.
2. *The Jazz Singer* is considered the first musical.
3. The most popular dance team in musicals were composed of Ginger Rogers and Fred Astaire.
4. A singing family face Nazism in *The Sound of Music.*
5. "Summer Nights" are sung by John Travolta and Olivia Newton-John in the musical film *Grease*.
6. Thirty-six hours are the time period covered in *A Hard Day's Night,* a musical featuring the Beatles.
7. The band display a zany comedy style.
8. *The Commitments* are a contemporary musical.
9. An Irish rock group are at the center of this movie.
10. The cast of most musicals is usually quite big.

LESSON 6

Special Sentence Problems

1 Here's the Idea

Making a verb agree with its subject can be tricky when the subject is difficult to identify.

Questions

In many questions, subjects follow verbs or come between parts of verb phrases. To find the subject in such a question, rewrite the question as a statement. Use the verb form that agrees with the subject of the statement.

Are comedians respected as much as serious actors?

Comedians are respected as much as serious actors.

Is comedy harder to perform than drama?

Comedy is harder to perform than drama.

Sentences Beginning with *Here* or *There*

In sentences beginning with *here* or *there,* those words rarely function as subjects. The subjects usually follow the verbs.

There are many famous comedies in the history of film.

Here is a video full of funny scenes.

Inverted Sentences

In an inverted sentence, the subject follows the verb. Do not confuse a word in an initial phrase with the subject.

Even more touching than the dramatic actors are the clowns.

The clowns are even more touching than the dramatic actors.

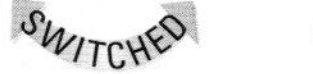

Over the wall scrambles the runaway thief.

The runaway thief scrambles over the wall.

SUBJECT-VERB

Predicate Nominatives

In a sentence containing a predicate nominative, the verb must agree with the subject, not with the predicate nominative.

Jan's main passion is the comedies of Robin Williams.

AGREE — PREDICATE NOMINATIVE

The comedies of Robin Williams are Jan's main passion.

AGREE — PREDICATE NOMINATIVE

Relative Pronouns as Subjects

When a relative pronoun (*who, which,* or *that*) is the subject of an adjective clause, its number is determined by the number of the word it refers to.

An actor who plays both comedy and drama is unusual.

REFERS TO

Actors who play both comedy and drama are unusual.

Don't be fooled by *don't* and *doesn't.* These words are contractions made up of a helping verb (*do* or *does*) and the word *not.* The helping verb should agree with the subject, as usual.

Comedians don't usually win Oscars.

Sammi doesn't think that makes any sense.

2 Why It Matters in Writing

When you write, you probably start sentences with *here* and *there* and use predicate nominatives without thinking, just as you do when talking. Check for subject-verb agreement as you revise.

STUDENT MODEL

In *Love and Marriage,* television and film star Bill Cosby tells the story of his courtship. There are some serious moments in the book, but parts of it ~~is~~ are sheer comedy. Here ~~are~~ is one of the funny parts: when he tries to take out one girl to make another one jealous, both girls catch on.

❸ Practice and Apply

A. CONCEPT CHECK: Special Sentence Problems

For each sentence, write the correct verb form in parentheses. Then write the subject with which the verb agrees.

The Great Stone Face

1. (Does, Do) Buster Keaton outshine Charlie Chaplin as a film comedian?
2. Revealed in over 40 movies (is, are) Keaton's unique comic character.
3. Keaton's films, which often (includes, include) elements of absurdity, seem modern today.
4. Battles against modern technology (is, are) the subject of many of Keaton's films.
5. (Doesn't, Don't) the greatest chase scene in comedy occur in Keaton's *The General?*
6. Keaton conceived some comedic moments that (is, are) still imitated today.
7. Through all the films (runs, run) Keaton's stone-faced comedy.
8. There (is, are) only one movie that shows Keaton laughing.
9. (Is, Are) "The Great Stone Face" a good nickname for Keaton?
10. Down the faces of Keaton's audiences always (pours, pour) tears of laughter.

➜ **For a SELF-CHECK and more practice, see the EXERCISE BANK, p. 326.**

Rewrite each inverted sentence and question as a declarative sentence in which the subject precedes the verb.

B. WRITING: Maintaining Agreement

The photo shows Michael Jordan facing the Monstars in the movie *Space Jam.* Write five sentences describing the scene, using sentence forms discussed in this lesson.

Working Portfolio

Return to the group you joined for the **Write Away** on page 154. Take out the sentence loops and work together to check subject-verb agreement. Revise if necessary.

Real World Grammar

Movie Review

A local library is setting up a database of movie reviews and has asked students to contribute to it. Because reviews are written in the present tense, errors in subject-verb agreement can easily creep in. Read Rayla's review of the movie *Glory*. The comments were made by the video librarian, who asked Rayla to correct some errors that might confuse readers.

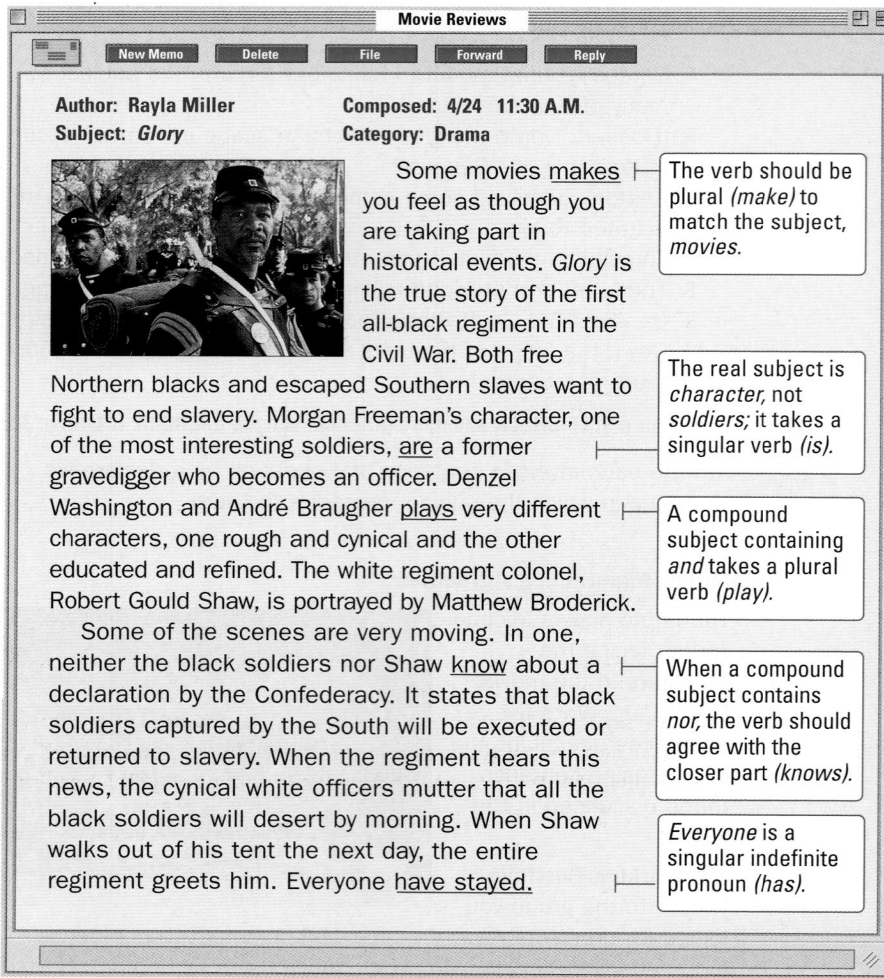

Movie Reviews

New Memo | Delete | File | Forward | Reply

Author: Rayla Miller **Composed: 4/24 11:30 A.M.**
Subject: *Glory* **Category: Drama**

Some movies <u>makes</u> you feel as though you are taking part in historical events. *Glory* is the true story of the first all-black regiment in the Civil War. Both free Northern blacks and escaped Southern slaves want to fight to end slavery. Morgan Freeman's character, one of the most interesting soldiers, <u>are</u> a former gravedigger who becomes an officer. Denzel Washington and André Braugher <u>plays</u> very different characters, one rough and cynical and the other educated and refined. The white regiment colonel, Robert Gould Shaw, is portrayed by Matthew Broderick.

Some of the scenes are very moving. In one, neither the black soldiers nor Shaw <u>know</u> about a declaration by the Confederacy. It states that black soldiers captured by the South will be executed or returned to slavery. When the regiment hears this news, the cynical white officers mutter that all the black soldiers will desert by morning. When Shaw walks out of his tent the next day, the entire regiment greets him. Everyone <u>have stayed.</u>

The verb should be plural *(make)* to match the subject, *movies.*

The real subject is *character,* not *soldiers;* it takes a singular verb *(is).*

A compound subject containing *and* takes a plural verb *(play).*

When a compound subject contains *nor,* the verb should agree with the closer part *(knows).*

Everyone is a singular indefinite pronoun *(has).*

Using Grammar in Writing

Agreement in number	Watch out for plural subjects that don't look plural. Examples include plural nouns that don't end in *-s* (*children, mice, deer*) and collective nouns that refer to groups acting as individuals (*the committee take their seats*).
Words between subjects and verbs	When you add a detail by inserting a phrase after the subject of a sentence, make sure the verb agrees with the sentence's real subject.
Compound subjects	When using compound subjects to compare or contrast or to combine sentences, make sure the verbs agree with the subjects.
Indefinite pronouns	When you use an indefinite-pronoun subject to make a generalization, make sure the verb agrees in number with the pronoun.

PRACTICE AND APPLY: Editing and Proofreading

Here is another review of a popular movie. Correct the sentences that contain errors in subject-verb agreement. If a sentence contains no errors, write *Correct.*

STUDENT MODEL

The Fugitive

(1) Good characters, a fast-moving plot, and suspense is all part of *The Fugitive.* **(2)** Dr. Richard Kimble, a convicted murderer, escapes from a prison train. **(3)** He try to prove his innocence and stay ahead of U.S. Marshal Samuel Gerard. **(4)** Kimble sneaks into two hospitals and a federal building. **(5)** A sewer and a St. Patrick's Day parade is places he hides from Gerard. **(6)** Straight over a huge dam plunge Kimble in one scene. **(7)** Is these believable situations? **(8)** It don't really matter, because the story is so exciting. **(9)** Kimble and Gerard are portrayed by the actors Harrison Ford and Tommy Lee Jones. **(10)** The work of these two actors have always been of high quality. **(11)** Does Kimble prove his innocence? **(12)** Doesn't you want to find out for yourself?

SUBJECT-VERB

Mixed Review

A. Agreement in Number Read the following review of a movie that introduced new animation techniques. Then answer the questions below it.

PROFESSIONAL MODEL

(1) *Who Framed Roger Rabbit* is the kind of movie that gets made once in a blue moon. . . . **(2)** This movie is not only a great entertainment, but a breakthrough in craftsmanship—the first film to convincingly combine real actors and animated cartoon characters in the same space in the same time and make it look real.

(3) I've never seen anything like it before. **(4)** Roger Rabbit and his cartoon comrades cast real shadows. **(5)** They shake the hands and grab the coats and rattle the teeth of real actors. **(6)** They change size and dimension and perspective as they move through a scene, and the camera isn't locked down in one place to make it easy, either—**(7)** the camera in this movie moves around like it's in a 1940s thriller, **(8)** and the cartoon characters look three-dimensional and seem to be occupying real space.

—Roger Ebert, review of *Who Framed Roger Rabbit*

CHAPTER 7

1. In sentence 1, find the first verb. Is it singular or plural?
2. In sentence 2, find the two predicate nominatives. Is the verb singular or plural?
3. What are the subject and the verb in sentence 3?
4. In sentence 4, why is the verb *cast* in the plural?
5. What three verbs agree with the subject *They* in sentence 5?
6. Identify the first subject and verb in sentence 6.
7. Identify the first subject and verb in sentence part 7. What phrase appears between the subject and the verb?
8. In sentence part 8, what is the subject of the verbs *look* and *seem?*

B. Additional Agreement Problems Write the verb form that agrees with the subject of each sentence.

1. John Sayles, the director of many independent films, (has, have) written numerous horror movies.
2. The money paid for these scripts (helps, help) finance Sayles's independent films.
3. Sixty thousand dollars (is, are) what Sayles spent on his popular film about college activists, *Return of the Secaucus 7*.
4. Both *Matewan* and *Eight Men Out* (deals, deal) with injustices in American society.
5. Many of the same actors (appears, appear) repeatedly in Sayles's films.

Mastery Test: What Did You Learn?

Choose the letter of the best revision for each underlined section.

> Science fiction movies, which remain wildly popular, inspires (1) speculation about life on other worlds. The idea of extraterrestrial beings comfort some people and scares (2) others. *E.T. the Extra-Terrestrial,* one of the most popular movies ever made, introduce a charming creature that delight (3) audiences. *Aliens* feature a species far different from the lovable E.T. and frighten (4) some with its vision. Many prefer *Star Wars* and find (5) its community of humans and nonhumans intriguing. Whether you see aliens as "cat people" or as robots, you will find a compelling extraterrestrial vision in science fiction films.

1. A. movies, which remain wildly popular, inspire
   B. movies, which remains wildly popular, inspires
   C. movies, which remains wildly popular, inspire
   D. Correct as is

2. A. comforts some people and scare
   B. comforts some people and scares
   C. comfort some people and scare
   D. Correct as is

3. A. introduces a charming creature that delight
   B. introduces a charming creature that delights
   C. introduce a charming creature that delights
   D. Correct as is

4. A. features a species far different from the lovable E.T. and frightens
   B. features a species far different from the lovable E.T. and frighten
   C. feature a species far different from the lovable E.T. and frightens
   D. Correct as is

5. A. prefers *Star Wars* and find
   B. prefers *Star Wars* and finds
   C. prefer *Star Wars* and finds
   D. Correct as is

Student Help Desk

Subject-Verb Agreement at a Glance

Subjects and verbs must always agree in number.

- **A singular subject takes a singular verb.**
- **Plural subjects take plural verbs.**

CHAPTER 7

Phrases Between Subjects and Verbs

If You See	Use This Kind of Verb	Example
Singular subject + phrase + verb	singular	**Nora** on her best days **reads** three scripts.
Plural subject + phrase + verb	plural	**The Nelsons,** partners in movie production, **choose** only the best ones.

Compound Subjects

Double Exposure

If You See	Use This Kind of Verb	Example
and	plural	**Zoe and Zack watch** three movies a week.
or, nor	singular or plural, to agree with the part nearest the verb	**Neither Zoe nor Zack has** time for more. **Neither Zoe nor her friends have** time for more.

Indefinite-Pronoun Subjects

Cast of Thousands

If You See	Use This Kind of Verb	Example
another, anybody, anyone, everyone, everything, neither, nobody, someone	singular	**Everyone** in the cast **arrives** at eight in the morning.
both, few, many, several	plural	**Few** of the costumes **are done.**
all, any, more, most, none, some	singular or plural, depending on whether the pronoun refers to one or more than one	**Most wear** their own clothes until the final rehearsal.

SUBJECT–VERB

The Bottom Line

Checklist for Subject-Verb Agreement

Have I . . .

- ____ correctly identified the subjects of all sentences, including questions?
- ____ made each verb agree in number with its subject?
- ____ recognized that intervening phrases do not affect the number of verbs?
- ____ used correct verb forms with compound subjects?
- ____ used correct verb forms with indefinite-pronoun subjects?
- ____ used correct verb forms with collective-noun subjects?
- ____ used correct verb forms with titles and amounts?
- ____ made verbs agree with the subjects rather than with predicate nominatives?
- ____ used correct verb forms with relative-pronoun subjects?
- ____ used *don't* and *doesn't* correctly?

Chapter 8

Using Pronouns

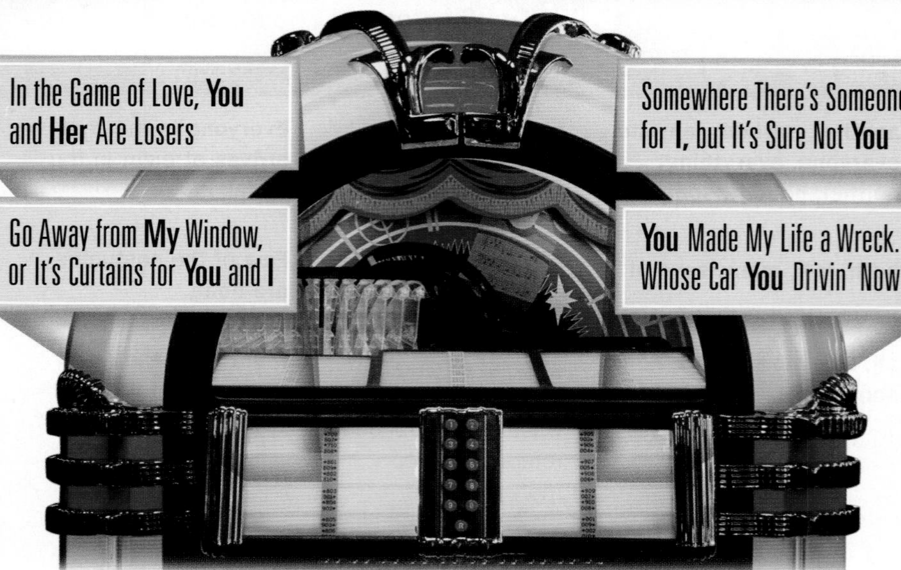
In the Game of Love, **You** and **Her** Are Losers
Somewhere There's Someone for **I**, but It's Sure Not **You**
Go Away from **My** Window, or It's Curtains for **You** and **I**
You Made My Life a Wreck. Whose Car **You** Drivin' Now?

Theme: Music and Musicians

What's Wrong with This Song?

Some country music songs have long and humorous titles like those listed in the jukebox. Many of these songs tell sad stories of heartbreak and betrayal. Unfortunately, whoever wrote the songs above has more than just a broken heart to be sad about—this person doesn't know how to use pronouns correctly! Can you figure out what the pronoun errors are in these song titles?

Using pronouns correctly may not be important for song titles, but you would not want to make these same errors in your own writing. In this chapter you will learn about different pronoun forms and when to use them.

Write Away: Titles for Tunes

Make up two or three song titles of your own. Use pronouns correctly in each title. Put your titles in your **Working Portfolio.**

Diagnostic Test: What Do You Know?

Choose the best way to rewrite each underlined word or word group.

When you listen to music, do you think about its (1) origins? People typically respond to this question by saying, "My friends and me (2) don't think about this. We (3) just like the music." Music has been an important part of ours (4) existence since the beginning of humankind. Historians tell scholars and we (5) that humans began to sing as soon as them (6) developed language. Like us, people in ancient civilizations used they're (7) voices to express feelings. However, most ancient music was not meant to entertain. Ancient musicians played them (8) mainly during important ceremonies. The ancient people whom (9) were most interested in music were the early Greeks. They thought music had a positive role in the education of young people. They also believed that young people who (10) listened to good music would become better adults.

1. A. it's
   B. it is
   C. their
   D. Correct as is

2. A. My friends and us
   B. My friends and I
   C. Me and my friends
   D. Correct as is

3. A. Us
   B. Them
   C. You
   D. Correct as is

4. A. our
   B. theirs
   C. their
   D. Correct as is

5. A. scholars and I
   B. scholars and they
   C. scholars and us
   D. Correct as is

6. A. they
   B. their
   C. it
   D. Correct as is

7. A. there
   B. theirs
   C. their
   D. Correct as is

8. A. they
   B. it
   C. its
   D. Correct as is

9. A. whomever
   B. who
   C. whose
   D. Correct as is

10. A. whom
    B. whoever
    C. whomever
    D. Correct as is

LESSON 1

Pronoun Cases

1 Here's the Idea

Personal pronouns take on different forms depending on how they are used in sentences. These forms are called cases.

There are three pronoun cases: the nominative case, the objective case, and the possessive case. The chart below shows personal pronouns sorted by case, number, and person.

Personal Pronouns

	Nominative	Objective	Possessive
Singular			
First person	I	me	my, mine
Second person	you	you	your, yours
Third person	he, she, it	him, her, it	his, her, hers, its
Plural			
First person	we	us	our, ours
Second person	you	you	your, yours
Third person	they	them	their, theirs

CHAPTER 8

2 Why It Matters in Writing

The most common errors in writing concern pronouns. Be sure to check your writing for pronoun errors and correct any you find. In this chapter, you will learn the reasons for the corrections shown in the model below.

STUDENT MODEL

My friends and ~~**me**~~ I are musicians in a Tejano band. Tejano music comes from the region of Texas that is close to the Texas-Mexico border. **It** is a combination of musical traditions from Spain, Mexico, Germany, and Poland. Different Tejano bands have taken ~~**its**~~ their influences from polkas, waltzes, rock and roll, and other kinds of music. **Our** band has a modern sound, although ~~**you**~~ we sometimes play older styles of Tejano music.

LESSON 2 Nominative and Objective Cases

1 Here's the Idea

Writers often mix up the nominative and the objective cases of pronouns. To figure out which pronoun form to use, you first need to figure out how the pronoun functions in the sentence.

The Nominative Case

▶ **The nominative form of a personal pronoun is used when a pronoun functions as a subject or a predicate nominative.**

We saw Bonnie Raitt in concert. She played the guitar.
(We — SUBJECT; She — SUBJECT)

Nominative Pronoun Forms

	First Person	Second Person	Third Person
Singular	I	you	he, she, it
Plural	we	you	they

A nominative pronoun may be used as part of a compound subject.

Jerry and he went to the concert.
COMPOUND SUBJECT

Use the chart below to help you choose the correct pronoun case in a compound subject.

Here's How **Choosing the Correct Case**

Arlo and (I, me) sang a song.

1. Try each part of the compound subject alone in the sentence.

   Arlo sang a song.

   I sang a song. (CORRECT)

   Me sang a song. (INCORRECT)

2. Choose the correct case for the sentence.

   Arlo and I sang a song.

When a nominative pronoun is used as a predicate nominative, it is called a **predicate pronoun**. A predicate pronoun immediately follows a linking verb and identifies the subject of the sentence.

It was they who stood up and cheered.
(It — SUBJECT; was — LINKING VERB; they — PREDICATE PRONOUN)

PRONOUNS

You may not use these forms in everyday speech, but you should use them in formal writing, such as applications and reports.

The Objective Case

The objective form of a personal pronoun is used when the pronoun functions as a direct object, an indirect object, or an object of a preposition.

Rena called her. (DIRECT OBJECT)

Rena lent me the CD. (INDIRECT OBJECT)

Rena gave the poster to us. (OBJECT OF A PREPOSITION)

Objective Pronoun Forms

	First Person	Second Person	Third Person
Singular	me	you	him, her, it
Plural	us	you	them

CHAPTER 8

An objective pronoun is used as part of a compound object.

- Direct object **We heard Sam and her in concert.**
- Indirect object **Charlie wrote Sonya and me a song.**
- Object of a preposition **Play your banjo for their class and us.**

To make sure you are using the correct pronoun case in a compound object, look at each part of the object separately.

Here's How Choosing the Correct Case

Yuki played a song for Holly and (he, him).

1. Try each part of the compound object alone in the sentence.
   Yuki played a song for Holly.
   Yuki played a song for he. (INCORRECT)
   Yuki played a song for him. (CORRECT)
2. Choose the correct case for the sentence.
   Yuki played a song for Holly and him.

Writers often mistakenly use the nominative case after the preposition *between*. Always use the objective case after this preposition.

INCORRECT: **The musician stood between he and I.**

CORRECT: **The musician stood between him and me.**

❷ Why It Matters in Writing

Many people incorrectly assume that *I* always sounds better than *me.* Remember that *I* is correct only if the pronoun's function calls for the nominative case.

STUDENT MODEL

My aunt invited my friend Sharon and ~~I~~ me to a jazz concert. My aunt and I are big fans of jazz piano. After the concert, Sharon took a picture of one of the musicians and ~~I~~ me.

❸ Practice and Apply

A. CONCEPT CHECK: Nominative and Objective Cases

For each sentence, write the correct pronoun from those in parentheses. Then identify the pronoun as nominative (N) or objective (O).

***Cats* on Broadway**

1. The composer Andrew Lloyd Webber has given (we, us) many wonderful musicals.
2. It is (he, him) who wrote the long-running musical *Cats.*
3. Lloyd Webber first got the idea for writing this show when (he, him) bought a book of poems by T. S. Eliot in an airport bookstore.
4. Lloyd Webber's mother used to read these poems to (he, him) when he was a child.
5. Eventually, his friend Trevor Nunn and (he, him) turned Eliot's poems into a musical.
6. Choreographers, costume designers, and other creative people worked with (they, them) to develop the show.
7. As the story opens, several cats have gathered in a junkyard where (they, them) take turns singing about themselves.
8. One of the cats is named Grizabella. It is (her, she) who sings the classic song "Memory."
9. Andrew Lloyd Webber is a very successful composer, although some critics have given (he, him) and his shows poor reviews.
10. His fans are loyal to (he, him) and his work. Many have seen *Cats* more than once.

➜ **For a SELF-CHECK and more practice, see the EXERCISE BANK, p. 326.**

B. EDITING: Using Pronoun Cases Correctly

Replace each underlined noun with a nominative or an objective pronoun.

A Young Performer

Concert violinist Midori began playing violin when **(1)** Midori was only a little girl of three. Zubin Mehta, the man who was conductor of the New York Philharmonic orchestra, first heard the young violinist play when **(2)** the young violinist was 11. Her poise and talent impressed **(3)** Zubin Mehta. It was **(4)** Zubin Mehta who gave Midori the opportunity to be a soloist in the Philharmonic's traditional New Year's Eve concert. The audience was amazed at the young girl's talent, and **(5)** the audience members gave **(6)** Midori a standing ovation. Audiences have always been impressed by Midori's maturity and sense of calm on stage. When Midori was 14, concert-goers in Massachusetts heard the Boston Symphony and **(7)** Midori. During the concert, a string on Midori's violin broke twice. **(8)** Midori simply borrowed another violin each time, and **(9)** Midori kept playing. Musical ability seems to run in Midori's family: her mother and **(10)** Midori are both violinists. In fact, Midori's mother was her first violin teacher.

CHAPTER 8

C. WRITING: Sentences with Pronouns

Sidewalk Concert

Imagine that you are part of the scene in the photograph below. You might be one of the musicians, the plant store owner, or a customer. Write five sentences about the photograph using the compound subjects and objects below.

Example: my friends and I

Answer: On Saturdays, my friends and I perform in front of the plant store.

1. the two violinists and me
2. the customers and I
3. my friends and me
4. us and our instruments
5. other musicians and they

The Possessive Case

1 Here's the Idea

Personal pronouns that show ownership or relationships are in the possessive case.

Possessive Pronoun Forms

	First Person	Second Person	Third Person
Singular	my, mine	your, yours	his, her, hers, its
Plural	our, ours	your, yours	their, theirs

Possessive pronouns can be used in two ways.

1. A possessive pronoun can be used in place of a noun. The pronoun can function as a subject or an object.

   Where are the earplugs?
   Let me borrow yours. Mine are upstairs.
   DIRECT OBJECT ↑ ↑ SUBJECT

2. A possessive pronoun can be used as an adjective to modify a noun or a gerund. The pronoun comes before the word it modifies.

   Jeb is playing his bongo drums. NOUN ↑ **Our complaining doesn't help.** ↑ GERUND

Don't confuse gerunds with present participles. These verbals both end in *-ing*, but a possessive pronoun is used only before a gerund (acting as a noun) and not before a participle.

POSSESSIVE
His playing has improved since last year.
↑ GERUND

We heard him playing in the auditorium.
OBJECTIVE ↑ ↑ PRESENT PARTICIPLE

For more information on gerunds and present participles, see pp. 71–74.

Some contractions and possessive pronouns sound alike, but they have different spellings and meanings. Be sure to use all of these words correctly.

- **You're** a songwriter. [*you are*]
- **They're** ballads. [*they are*]
- **There's** the CD player. [*there is*]
- **It's** bothering my dog. [*it is*]
- **Your** songs are great.
- **Their** ballads are famous.
- The CD player is **theirs**.
- Listen to **its** howling.

PRONOUNS

❷ Why It Matters in Writing

It's easy to confuse contractions and possessive pronouns. Be sure to look for and correct these errors in your work.

STUDENT MODEL

George Clinton is the mastermind behind the two greatest funk bands—Parliament and Funkadelic. ~~They're~~ Their music is influenced by gospel, doo-wop, and jazz. It's more dance-oriented than rock is.

❸ Practice and Apply

CONCEPT CHECK: The Possessive Case

Write the correct form of the pronoun from those given in parentheses.

The Beatles

1. As a young teenager, John Lennon said to his aunt, "You throw (my, mine) poetry out and you'll regret it when I'm famous."
2. Did Lennon know that someday (he, his) songs would make him a star?
3. In 1956, Lennon met Paul McCartney, and the two musicians worked together to improve (they're, their) playing.
4. With other musicians, Lennon and McCartney formed a band called the Quarrymen, which they named after (their, theirs) high school.
5. Many young people heard (them, their) playing in music clubs.
6. The group changed (it's, its) name to the Beatles in 1960.
7. One British newspaper editorial said this about the Beatles: "If they don't sweep (your, you're) blues away, brother you're a lost cause."
8. In 1964, the Beatles came to the United States, and (them, their) singing made teenagers go crazy.
9. More than one teenage girl waiting outside a theater fainted at the sight of (her, hers) musical idols driving by.
10. In a time like (our, ours), can you think of a music group that makes fans respond this way?

➜ **For a SELF-CHECK and more practice, see the EXERCISE BANK, p. 327.**

Using *Who* and *Whom*

1 Here's the Idea

The case of the pronoun *who* is determined by the pronoun's function in a sentence.

Forms of *Who* and *Whoever*	
Nominative	who, whoever
Objective	whom, whomever
Possessive	whose, whosever

Who and *whom* can be used to ask questions and to introduce subordinate clauses.

Who and *Whom* in Questions

Who is the nominative form. In a question, *who* is used as a subject or as a predicate pronoun.

Who wrote the song "This Land Is Your Land"?
SUBJECT

The writer was who?
PREDICATE PRONOUN

Whom is the objective form. In a question, *whom* is used as a direct or indirect object of a verb or as the object of a preposition.

Whom did you ask?
DIRECT OBJECT

From whom did you get the information?
OBJECT OF PREPOSITION

Here's How **Choosing *Who* or *Whom* in a Question**

(Who, Whom) are you speaking to?

1. Rewrite the question as a statement.

   You are speaking to (who, whom).

2. Figure out whether the pronoun is used as a subject, an object, a predicate pronoun, or an object of a preposition and choose the correct form. The pronoun in the sentence above is the object of a preposition. The correct form is *whom.*

   You are speaking to whom.

3. Use the correct form in the question.

   Whom are you speaking to?

Who and *Whom* in Subordinate Clauses

Who and *whom* are also used to introduce subordinate clauses. To choose the correct form, you must figure out how the pronoun is used in the clause. *Who* should be used when the pronoun functions as the subject of a subordinate clause.

Pete Seeger is a singer who cares about the environment.
SUBJECT SUBORDINATE CLAUSE

Whom should be used when the pronoun functions as a direct object, an indirect object, or an object of a preposition.

Bob Dylan is one singer whom Pete Seeger influenced.
DIRECT OBJECT SUBORDINATE CLAUSE

Use the chart below to help you figure out whether to use *who* or *whom* in a subordinate clause.

Here's How Choosing *Who* or *Whom* in a Clause

Pete Seeger is a singer (who, whom) I admire.

1. Identify the subordinate clause in the sentence.
   (who, whom) I admire
2. Figure out how the pronoun is used in the clause. Is it a subject or an object? You may have to rearrange the clause to figure this out.
   I admire (who, whom).

   The pronoun is a direct object in the clause. The correct form is *whom.*

   I admire whom.
3. Use the correct form in the clause.
   Pete Seeger is a singer whom I admire.

2 Why It Matters in Writing

You will be expected to use *who* and *whom* correctly in formal writing, such as application letters, term papers, and reports. Don't assume that *whom* is just a more formal version of *who*. Choose the form that fits the way the pronoun is used.

Peanuts by Charles Schulz

❸ Practice and Apply

A. CONCEPT CHECK: Using *Who* and *Whom*

Write the correct form of the pronoun from those given in parentheses.

Pete Seeger: American Troubadour

1. (Who, Whom) is known as "America's tuning fork"?
2. Pete Seeger is a musician (who, whom) many regard as America's greatest folksinger.
3. Seeger is a musician for (who, whom) music has many purposes: to entertain, to bring people together, and to spread ideas.
4. At 16, Seeger heard folk music for the first time when he attended a music festival with his father, (who, whom) was a music historian and scholar.
5. Seeger listened closely to the musicians (who, whom) played the 5-string banjo, and he fell in love with this instrument.
6. As a young man, Seeger traveled thousands of miles around the country, learning new folksongs and playing his banjo for (whoever, whomever) would pay him or give him food.
7. Woody Guthrie and Leadbelly are two other great musicians (who, whom) Seeger admired.
8. For (who, whom) has Seeger played? He has played for audiences in concert halls and auditoriums all over.
9. He plays for (whoever, whomever) is interested in listening.
10. (Who, Whom) will he entertain next?

➜ **For a SELF-CHECK and more practice, see the EXERCISE BANK, p. 328.**

B. REVISING: Correcting *Who* and *Whom* Errors

Rewrite the following paragraph. Correct any errors in the use of *who* and *whom*.

New Talent, Ancient Music

Do you know whom Anoushka Shankar is? Many people don't yet, but they might know her father. Ravi Shankar is an Indian classical music master and teacher who made Indian sitar music known in the United States. Who did he teach? One of his students was former Beatle George Harrison. Now Anoushka has become a talented sitar player, taught by her father who she gives concerts with. Anoushka, who recorded her first CD when she was 17, began studying Indian music when she was 9. Who does she get her inspiration from? It comes from her father.

Pronoun-Antecedent Agreement

1 Here's the Idea

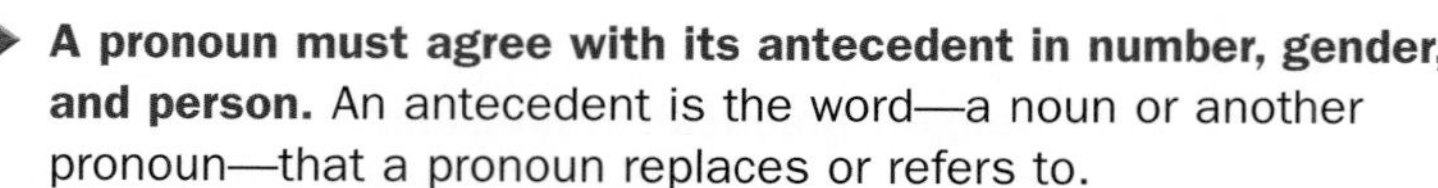

A pronoun must agree with its antecedent in number, gender, and person. An antecedent is the word—a noun or another pronoun—that a pronoun replaces or refers to.

Agreement in Number

Most of the time, making a pronoun agree in number with its antecedent is easy: a plural antecedent takes a plural pronoun, and a singular antecedent takes a singular pronoun.

Here are three trouble spots that confuse writers and readers.

1. A collective noun, such as *team*, *audience*, *herd*, or *family,* may be referred to by either a singular or a plural pronoun. The collective noun's number is determined by its meaning in the sentence.

Use a singular pronoun to refer to a collective noun whose parts act as a single unit.

The orchestra will give its final performance tonight.
(The orchestra is acting as a single unit.)

Use a plural pronoun to refer to a collective noun whose parts act individually.

The orchestra have tuned up their instruments.
(The orchestra members are acting individually.)

2. A plural pronoun is used to refer to nouns or pronouns joined by *and.*

REFERS TO

Marla and Denise played their trumpets together.

3. A pronoun that refers to nouns or pronouns joined by *or* or *nor* should agree with the noun or pronoun nearest to it.

REFERS TO

Neither the conductor nor the musicians have taken their places on stage. PLURAL PRONOUN

CHAPTER 8

Agreement in Gender

The gender of a pronoun must be the same as the gender of its antecedent. The chart below shows pronouns by gender.

Pronoun Gender		
Feminine	**Masculine**	**Neuter**
she, her, hers	he, him, his	it, its

When the antecedent of a singular pronoun could be either feminine or masculine, you can use the phrase *his or her.*

Each musician played his or her solo.

If using *his or her* sounds awkward, try making both the pronoun and its antecedent plural.

All the musicians played their solos.

Agreement in Person

The person of a pronoun must match the person of its antecedent.

All students should bring ~~your~~ their favorite CD to class.

The pronouns *one, everyone,* and *everybody* are third person and singular. They are referred to by *he, him, his, she, her,* and *hers.*

Everyone has his or her favorite recordings.

❷ Why It Matters in Writing

Using the correct pronoun when a collective noun is the antecedent will give your readers information about whether the group is behaving as one unit or as individuals.

STUDENT MODEL

The **Bristol High School Jazz Band** finished recording **its** first CD this week. The recording session was the prize for winning the All-County Jazz Band Contest. The **band** were thrilled when **they** learned about the unusual prize.

PRONOUNS

❸ Practice and Apply

A. CONCEPT CHECK: Pronoun-Antecedent Agreement

Write the correct pronoun from those given in parentheses.

Jazz in the Family

1. The Marsalis family is unusual because five out of eight of (their, its) members are professional musicians.
2. Everyone in this family has (his or her, their) own special talent.
3. Ellis Marsalis, a musician and educator, shared a love of jazz with (his, their) sons.
4. Before Dolores Marsalis married Ellis Marsalis and became the mother of six sons, (she, he) was a jazz singer.
5. Like (their, his) father, Wynton, Branford, Delfeayo, and Jason Marsalis are jazz musicians.
6. Even in high school, these musicians understood that (they, you) had to take music seriously to succeed.
7. Wynton and Branford were taught piano by (his, their) father.
8. Neither Branford nor his brothers chose piano as (his, their) main instrument.
9. The Marsalis brothers learned from (his, their) father that playing music requires education, discipline, and inspiration.
10. New Orleans, a city famous for (their, its) jazz, is the Marsalises' hometown.

➜ **For a SELF-CHECK and more practice, see the EXERCISE BANK, p. 328.**

B. REVISING: Agreement with Collective Nouns

Rewrite each sentence below so that the pronouns agree with their collective noun antecedents. Write *Correct* if there is no error.

All That Jazz

1. Last Saturday night, the jazz band gave their first performance.
2. Before the concert, the band unpacked its instruments.
3. The audience showed its approval by giving the musicians a standing ovation.
4. The jazz group played one more song for their audience.
5. After the concert, the group went its separate ways.

CHAPTER 8

Indefinite Pronouns as Antecedents

1 Here's the Idea

An indefinite pronoun may be the antecedent of a personal pronoun.

Making sure that a personal pronoun agrees in number with an indefinite pronoun can be difficult. This is true because the number of the indefinite pronoun is not always obvious. Refer to the chart below when you are trying to determine the number of an indefinite pronoun.

Indefinite Pronouns

Singular		Plural	Singular or Plural
another	everything	both	all
anybody	much	few	any
anyone	neither	many	more
anything	nobody	several	most
each	no one		none
either	nothing		some
everybody	one		
everyone	somebody		
	someone		
	something		

PRONOUNS

Singular Indefinite Pronouns

Use a singular personal pronoun to refer to a singular indefinite pronoun.

REFERS TO

Each of the instruments has its own special sound.
SINGULAR INDEFINITE PRONOUN — SINGULAR PERSONAL PRONOUN

The phrase *his or her* is considered a singular personal pronoun.

Everyone brought his or her clarinet.

One or more nouns may come between a personal pronoun and its indefinite pronoun antecedent. Make sure the personal pronoun agrees with the indefinite pronoun, not with a noun.

INCORRECT: **One of the musicians played their trumpet off key.**
(The personal pronoun agrees with the noun, not the indefinite pronoun.)

CORRECT: **One of the musicians played her trumpet off key.**
(The personal pronoun agrees with the indefinite pronoun.)

Plural Indefinite Pronouns

Use a plural pronoun to refer to a plural indefinite pronoun.

REFERS TO

Both of the pianists played their own compositions.
PLURAL INDEFINITE PRONOUN — PLURAL PERSONAL PRONOUN

Few of us brought our sheet music.

Singular or Plural Indefinite Pronouns

Some indefinite pronouns can be singular or plural. Use the meaning of the sentence to determine whether a personal pronoun that refers to an indefinite pronoun should be singular or plural.

If the indefinite pronoun refers to a portion of a whole, use a singular personal pronoun.

Some of the music has lost its appeal.

If the indefinite pronoun refers to members of a group, use a plural personal pronoun.

Some of the musicians play their instruments.

Indefinite pronouns that end in *one, body,* or *thing* are always singular.

CHAPTER 8

2 Why It Matters in Writing

If the personal pronouns and indefinite-pronoun antecedents in your sentences don't agree, your writing will be very confusing for readers.

STUDENT MODEL

Each of the instruments of the modern orchestra has ~~their~~ its own particular history. The violin is related to two three-stringed instruments, the rebec and the Polish fiddle, played in the 1500s. Both of these had ~~its~~ their limitations.

3 Practice and Apply

A. CONCEPT CHECK: Indefinite Pronouns as Antecedents

Find and correct the errors in agreement in these sentences. Write *Correct* if there is no error.

The Electric Guitar

1. Even before guitars became electric, most of the large jazz orchestras included a guitarist among its musicians.
2. Several of the early jazz and blues guitarists, such as Charlie Christian, wanted to make his guitars louder.
3. Early on, some of these musicians used a vibrating metal disc to make its guitars produce more sound.
4. At first, none of the early inventors knew exactly how to make an electric guitar, so he or she experimented with different materials and designs.
5. Each of the inventors contributed their own ideas to the creation of the electric guitar.
6. All of this experimenting served its purpose.
7. By the late 1930s, several of the guitar manufacturers in the United States were producing its first line of electrics.
8. Some of the guitars made by one manufacturer were called Frying Pans because of its shape.
9. Few of the creators of the electric guitar knew how their instrument would change popular music.
10. By the 1950s, anyone who could play electric guitar could start their own rock 'n' roll band.

➜ **For a SELF-CHECK and more practice, see the EXERCISE BANK, p. 329.**

B. EDITING: Agreement with Indefinite Pronouns

Find the five agreement errors in the paragraph below. Rewrite the sentences in which they occur to correct the errors.

Sounds of Bali

A gamelan is the traditional orchestra of the Indonesian island of Bali. Although everyone in the orchestra plays their own instrument, the gamelan sounds like one instrument played by many musicians. This is because each of the gamelans has their own special tuning. A single orchestra is made up of gongs, drums, xylophones, flutes, and stringed instruments. Most of the instruments make its sound through percussion, or striking. Many of the gamelan musicians play his or her instruments with wooden mallets or hammers. Anyone who goes to Bali should attend a gamelan performance during their visit.

Other Pronoun Problems

1 Here's the Idea

A pronoun may be used with an appositive, in an appositive, or in a comparison. You can learn techniques that will help you use pronouns correctly in each of these situations.

Pronouns and Appositives

The pronoun *we* or *us* is sometimes followed by an appositive, a noun that identifies the pronoun.

We pianists will have to rent pianos.
APPOSITIVE

The conductor pointed toward us violinists.
APPOSITIVE

Use the chart below to figure out whether to use *we* or *us* in front of an appositive.

CHAPTER 8

Here's How Using Pronouns with Appositives

The oboe players are having lunch with (we, us) cellists.

1. Drop the appositive from the sentence.

   The oboe players are having lunch with (we, us).

2. Determine whether the pronoun is a subject or an object. In this sentence, the pronoun is the object of the preposition *with.*
3. Write the sentence, using the correct case.

   The oboe players are having lunch with us cellists.

Sometimes a pronoun is used in an appositive. The pronoun helps to identify the noun in front of the appositive.

The sopranos, Eva and I, sang a duet.
APPOSITIVE

The pronoun's case is determined by the function of the noun it identifies. In the sentence above, the noun *sopranos* is the subject, so the pronoun in the appositive *Eva and I* is a nominative pronoun.

Use the chart on the next page to help you figure out which case to use when a pronoun is in an appositive.

Here's How **Using Pronouns in Appositives**

Holly sang for the two tenors, Marcello and (he, him).

1. Rewrite the sentence with the appositive by itself.

   Holly sang for Marcello and (he, him).

2. Then try each part of the appositive alone with the verb.

   Holly sang for Marcello. Holly sang for (he, him).

3. Determine whether the pronoun is a subject or an object. In this sentence, the pronoun is the object of the preposition *for.*

4. Write the sentence using the correct case.

   Holly sang for the two tenors, Marcello and him.

PRONOUNS

Pronouns in Comparisons

A comparison can be made by using *than* or *as* to begin a clause.

Lily has more CDs than she has.

Carlos plays the saxophone as fast as I play.

When words are left out of such a clause, the clause is said to be **elliptical.**

Lily has more CDs than she.

Fill in the words missing from the elliptical clause to help you choose the correct pronoun case.

You can play as well as (he, him). [can play]

You can play as well as he.

"WHEN I WAS YOUR AGE I WAS JUST AS OLD AS YOU ARE."

www.CartoonStock.com

❷ Why It Matters in Writing

If you use pronouns incorrectly in comparisons, your readers may be confused or misled.

❸ Practice and Apply

A. CONCEPT CHECK: Other Pronoun Problems

Choose the correct pronoun from those in parentheses.

The Emperor's Daughter and the Unknown Prince

(1) (We, Us) music lovers are big fans of the opera *Turandot,* written by Puccini. The opera is about a clever princess named Turandot who meets a prince even more clever than **(2)** (she, her). Turandot has promised to marry any prince who can answer three riddles. The Prince of Persia and twelve other suitors have failed the test. Those unfortunate men, the twelve suitors and **(3)** (he, him), have been beheaded. An unknown prince believes he can do better than **(4)** (them, they). Turandot feels confident that no one will be smarter than **(5)** (her, she).

In a scene that is particularly entertaining to **(6)** (we, us) audience members, the ghosts of the slain suitors come back to warn the unknown prince. After answering the riddles correctly, the prince tells an unhappy Turandot that if she can guess his name, he will not press her to marry him. Only three people—his father, his servant, and **(7)** (him, he)—know that his name is Calaf. The princess orders her subjects to discover the prince's identity. They are as unsuccessful as **(8)** (she, her). Finally the prince reveals his name. Unexpectedly, Turandot agrees to marry Calaf. The happy couple, Calaf and **(9)** (her, she), declare their love to the crowd in the courtyard. It seems that no one has ever been as happy as **(10)** (they, them).

→ **For a SELF-CHECK and more practice, see the EXERCISE BANK, p. 329.**

B. WRITING: Pronouns and Appositives

Supply the correct pronouns needed in the following paragraph. Write them on a separate piece of paper.

West Side Story

Last night, ___(1)___ drama students gave a performance of *West Side Story.* This musical, set in the 1950s, is an updated version of Shakespeare's *Romeo and Juliet.* Through music and dialogue, the cast, my fellow actors and ___(2)___, told the story of two teenagers who fall in love. Like Romeo and Juliet, Tony and Maria are prevented from being together by their friends and families. At one point in the show, the main characters, Tony and ___(3)___, sing a beautiful duet. For ___(4)___ actors, there are lots of great songs in this show.

CHAPTER 8

Pronoun Reference

❶ Here's the Idea

If a pronoun's antecedent is missing or unclear, or if there is more than one antecedent, readers will be confused.

Indefinite Reference

Indefinite-reference problems occur when a pronoun's antecedents are not expressed. Writers often make the mistake of using the pronouns *it*, *they*, and *you* without clear reference. You can eliminate indefinite-reference problems by rewriting the sentences in which the pronouns appear.

Indefinite Reference

Awkward	Revised
In the article, it claims that the new Pink Blur CD is terrific.	The article claims that the new Pink Blur CD is terrific.
They state in the article that the songs are fresh and exciting.	The writer states in the article that the songs are fresh and exciting.
On the new CD, you have more slow songs.	The new CD has more slow songs on it.

PRONOUNS

General Reference

General-reference problems occur when the pronouns *it*, *this*, *that*, *which*, and *such* are used to refer to general ideas rather than to specific noun antecedents. Correct such problems by adding a clear antecedent or by rewriting the sentence without the pronoun.

General Reference

Awkward	Revised
Trudy practices the guitar every day. This has improved her playing.	Trudy practices the guitar every day. Practicing has improved her playing.
Malcolm broke a guitar string, which ended the band's rehearsal.	The band's rehearsal ended because Malcolm broke a guitar string.

Ambiguous Reference

Ambiguous means "having more than one possible meaning." An ambiguous-reference problem occurs whenever more than one word might be a pronoun's antecedent. You can eliminate ambiguous references by revising the sentences.

Ambiguous Reference

Awkward	Revised
Jeb talked to Max while he listened to music.	While Jeb listened to music, he talked to Max. **or** While Max listened to music, Jeb talked to him.
Carol told Rita that she was the next singer to perform.	Rita was the next singer to perform, and Carol told her to get ready.

CHAPTER 8

2 Why It Matters in Writing

Readers will be confused and frustrated by cases of general, indefinite, or ambiguous reference in your writing. Make your writing as clear as possible by eliminating these problems.

STUDENT MODEL

DRAFT

Bob Marley and Bunny Wailer listened to the records of other reggae music groups before they recorded their music.

REVISION

Before Bob Marley and Bunny Wailer recorded their music, they listened to the records of other reggae music groups.

3 Practice and Apply

A. CONCEPT CHECK: Pronoun Reference

Rewrite the following sentences to correct indefinite, ambiguous, and general pronoun references.

Reggae Sunsplash

1. In a recent magazine article, it explains that Reggae Sunsplash began as an annual music festival in Jamaica.

2. They say that the popular festival now tours Europe and the United States.
3. The biggest reggae bands in the world play at Sunsplash. That explains why the event has been called "the mother of all reggae festivals."
4. Music is important at the festival, but you also have Jamaican crafts and foods as part of the experience.
5. Bob Marley and the Wailers, Third World, and Toots and the Maytals played at the 1979 festival. This attracted large crowds.
6. When the bands began playing for the fans, they immediately started dancing.
7. One year, the weather during the festival was so wet that a local reporter called it "Reggae Mud-Splash."
8. Bob Marley is reggae's greatest legend, which is why the festival organizers decided to create Bob Marley week.
9. On the Sunsplash Web site, they explain that the Bob Marley Foundation helped organize this tribute.
10. Bob Marley died in 1981, and now his son Ziggy plays with his band at the festival.

→ **For a SELF-CHECK and more practice, see the EXERCISE BANK, p. 330.**

PRONOUNS

B. REVISING: Pronoun Reference Problems

The four underlined pronouns below have missing or unclear antecedents. Revise the paragraph to eliminate the problems.

Reggae's Next Generation

Bob Marley's son Ziggy Marley formed a reggae band with his sisters and brothers. The Melody Makers sing about history, human struggles, and the problems that all people face. This may explain why the band is popular around the world. On the Melody Makers' Web site, you have information about the four Marley siblings who make up the band: Cedella, Sharon, Stephen, and Ziggy. Many people associate the Melody Makers with their father's music and reputation. Although the Melody Makers are influenced by the music of Bob Marley, they have a sound all their own.

Ziggy Marley

Real World Grammar

School Newspaper Article

To be a successful sports reporter on your school newspaper, you need to know the rules of the games you write about. However, no matter how accurate your articles are, readers will be confused if your writing contains pronoun errors. Because sports articles often are about teams (collective nouns) and a number of individuals, it's easy to make these errors. Follow the basic rules of pronoun use to make your articles clear. Here's one high-school sports reporter's rough draft of an article.

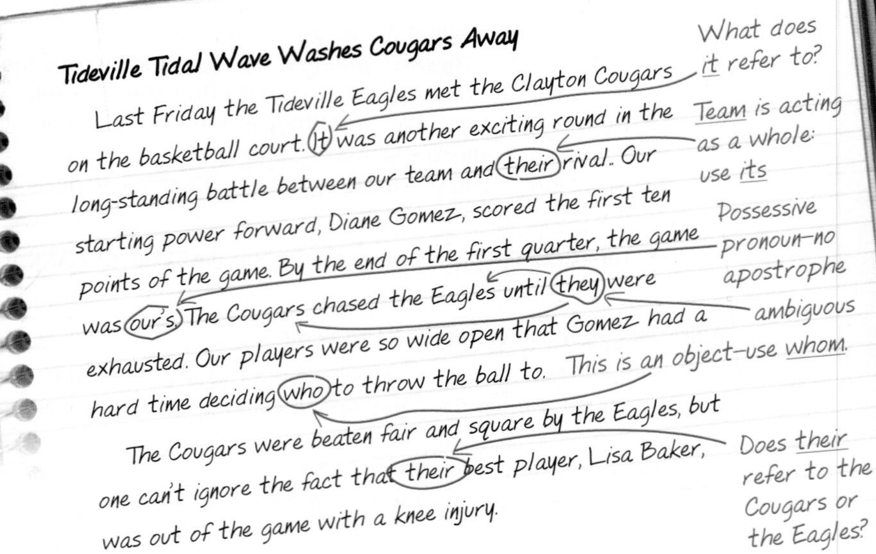

Tideville Tidal Wave Washes Cougars Away

Last Friday the Tideville Eagles met the Clayton Cougars on the basketball court. It was another exciting round in the long-standing battle between our team and their rival. Our starting power forward, Diane Gomez, scored the first ten points of the game. By the end of the first quarter, the game was our's. The Cougars chased the Eagles until they were exhausted. Our players were so wide open that Gomez had a hard time deciding who to throw the ball to.

The Cougars were beaten fair and square by the Eagles, but one can't ignore the fact that their best player, Lisa Baker, was out of the game with a knee injury.

What does it refer to?
Team is acting as a whole: use its
Possessive pronoun—no apostrophe
ambiguous
This is an object—use whom.
Does their refer to the Cougars or the Eagles?

Using Grammar in Writing

After you draft an article, review it to make sure you have used pronouns correctly.

Indefinite reference	• Give every pronoun a specific and stated antecedent.
Pronoun-antecedent agreement	• Make sure pronouns agree with their antecedents in person, number, and gender.
Possessive pronouns	• Avoid confusing contractions with possessive pronouns.
Who* and *Whom	• Use the nominative form *who* as a subject and the objective form *whom* as an object.

Tideville Tidal Wave Washes Cougars Away

By Natalie Young

Last Friday the Tideville Eagles met the Clayton Cougars on the basketball court. The game was another exciting round in the long-standing battle between our team and its rival. Our starting power forward, Diane Gomez, scored the first ten points of the game. By the end of the first quarter, the game was ours. The Cougars were exhausted from chasing the Eagles. Our players were so wide open that Gomez had a hard time deciding whom she should throw the ball to.

The Cougars were beaten fair and square by the Eagles, but one can't ignore the fact that the Cougars' best player, Lisa Baker, was out of the game with a knee injury.

PRONOUNS

PRACTICE AND APPLY: Revising

You are the editor of your school newspaper. One of your reporters has just handed you the article below. You need to check the article for pronoun errors before you publish it. Use the four pronoun tips to revise the article.

It is no surprise that our volleyball team will be playing in the state championships. Linda Buffington, the team coach, said the girls have been practicing hard. I asked Coach Buffington whom should get the credit when a team wins a title. After all, not every player is a star, and some players do stand out above the rest. "Its true that every team has it's strengths and weaknesses," said the coach. "Its also true that every team member contributes something important to the team."

Mixed Review

A. Using Pronouns Read the passage. Write the correct pronoun from the choices given in parentheses.

People often don't think about **1.** (who, whom) is playing drums in a jazz or rock band. Although drums cannot produce a melody line, they are essential in jazz and popular music. Before the development of jazz, drums were used mainly in marching and classical music. Many of the first jazz drummers didn't have **2.** (his or her, their) own drums. They borrowed **3.** (they're, their) instruments from circus orchestras and marching bands.

Early on, a jazz band hired **4.** (their, its) drummer mainly to impress an audience. Jimmy Crawford and Sonny Greer were two drummers who made **5.** (their, his) mark on jazz in the early 1920s. **6.** (They, Them) and other drummers added loud kettledrums to their sets to make more noise. In the 1930s, some of the jazz drummers in New Orleans and other cities began decorating **7.** (their, his) drum sets with pictures of landscapes or portraits of the bandleader.

Before the 1940s, a jazz drummer's task was simply to keep the beat of the music. Talented drummers like Max Roach changed this. It was **8.** (him, he) who influenced the way jazz drummers play today. Instead of simply keeping rhythm, **9.** (he, him) and other drummers created new playing styles. **10.** (His, Him) playing helped shape the style of jazz known as bebop.

B. Indefinite, General, and Ambiguous References The seven underlined pronouns in the following passage have indefinite, general, or ambiguous references. Rewrite the paragraph to eliminate the reference problems.

In a magazine article about New Orleans, it says that jazz funerals are a cultural tradition in this city. During a jazz funeral, a brass band plays as friends and family walk to the cemetery. In the article, they explain that the band plays sad, serious music and everyone walks slowly at first. However, this changes later on. After you leave the cemetery, the band plays a different kind of music. First the trumpeter plays two notes on his instrument, which means that it's time to play a lively song. The mourners dance behind the band as they hold up colorful umbrellas. Newer brass bands are changing these traditions, but some of them are still followed.

Mastery Test: What Did You Learn?

Choose the best way to rewrite each underlined word or word group.

As the opera *H.M.S. Pinafore* opens, the ship's crew welcomes aboard a woman named Little Buttercup. It is her (1) who sells candy and other small items to they and other sailors (2). A sailor named Ralph Rackstraw tells the crew and she (3) that he wants to marry the captain's daughter, Josephine. Unfortunately, Josephine must marry Sir Joseph, a navy official. Josephine's father and he (4) have agreed on the marriage. However, Josephine is in love with Ralph Rackstraw, even though your (5) position is not as powerful as Sir Joseph's. Josephine and Ralph plan they're (6) secret wedding. The captain and Sir Joseph become upset when a spy tells him (7) about this plan. Sir Joseph asks Josephine, "Have you lost your (8) mind?" Who (9) does Josephine finally marry? She marries Ralph, and the captain marries someone whom (10) has been very kind to him—Little Buttercup.

1. A. they
   B. she
   C. hers
   D. Correct as is

2. A. other sailors and they
   B. he and other sailors
   C. them and other sailors
   D. Correct as is

3. A. she and the crew
   B. the crew and hers
   C. the crew and her
   D. Correct as is

4. A. him
   B. his
   C. her
   D. Correct as is

5. A. their
   B. his
   C. her
   D. Correct as is

6. A. their
   B. theirs
   C. them
   D. Correct as is

7. A. his
   B. them
   C. they
   D. Correct as is

8. A. yours
   B. you're
   C. my
   D. Correct as is

9. A. Whom
   B. Whomever
   C. Whoever
   D. Correct as is

10. A. whose
    B. who
    C. whoever
    D. Correct as is

PRONOUNS

Student Help Desk

Pronouns at a Glance

Nominative Case		Objective Case		Possessive Case	
I	we	me	us	my/mine	our/ours
you	you	you	you	your/yours	your/yours
he	they	him	them	his	their/theirs
she		her		her/hers	
it		it		its	

Nominative Case

Use this case when

- the pronoun is a **subject**
- the pronoun is a **predicate nominative**

Objective Case

Use this case when

- the pronoun is the **direct object of a verb**
- the pronoun is the **indirect object of a verb**
- the pronoun is the **object of a preposition**

Possessive Case

Use this case for

- pronouns that show **ownership or relationship**

CHAPTER 8

Pronoun-Antecedent Agreement

Let's Not Disagree

A pronoun should agree with its antecedent in number, gender, and person.

Agreement in Number

Joan played **her** guitar in the garage. **(singular)**

Dad and Uncle Ralph brought **their** banjos to the picnic. **(plural)**

Agreement in Gender

Beatrice bought **her** drums in Jamaica. **(feminine)**

Mr. Zamorano has a 12-string guitar, which **he** played for us. **(masculine)**

The **trumpet** fell, and now **it** is dented. **(neuter)**

Agreement in Person

I brought **my** kazoo to class today. **(first person)**

You should play **your** tuba in the talent show. **(second person)**

Carly and Lucy sing nicely, although **they** don't like to perform. **(third person)**

In a Pickle with a Pronoun?

Pronoun Problems

Here are some tips for choosing the correct pronoun case in difficult situations:

Problem: A pronoun is part of a compound structure.

Example: Please give the cymbals to Lana and (me, ~~I~~).

Solution
- Drop the other part of the compound.
- Figure out how the pronoun functions in the sentence.

Problem: A pronoun is used in an elliptical clause of comparison.

Example: I play guitar better than (~~him~~, he).

Solution
- Add the missing words to the elliptical clause.

Problem: A pronoun is used with an appositive.

Example: Please give (~~we~~, us) dancers more time to rehearse.

Solution
- Drop the appositive from the sentence.
- Figure out how the pronoun functions in the sentence.

Problem: A pronoun is used in an appositive.

Example: The directors, Yoshi and (~~me~~, I), have a meeting today.

Solution
- Drop the words identified by the appositive.
- Try each part of the appositive separately in the sentence.

PRONOUNS

The Bottom Line

Checklist for Using Pronouns

Have I . . .

____ used the nominative case for pronouns functioning as subjects or predicate nominatives?

____ used the objective case for pronouns functioning as objects?

____ used the possessive case for pronouns to show ownership?

____ used *who* and *whom* correctly?

____ made all pronouns agree with their antecedents in number, gender, and person?

____ used the correct cases of pronouns in compound structures?

____ used the correct cases of pronouns in comparisons and appositives?

____ eliminated any pronoun-reference problems?

Using Modifiers

Theme: Money

Oh, No!

Imagine you were given one wish and only three seconds to say what you wanted. You might name the first thing that came into your head: something to drive! You've been needing a practical, low-mileage car to drive to school or work. You wouldn't mind if it were also sporty. Your wish is granted—with the vehicle shown above.

What went wrong? You forgot to say what *kind* of vehicle. You need to use modifiers, such as adjectives and adverbs, to translate the image in your head into words. That way, when you write, if not in life, you'll get across what you want.

Write Away: Making a Wish

Describe in great detail something you would really like to have, so that another person could make an accurate drawing from what you write. Save your description in your **Working Portfolio.**

Diagnostic Test: What Do You Know?

Choose the best way to rewrite each underlined word or group of words.

Recently the U.S. Treasury did a real good (1) job redesigning the country's paper money. The goal was to make currency more harder (2) to counterfeit. The $100 bill was the more likely (3) choice for the first redesign. That there (4) bill still has Benjamin Franklin's portrait. However, the portrait is now bigger (5) and off-center. You can't hardly (6) notice the other changes, which include a watermark, a security thread, and color-shifting ink.

Now store clerks can spot a fake real easy (7). The baddest (8) news for counterfeiters is that it would cost them very much to print fake bills with these security features. American bills are now harder to counterfeit than the currency of any country (9). Americans can feel well (10) about the physical safety of their money.

1. A. real well
   B. really well
   C. really good
   D. Correct as is
2. A. most harder
   B. harder
   C. hardest
   D. Correct as is
3. A. most likeliest
   B. most likely
   C. likelier
   D. Correct as is
4. A. That
   B. This here
   C. These
   D. Correct as is
5. A. more bigger
   B. more big
   C. biggest
   D. Correct as is
6. A. can hardly
   B. don't hardly
   C. can't scarcely
   D. Correct as is
7. A. really easy
   B. really easily
   C. real easily
   D. Correct as is
8. A. badder
   B. worst
   C. most bad
   D. Correct as is
9. A. than any currency
   B. than the currency of another country
   C. than the currency of any other country
   D. Correct as is
10. A. good
    B. more good
    C. more well
    D. Correct as is

MODIFIERS

Using Adjectives and Adverbs

CHAPTER 9

1 Here's the Idea

Modifiers are words that describe or give more specific information about—or modify—the meanings of other words. Adjectives and adverbs are common modifiers.

Adjectives

Adjectives modify nouns and pronouns. They answer the questions *which one, what kind, how many,* and *how much.*

PROFESSIONAL MODEL

John August Sutter was a short, fat, kindly man whom everyone in California knew for his hospitality. He had come to America from Switzerland in 1834, and catching the western fever, had traveled across the plains. . . . The Mexican governor welcomed his plan to develop the country and granted him some land.

—"Gold Is Found and a Nation Goes Wild"

WHAT KIND
WHICH ONE
HOW MUCH

Notice that more than one adjective may modify the same noun or pronoun. (For more on punctuating a series of adjectives, see page 224.) Proper adjectives, like *Mexican,* are capitalized.

Other words can often be used as adjectives.

Other Words Used as Adjectives	
Nouns	**stone** wall, **Bob's** cabin
Possessive pronouns	**my** book, **your** song, **his** plan, **their** garden,
Demonstrative pronouns	**this** road, **that** farm, **these** trees, **those** flowers
Participles	**shining** light, **falling** price, **locked** gate, **deserted** look
Indefinite pronouns	**all** signs, **each** direction, **few** options, **many** turns, **much** snow, **several** days, **some** hope
Numbers	**one** time, **10** minutes

Most adjectives come before the words they modify. **Predicate adjectives,** however, follow a linking verb and modify the subject of a clause.

MODIFY

The gold was pure and shiny.
PREDICATE ADJECTIVES

Adverbs

Adverbs modify verbs, adjectives, and other adverbs. They answer the questions *when, where, how,* and *to what extent.*

MODIFIES

Prospectors eagerly searched for gold. (MODIFIES VERB)

MODIFIES

The search was often dangerous. (MODIFIES ADJECTIVE)

MODIFIES

Nuggets accumulated very slowly. (MODIFIES ADVERB)

An adverb can be placed before or after a verb it modifies.

MODIFIES MODIFIES

They slowly examined the rocks and shouted triumphantly.

Place modifiers like *only* close to the words they modify (see page 224). Changing their position changes their meaning.

They only thought about gold. (THEY DID NOTHING ELSE.)

They thought only about gold. (THEY THOUGHT OF NOTHING ELSE.)

2 Why It Matters in Writing

Adjectives used in groups efficiently add details about a setting. Adverbs can indicate changes over time.

LITERARY MODEL

It was a lovely region, woodsy, balmy, delicious, and had once been populous, long years before, but now the people had vanished.

—Mark Twain, "The Californian's Tale"

ADJECTIVES
ADVERBS

MODIFIERS

❸ Practice and Apply

A. CONCEPT CHECK: Using Adjectives and Adverbs

For each sentence, find the modifiers (ignoring *a, an,* and *the*) and indicate whether they are used as adjectives or adverbs.

California Dreaming

1. In 1848, a mechanic named James Marshall noticed a shiny glint in the sparkling waters of the American River's south fork.
2. His lucky discovery—gold—eventually led to bad luck for his kindly boss, John Sutter.
3. Sutter was generous and openhanded and the proud owner of 49,000 acres of prime gold-mining land.
4. Before he knew it, word of the abundant gold spread across the country to Washington, D.C.
5. There President Polk told Congress that any hard-working miner might find untold wealth in the California territory.
6. Soon afterward, an estimated 100,000 people swarmed Sutter's pristine land.
7. In the first year, about 10,000 miners died because of inadequate shelter, poor food, too few medical supplies, rough crime, and frontier "justice."
8. They trashed Sutter's land, butchered his cattle, and even challenged his land ownership.
9. During the next five years, gold worth more than $285 million was mined in California, but poor Sutter quickly went bankrupt.
10. His was not the only sad story from the California gold rush; still, the gold rush did lay a solid foundation for the state's future economic prosperity.

→ **For a SELF-CHECK and more practice, see the EXERCISE BANK, p. 331.**

B. WRITING: Describing with Modifiers

The Art of Mining

Two artists who went West with the gold rush painted this picture. Write a descriptive paragraph about the picture, using as many adjectives and adverbs as possible.

Miners in the Sierras (1851-52) Charles Christian Nahl and Frederick August Wenderoth. National Museum of American Art, Washington DC/Art Resource, NY

CHAPTER 9

LESSON 2

Problems with Modifiers

❶ Here's the Idea

Here are several common problems you can have using modifiers.

STUDENT MODEL

My grandfather collects coins, which he calls a **scholar** pursuit. He says it's a good hobby, and he feels **badly** that I don't take a greater interest in it. He's most interested in old coins because they have stories to tell. Most of **them** coins contain real precious metals. Coins minted today in the United States **don't have no** gold or silver in them.

Should be *scholarly,* an adjective despite its *-ly* ending.

Should be the adjective *bad,* not the adverb *badly.*

Should be the adjective *those,* not the pronoun *them.*

Should be a single negative.

MODIFIERS

Adverb or Adjective?

It is easy to confuse adjectives and adverbs. For example, you might think that all words that end in *-ly* are adverbs, but some *-ly* words—such as *lovely* and *lonely*—function as adjectives.

Collecting lovely coins can be a lonely hobby.

Many words have both adjective and adverb forms. If you're not sure which form of a word to use, look at the word that it modifies. If the modified word is a noun or a pronoun, use the adjective form. If it's a verb, an adjective, or an adverb, use the adverb form.

MODIFIES MODIFIES

Real coins can be really difficult to identify.

MODIFIES MODIFIES

The careful collector examines them carefully.

Some words can function as either adjectives or adverbs depending on how they are used.

Kim earns an hourly wage at the clock store. (ADJECTIVE)

The grandfather clock chimes hourly. (ADVERB)

Two pairs of modifiers—*good* and *well*, *bad* and *badly*—cause writers special problems.

Good = Adjective

Maria is a good coin collector.

She feels good when she finds an old coin.

Well = Adjective or Adverb

She missed a convention because she didn't feel well.
ADJECTIVE

She handled her disappointment well.
ADVERB

Bad = Adjective

Once she made a bad investment in coins.

I felt bad for her.

Badly = Adverb

That time she was cheated badly.

CHAPTER 9

Never write "I feel badly" when referring to a state of mind or health. You are saying that you literally feel (touch things) poorly.

Double Negatives

A negative is a word that negates, or cancels, something. *No, not, none, never*, and contractions and expressions using these words are all negatives. In business and school writing, you should avoid **double negatives,** that is, the use of two negative words in a clause.

Nonstandard: Most coins don't contain no gold.

Standard: Most coins don't contain any gold.

Standard: Most coins contain no gold.

For this purpose, the words *hardly, barely,* and *scarcely* are considered negatives. Don't combine one of these words with another negative.

You can't hardly use a penny these days.

This, That, These, and *Those*

This, that, these, and *those* are demonstrative pronouns that can be used as adjectives. Three rules cover all situations.

1. These words must agree in number with the words they modify.

   This hobby is educational. (SINGULAR)

   These coins are old. (PLURAL)

2. Never use *here* or *there* with one of these words. The adjective already points out which one; it doesn't need any help.

   This ~~here~~ coin is a Lincoln penny from 1909.

3. Never use the pronoun *them* as an adjective in place of *these* or *those*.

   Nonstandard: **Them pennies are rare and valuable.**

   Standard: **Those pennies are rare and valuable.**

MODIFIERS

2 Why It Matters in Writing

When you write dialogue, you may have characters use modifiers in nonstandard ways, just as people use modifiers in everyday speech. You should eliminate nonstandard constructions in more formal writing, however.

STUDENT MODEL

Draft Loan Application

I'm applying for this ~~here~~ loan to pay my tuition. I'm doing very ~~good~~ well in school, even though ~~them~~ those classes are hard. I have a part-time job now that pays practical(ly) all my other expenses. I've already been promised a good job after graduation. I'm enclosing a payment plan to show how quick(ly) I'll be able to pay you back. I can't hardly wait for your decision. Thank you.

3 Practice and Apply

A. CONCEPT CHECK: Problems with Modifiers

For each sentence, choose the correct modifier.

How Many Watermelons Does That Shirt Cost?

1. When there wasn't (any, no) paper or metal money, people used various kinds of objects as currency.
2. They also used barter, which meant trading things they had for things they wanted (bad, badly).
3. Barter didn't work too (good, well).
4. You had to carry around (real, really) big bags of items you were willing to part with.
5. Then you had to find someone who wanted your things and was willing to part with (those, them) things that you wanted.
6. How (like, likely) is that?
7. You probably wouldn't (ever, never) go anywhere.
8. With the invention of coins, people could buy things (easy, easily).
9. They could just say, "I'd like (that, that there) shirt" and hand over some money instead of, say, a watermelon or a chicken.
10. Gold and silver made (good, well) money for many cultures.

→ **For a SELF-CHECK and more practice, see the EXERCISE BANK, p. 332.**

B. EDITING AND PROOFREADING: Fixing Problems with Modifiers

Rewrite these sentences, correcting errors in the use of modifiers.

The Invention of Money

(1) The earliest known coins appeared near 9,000 years ago in what is now Turkey. **(2)** The Chinese didn't never use any metal but copper for their early coins. **(3)** The sizes, weights, and values of coins were actual standardized under the Roman Empire. **(4)** Other types of money have worked good for other cultures. **(5)** Cowrie shells served as money for an awfully lot of people from Africa to the Americas. **(6)** These here shells were durable and easy to carry. **(7)** In North America, many tribes used a conveniently kind of shell bead called wampum. **(8)** Women made wampum by breaking clam shells into pieces and careful drilling holes in them. **(9)** They strung them beads as necklaces or made belts of them. **(10)** It wasn't hardly a big step from shells to metals.

LESSON 3 Using Comparisons

1 Here's the Idea

Modifiers can be used to compare two or more things.

Three Degrees of Comparison

An adjective or adverb **modifies** one word.	Bus A is **long.**
The **comparative** compares two persons, places, or things.	Bus B is **longer** than Bus A.
The **superlative** compares three or more persons, places, or things.	Bus C is the **longest** of the three. It is the **longest** bus of all.

MODIFIERS

Regular Comparisons

Most modifiers are changed in regular ways to show comparisons.

Regular Comparisons

Rule	Modifier	Comparative	Superlative
To a one-syllable word, add ***-er*** or ***-est.***	cheap kind	cheap**er** kind**er**	cheap**est** kind**est**
For most two-syllable words, add ***-er*** or ***-est.***	simple fancy	simpl**er** fanci**er**	simpl**est** fanci**est**
For most words of more than two syllables and words ending in *ly,* use ***more*** and ***most.***	expensive wonderful kindly	**more** expensive **more** wonderful **more** kindly	**most** expensive **most** wonderful **most** kindly

Negative Comparisons To make a negative comparison, use *less* and *least.*

I'm less wasteful than Matt.

Jody is the least wasteful of all my friends.

Irregular Comparisons

Some modifiers, like *bad,* have irregular comparative and superlative forms.

It was a bad day when my car broke down.

It was a worse day when I found out I needed a new battery.

The worst news was that the engine block was cracked.

Common Irregular Comparative Forms

Modifier	Comparative	Superlative
bad	worse	worst
good	better	best
ill	worse	worst
little	less, lesser	least
many	more	most
much	more	most
well	better	best

CHAPTER 9

When a 2-syllable word sounds awkward with the *-er* and *-est* endings, use *more* and *most* or *less* and *least,* as with longer words. For example: thankful, more thankful, least thankful.

2 Why It Matters in Writing

Comparative and superlative forms greatly expand your power to describe. To say a building is *tall* paints a vague picture; to say it is *taller* than the Washington Monument makes the image more exact.

LITERARY MODEL

Every place they passed through looked nastier than the last, partly on account of the dismal light, partly because people had given up bothering to take a pride in their boroughs. And then, just as they were entering a village called Molesworth, the dimmest, drabbest, most insignificant huddle of houses they had come to yet, the engine coughed and died on them.

—Joan Aiken, "Searching for Summer"

COMPARATIVE

SUPERLATIVES

3 Practice and Apply

A. CONCEPT CHECK: Using Comparisons

Choose the correct form of comparison for each sentence.

Simplify, Simplify

1. Americans spend money (fast, faster) than any other culture.
2. Since 1950, Americans have used resources (more, most) quickly than the total of everyone who ever lived before then.
3. Many Americans are (prouder, proudest) of their ability to give their children material things.
4. But some people are saying we'd appreciate life more if we spent money (less freely, least freely).
5. They say we'd be (happier, more happy) if we bought less.
6. Spending (carefully, more carefully) than they do now would help people stay out of the rat race.
7. Then they could be (frantic, less frantic) about their jobs and spend more time doing things they enjoy.
8. People who've gotten out of the spending race say they're (calm, calmer) and (serener, more serene) than before.
9. "Buy Nothing Day" is the (newer, newest) holiday.
10. The (better, best) way of all to simplify our lives might be to spend money less freely.

➜ **For a SELF-CHECK and more practice, see the EXERCISE BANK, p. 332.**

MODIFIERS

B. WRITING: Describing a Graph

Government Spending
The pie graph shows an average state government's budget. Referring to the graph, fill in the blanks in the following sentences with comparative or superlative forms of adjectives, such as *greater* or *greatest*.

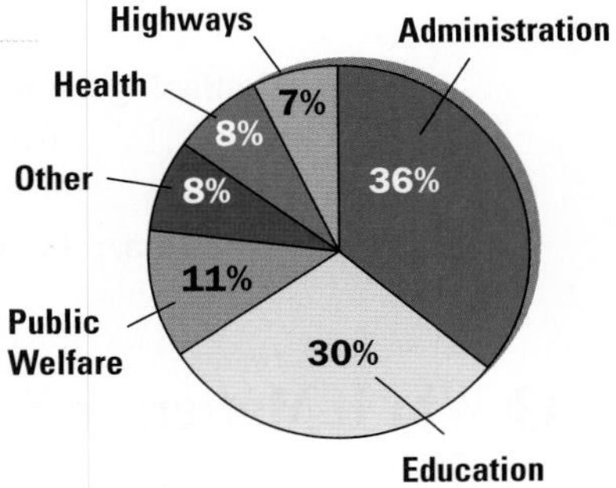

Source: *Statistical Abstract of the United States,* 1991

1. A typical state spends a ________ amount on welfare than on education.
2. The government spends a ________ amount on health than on highways.
3. The government spends the ________ amount of all on administration.
4. The ________ amount is spent on highways.

Problems with Comparisons

1 Here's the Idea

Writers sometimes make the mistake of using a double comparison or an illogical comparison.

Double Comparisons

Don't use both ways of forming comparisons or superlatives at once: *-er* and *more* or *-est* and *most.*

Nonstandard: **It's more wiser to save money than to spend it.**

Standard: **It's wiser to save money than to spend it.**

Nonstandard: **The most simplest way to shop is with a list.**

Standard: **The simplest way to shop is with a list.**

CHAPTER 9

Illogical Comparisons

Illogical or confusing comparisons can result if you unintentionally compare something to itself or compare two unrelated things.

Illogical: **Mariko thinks the quarter is prettier than any coin.** (A quarter *is* a coin, so it can't be prettier than any coin.)

Clear: **Mariko thinks the quarter is prettier than any other coin.**

Confusing: **Isabel likes coins better than her sister.** (Does Isabel like coins more than she likes her sister, or does she like coins more than her sister does?)

Clear: **Isabel likes coins more than her sister does.**

2 Why It Matters in Writing

A double or an illogical comparison can be a sign of trying too hard to emphasize a point.

Nick was more concerned about money than anyone[else]**. So he worked ~~more~~ harder on his budget than I.**

3 Practice and Apply

A. CONCEPT CHECK: Problems with Comparisons

Choose the correct form of comparison for each sentence.

Rich and Poor

1. The distribution of income is one of the (biggest, most biggest) differences among countries.
2. The United States is richer than (any, any other) country.
3. The average U.S. income is (greater, more greater) than that of most countries.
4. By contrast, the African nation of Somalia is one of the world's (poorest, most poorest) countries.
5. At less than $226 a year, its average income is (lower, more lower) than incomes of almost any other country.
6. Some families live even (more cheaply, more cheaplier).
7. Because of a civil war, the nation's economy is now even (less healthy, less healthier).
8. Nearly 43 percent of the population lives in extreme poverty, and that figure is (higher, more high) for nomadic and rural communities.
9. The perecentage of children enrolled in primary school is the (lowest, most low) in the world.
10. The life expectancy of Somalis is also lower (than Americans, than that of Americans).

➜ **For a SELF-CHECK and more practice, see the EXERCISE BANK, p. 333.**

B. REVISING: Eliminating Problem Modifiers

Rewrite the following sentences, revising each double or illogical comparison.

The Income Gap

(1) Income is distributed unevenly within the United States; the rich are getting more richer. **(2)** The most wealthiest 10 percent of Americans receive more than 48.5 percent of the country's total income. **(3)** Therefore, they have more money to spend than any income group. **(4)** At the same time, the poverty rate rose more higher, from 12.5 percent in 2003 to 12.7 percent in 2004. **(5)** The income gap has been growing more wider over time.

Grammar in Literature

Modifiers and Lively Writing

In the passage below, O. Henry uses modifiers in several ways to help introduce the characters and start the action. Notice how each adjective and adverb functions to describe or give more specific information about the word it modifies.

CHAPTER 9

ONE THOUSAND DOLLARS

O. HENRY

"One thousand dollars," repeated Lawyer Tolman, solemnly and severely, "and here is the money."

Young Gillian gave a decidedly amused laugh as he fingered the thin package of new fifty-dollar notes.

"It's such a confoundedly awkward amount," he explained, genially, to the lawyer. "If it had been ten thousand a fellow might wind up with a lot of fireworks and do himself credit. Even $50 would have been less trouble."

"You heard the reading of your uncle's will," continued Lawyer Tolman, professionally dry in his tones. "I do not know if you paid much attention to its details. I must remind you of one. You are required to render to us an account of the manner of expenditure. . . . "

"You may depend upon it," said the young man, politely, "in spite of the extra expense it will entail. I may have to engage a secretary, I was never good at accounts."

Adverbs immediately characterize the lawyer's manner and define the mood.

Adjectives contribute sensory details and key information.

An **adverb** captures the manner of the second character in the scene and contrasts him to the first.

Here as earlier, an **adverb-adjective pair** offers specific information about the action while contributing rhythm and character to the writing style.

Adjectives and adverbs continue to deepen characterization and add details.

Using Modifiers to Create Specific Descriptions

Adverbs	Use adverbs to sketch a character quickly. Notice how the adverb *genially* does for the second character what *solemnly* and *severely* do for the first.
Adjectives	Use adjectives to convey useful information about quantity and quality in an economic way.
Adverb-adjective pairs	Use adverb-adjective pairs to deepen character. Pairs like *decidedly amused, confoundedly awkward,* and *professionally dry* describe and comment on the characters.

PRACTICE AND APPLY: Choosing Modifiers

Replace the underlined modifiers in the following passage with alternatives that would change the nature of the characters.

LITERARY MODEL

Our father was a **(1)** big man, **(2)** outgoing and **(3)** immensely active. We thought he was **(4)** immortal, but then **(5)** most children think that about their father. The **(6)** worst thing was that Mother thought he was **(7)** immortal too, and when he died, keeling over on the pavement between the **(8)** insurance offices where he worked, and the **(9)** company car into which he was just about to climb, there followed a period of **(10)** ghastly limbo. **(11)** Bereft, **(12)** uncertain, **(13)** lost, none of us knew what to do **(14)** next. But after the funeral and a little talk with the family lawyer, Mother **(15)** quietly pulled herself together and told us.

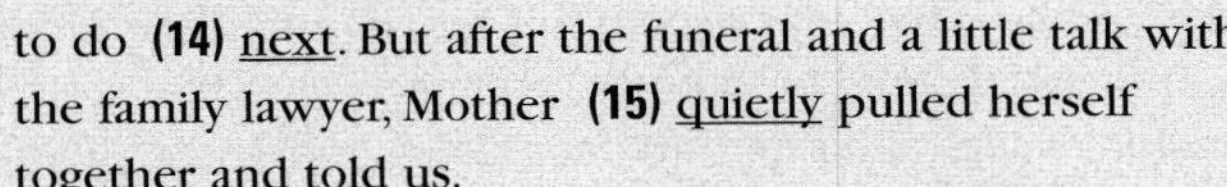

—Rosamunde Pilcher, "Lalla"

Mixed Review

A. Adjectives and Adverbs Read the following passage. Then answer the questions below it.

LITERARY MODEL

(1) Our greatest concern was how we were going to reach the fifty thousand black people of Montgomery, no matter how hard we worked. **(2)** The white press, in an outraged exposé, spread the word for us in a way that would have been impossible with only our own resources.

(3) As it happened, a white woman found one of our leaflets, which her black maid had left in the kitchen. **(4)** The irate woman immediately telephoned the newspapers to let the white community know what the blacks were up to. **(5)** We laughed a lot about this, and Martin later said that we owed them a great debt.

(6) On Sunday morning, from their pulpits, almost every African-American minister in town urged people to honor the boycott.

— Coretta Scott King, *Montgomery Boycott*

CHAPTER 9

1. In what form is the adjective *greatest* in sentence 1?
2. Is the word *hard* in sentence 1 an adjective or adverb? What does it modify?
3. In sentence 2, what word is a participle functioning as an adjective?
4. In sentence 2, what word does the adjective *impossible* modify?
5. What part of speech is *only* in sentence 2, and what does it modify?
6. What part of speech is *our* in sentence 3, and how is it being used?
7. What would be the comparative form of *irate* in sentence 4?
8. What does the word *immediately* modify in sentence 4?
9. What does the word *almost* modify in sentence 6?
10. What part of speech is *every* in sentence 6, and how is it being used?

B. Correcting Problems with Modifiers Read the following paragraph. If an underlined word or phrase is correct, write *Correct*. If there is a problem, write the word or phrase correctly.

What Makes Good Money?

Money **(1)** <u>doesn't have to have no</u> inherent value. It just has to be something people **(2)** <u>readily</u> accept in exchange for their products. The **(3)** <u>bestest</u> money should be durable, compact, divisible, in limited and fairly constant supply, and hard to counterfeit. **(4)** <u>These kind of things</u> wouldn't make good money: bananas, car tires, cows, and sand. Many cultures have used gold because it meets the standards **(5)** <u>better than any money</u>. Gold is one of the **(6)** <u>most longest-lasting</u> things around. But even **(7)** <u>that there</u> metal has its flaws. Gold is **(8)** <u>fair</u> heavy and **(9)** <u>easily</u> to counterfeit with coins **(10)** <u>only made partly</u> of gold.

Mastery Test: What Did You Learn?

Choose the best way to rewrite each underlined word or group of words.

It is considerable interesting (1) that the word *money* comes from the Latin word *moneta,* which means "she who advises or warns." Moneta was a name given to Juno, one of the ancient (2) Romans' most greatest (3) deities. She was more powerful than any goddess (4). Her followers sure (5) did worship her enthusiastically (6). They established a mint in the Temple of Juno Moneta. This here (7) word *moneta* came to mean "mint" and eventually "minted coins." The word *dollar* comes from the old German *Taler,* a silver coin first minted in Germany in 1519. The dollar has held up undeniably good (8) as the standard unit of account in the United States for over 200 years. The word *coin* comes from the Latin word *cuneus.* It originally didn't have no (9) meaning except "corner" or "wedge." Studying these kind (10) of word origins tells us much about how currency systems evolved.

1. A. considerable interestingly
   B. considerably interesting
   C. considerably interestingly
   D. Correct as is

2. A. ancientest
   B. most anciently
   C. too ancient
   D. Correct as is

3. A. most great
   B. greatest
   C. greater
   D. Correct as is

4. A. than anyone
   B. than any other goddess
   C. than another goddess
   D. Correct as is

5. A. surely
   B. more sure
   C. most sure
   D. Correct as is

6. A. more enthusiastic
   B. most enthusiastic
   C. enthusiastic
   D. Correct as is

7. A. That there
   B. Those
   C. This
   D. Correct as is

8. A. undeniably well
   B. undeniable good
   C. undeniable well
   D. Correct as is

9. A. hadn't no
   B. didn't have any
   C. scarcely had no
   D. Correct as is

10. A. this kinds
    B. these kinds
    C. those kind
    D. Correct as is

Student Help Desk

Modifiers at a Glance

	Modifier	Comparative	Superlative
Adjectives tell which one, what kind, how many, how much	cool	cooler	coolest
	generous	more generous less generous	most generous least generous
Adverbs tell when, where, how, to what extent	generously	more generously less generously	most generously least generously

CHAPTER 9

Adjectives in a Series Smooth Sailing

Use commas between adjectives when their order could be reversed without changing the meaning.

The **elegant, expensive** yacht sailed into view.
The **expensive, elegant** yacht anchored offshore.

Don't use commas to separate modifiers that could not be reversed.

The **miserly yacht** owner forgot to pay the crew.

Don't use commas to separate adjectives that describe color, age, size, or material.

The **old blue** rowboat sprang a leak.
The **new green fiberglass** canoe nearly sank.

Adverbs in Different Positions Safe Harbor

Place adverbs carefully to ensure they refer to the words they modify.

Almost everyone was on time to meet the ship. (Few were late.)
Everyone was **almost** on time to meet the ship. (No one was on time.)

Eliminate confusion in the placement of adverbs.

The captain considers steering **terribly** important. (Confusing)
The captain considers steering to be **terribly** important.

Recognizing Adverbs

Don't Be at Sea

Adverb Types	Adverbs	Example
Many adverbs are formed by adding *-ly* to adjectives.	angrily, critically, equally, finally, nicely, stubbornly, warmly	The harbor beckons **warmly.**
Some common adverbs do not end in *-ly.*	afterward, almost, also, even, here, instead, not, then, there, too, yet	We're **not there yet.**
Some nouns can function as adverbs.	home, outdoors, tomorrow, yesterday	We'll sail again **tomorrow.**

MODIFIERS

The Bottom Line

Checklist for Using Modifiers

Have I . . .

____ chosen adjectives and adverbs that contribute to lively descriptions?

____ used the correct forms of adjectives and adverbs?

____ avoided double negatives?

____ used *this, that, these,* and *those* correctly?

____ formed comparatives and superlatives correctly?

____ avoided illogical and confusing comparisons?

"This is Fluffy, my pet money."

Chapter 10

Capitalization

dearest granddaughter,

for safekeeping, i have hidden my valuable eleanor t jones oil painting beside the maple river at the bench.

your loving grandma

Theme: Trash or Treasure?

Which Is It?

Lucy had wondered for years what had happened to the oil painting that used to hang above her grandmother's fireplace. Finding this note solved part of the mystery.

Still, Lucy wasn't quite sure where to begin looking. Did *bench* mean bench, or did it mean BENCH for Bank of East North Central Highwood? Was the painting called *Beside the Maple River,* or was it buried beside the Maple River? Because her grandmother had not capitalized any words, Lucy could not know for sure.

Write Away: Treasured Possessions

Write a paragraph describing one of your favorite possessions. Choose something that has little value in terms of money but is important to you. Save your paragraph in your **Working Portfolio.**

Diagnostic Test: What Do You Know?

For each underlined group of words, choose the letter of the correct revision.

In the shop of mr. Martin Tytell (1), the writer Ian Frazier found untold treasures. He shared his discovery in "Typewriter Man" in *The Atlantic monthly* (2) magazine. In Tytell's shop, hundreds of manual and electric typewriters—some with russian, Greek, and Hebrew (3) alphabets—are lovingly preserved. Tytell remarked, "the (4) way these machines continue to function . . . is a miracle."

Not long ago, typewriters were considered junk, but now they can be found in museums, antique shows, and collectors' homes both east and west of the Mississippi river. (5) Some of their value comes from history. In the second World War (6), for example, the War Production Board (7) was in charge of typewriters. One shipment of 20,000 typewriters was sunk during the d-Day invasion of Normandy. (8) For many decades after the war, machines made by Remington, Hermes, Ibm (9), and countless others kept communications flowing from 8 A.M. to 5 p.m., Monday (10) through Friday.

1. A. Mr.
   B. martin
   C. tytell
   D. Correct as is

2. A. "Typewriter man"
   B. *atlantic*
   C. *Monthly*
   D. Correct as is

3. A. Russian
   B. greek
   C. hebrew
   D. Correct as is

4. A. tytell
   B. Remarked
   C. The
   D. Correct as is

5. A. East and West
   B. mississippi
   C. River
   D. Correct as is

6. A. Second
   B. world
   C. war
   D. Correct as is

7. A. The
   B. war
   C. board
   D. Correct as is

8. A. D-Day
   B. Invasion
   C. normandy
   D. Correct as is

9. A. remington
   B. hermes
   C. IBM
   D. Correct as is

10. A. a.m.
    B. P.M.
    C. monday
    D. Correct as is

CAPITALIZATION

People and Cultures

Here's the Idea

People's names and titles, the names of the languages they speak, and the names of the religions they practice are all proper nouns and should be capitalized.

Names and Initials

Capitalize people's names and initials.

Celia Cruz | Eldrick "Tiger" Woods | E. B. White
Frederick W. Douglass | Coretta Scott King | E. M. Forster

Personal Titles and Abbreviations

Capitalize titles and abbreviations of titles that are used before names or in direct address.

General Colin Powell | Dr. Brazelton
Secretary of State Madeleine Albright | Mrs. Wilson

Sgt. McDonald interviewed Professor Chandra about the stolen bead collection.

Capitalize the abbreviations of some titles even when they follow names.

Edward Jones, Sr. | Deborah Young, C.E.O. | Lewis Kent, Ph.D.

Capitalize a title of royalty or nobility only when it precedes a person's name.

King Olaf V | Sir Paul McCartney | Queen Margrethe II

The beaded gown was worn by Princess Catherine.

The dukes and duchesses attended the auction.

Family Relationships

▶ **Capitalize words indicating family relationships only when they are used as parts of names or in direct address.**

Aunt Angela   Cousin Steve   Grandpa Leon

My father bought Uncle Roy's crystal bead collection.

In general, do not capitalize a title when it follows a person's name or is used without a proper name.

Juanita, my aunt, gave us her handmade quilts.

The Pronoun *I*

▶ **Always capitalize the pronoun *I*.**

My cousin and I were overjoyed.

Ethnic Groups, Languages, and Nationalities

▶ **Capitalize the names of ethnic groups, races, languages, and nationalities, along with the adjectives formed from these names.**

Kurds	Native American	French
Hispanic	African American	Navajo

Religious Terms

▶ **Capitalize the names of religions, denominations or branches of religions, sacred days, sacred writings, and deities.**

Religious Terms	
Religions	Christianity, Buddhism, Islam
Denominations/branches	Baptist, Protestant, Shiite
Sacred days	Ramadan, Christmas, Rosh Hashanah
Sacred writings	Koran, Torah, Bible
Deities	God, Yahweh, Allah

Do not capitalize the words *god* and *goddess* when they refer to one of a group of gods, as in ancient mythology; but do capitalize the names of such gods.

The Greek god of war was Ares.

CAPITALIZATION

2 Practice and Apply

A. CONCEPT CHECK: People and Cultures

For each sentence, write the words that should be capitalized.

Beautiful Beaded Bowls

1. Diego j. pérez runs a native american cultural museum.
2. Last June, mr. pérez visited his niece, marta ríos, m.d., in Jalisco, Mexico, and discovered treasures.
3. He and dr. ríos visited huichol indian communities.
4. Although Pérez speaks spanish and english, he needed his niece to interpret the huichol language.
5. The huichols combine christianity with ancient beliefs.
6. Through the influence of roman catholic missionaries, some communities observe christian holidays.
7. Artisans make christmas ornaments to sell; but they also create *rukuri*, beaded gourd bowls, to honor ancient gods.
8. They coat the inside of a gourd with wax and prefer to make designs with czech or japanese seed beads.
9. "The rattlesnake, i believe, represents the fire god," said Pérez, pointing to one design.
10. "Recently, american and european dealers have begun selling the *rukuri*, but i think we must be careful not to exploit the huichol beliefs for profit," concluded mr. Pérez.

➜ **For a SELF-CHECK and more practice, see the EXERCISE BANK, p. 333.**

B. PROOFREADING: Correcting Capitalization

Find and correct 20 capitalization errors in the following passage.

Trinkets or Treasures?

(1) The debate started when grandma Eloise brought out her rare agate bead, which is revered by many himalayan peoples. **(2)** My Grandfather, an Engineer, and his friend, senator Brown, called it a trinket. **(3)** However, james kelly and dr. maggie drews said it had great value. **(4)** Grandma argued that in some asian cultures, beads were offered to appease the Gods. **(5)** Today, roman mosaic face beads and egyptian paste beads are valued highly, and the jewels and beads of empress Catherine II, of Russia, are considered treasures. **(6)** Yet not everyone agrees that the russian beaded flowers made for 18th-century europeans were valuable. **(7)** Nevertheless, i believe that even a seed pendant inscribed with a buddhist prayer is as much a treasure as catherine's jewels.

CHAPTER 10

LESSON 2

First Words and Titles

1 Here's the Idea

First words in sentences, most lines of poetry, quotations, and outline entries are capitalized. Greetings and closings in letters and important words in titles are capitalized.

Sentences and Poetry

Capitalize the first word of every sentence.

The critics turned up their noses at the new movie.

Capitalize the first word in every line of traditional poetry whether it begins a new sentence or not.

LITERARY MODEL

When I see birches bend to left and right
Across the lines of straighter darker trees,
I like to think some boy's been swinging them. . . .

—Robert Frost, "Birches"

Contemporary poetry often does not follow this convention.

Quotations

Capitalize the first word of a direct quotation when the quotation is a complete sentence and is not connected grammatically to the sentence in which it appears.

Ryan said, "Popular culture is mostly trash."

Ryan had a habit of saying that "popular movies are ridiculous."

In a divided quotation, do not capitalize the first word of the second part unless it starts a new sentence.

"It's not true," said Syd, "that pop culture is worthless."
"I agree," said Rosa. "That new movie is terrific."

Parts of a Letter

In a letter, capitalize the first word of the greeting, the word *Sir* or *Madam,* and the first word of the closing.

May 24, 2000

Dear Sir:

Thank you for your inquiry. Because of the renewed interest in twentieth-century popular culture, our entire stock of mechanical banks in mint condition has been depleted. I recommend you contact the Mechanical Bank Collectors of America for additional information.

Yours truly,

Jane Wrightwood

Outlines

Capitalize the first word of each entry in an outline, as well as the letters that introduce major subsections.

I. Fine arts
  A. European
    1. Artists
    2. Composers

Titles

Capitalize the first word, the last word, and all other important words in a title. Do not capitalize articles, conjunctions, or prepositions of fewer than five letters.

Titles	
Books	*Farewell to Manzanar, The Grapes of Wrath*
Plays and musicals	*Antigone, The Tragedy of Julius Caesar, Lion King*
Short stories	"A Sound of Thunder," "Sweet Potato Pie"
Poems	"Birches," "For the New Year, 1981," "The Sun"
Musical compositions	"I Will Always Love You," "Don't Worry; Be Happy"
Movies	*Jaws, The Sound of Music, The Breakfast Club*
Television shows	*Saturday Night Live, Nightline, All My Children*
Works of art	*Girl with Tear III, American Gothic, The Thinker*
Magazines and newspapers	*News Story, Entertainment Weekly, Ski and Sea, Lewistown Journal*
Games	Word for Word, Brain Battle, Sink or Swim

2 Practice and Apply

A. CONCEPT CHECK: First Words and Titles

For each sentence, write the words that should be capitalized.

Into the Classics

1. If a friend says, "parting is such sweet sorrow," he or she is quoting from the play *romeo and juliet.*
2. "it's possible," said Mr. Wilcox, "that popular culture can lead us to the classics."
3. For example, watching an episode of *Xena, warrior princess* could inspire someone to read *the Odyssey.*
4. The traditional poet Robert Herrick reminds us of the importance of taking time in these lines from one of his poems:

   Gather ye rosebuds while ye may,
   Old Time is still a-flying;
   and this same flower that smiles today
   tomorrow will be dying.
5. So after seeing a spoof of the painting *american gothic,* check out the original, because "old Time is still a-flying."

➜ **For a SELF-CHECK and more practice, see the EXERCISE BANK, p. 334.**

Write sentences patterned on items 1, 3, and 5, using other titles you know.

B. PROOFREADING: Capitalization Errors

Find and correct 15 capitalization errors in the following letter.

A Classic Look

(1) Dear miss Guided:

(2) in your letter in *The Evening Standard,* you said, "The fine arts are irrelevant and unfamiliar." **(3)** Susan Sontag once wrote, "interpretation makes art manageable, conformable. . . ." **(4)** You can't compare *The war of the worlds* to *The x-Files* or *The Marriage Of Figaro* to *Grease!* **(5)** don't be swayed by the critics. **(6)** "A critic is a man who knows the way," said Kenneth Tynan, "But can't drive the car." **(7)** You can appreciate *Masterpiece theatre* if you try. **(8)** Acquaint yourself with *As you like it* before you rent *Shakespeare In Love.*

(9) Sincerely Yours,

(10) Ann E. Chance

Places and Transportation

1 Here's the Idea

The names of specific places, celestial bodies, landmarks, and vehicles are capitalized.

Geographical Names

In geographical names, capitalize each word except articles and prepositions.

Type of Name	Example
Special terms	**S**outhern **H**emisphere, **N**orth **P**ole
Continents	**A**frica, **A**sia, **N**orth **A**merica
Bodies of water	**L**ake **E**rie, **A**tlantic **O**cean, **N**ile **R**iver
Islands	**G**alapagos **I**slands, **P**hilippines, **H**awaiian **I**slands
Mountains	**A**ndes, **M**ount **E**verest, **R**ocky **M**ountains
Other landforms	**E**nglish **C**hannel, **P**ainted **D**esert, **N**iagara **F**alls
World regions	**B**alkans, **S**outheast **A**sia, **L**atin **A**merica
Countries/nations	**E**l **S**alvador, **T**hailand, **E**ngland
States	**T**exas, **C**alifornia, **F**lorida
Counties/townships	**P**olk **C**ounty, **I**ngham **T**ownship
Cities/towns	**T**ulsa, **S**alt **L**ake **C**ity, **B**oston
Roads/streets	**P**ennsylvania **A**venue, **R**odeo **D**rive, **C**entral **S**treet

Regions and Directions

Capitalize the words *north, south, east,* and *west* when they name a particular region of the country or world or are parts of proper nouns.

The Willises held a garage sale before moving to **S**outh Dakota.

Garage sales are popular on the **W**est **C**oast, where they lived.

Do not capitalize compass directions or adjectives that indicate direction or a general location.

They drove east out of Nevada City, and then turned north.

Bodies of the Universe

▶ **Capitalize the names of planets and other specific objects in the universe.**

Hale-Bopp Comet Venus Milky Way Galaxy

Do not capitalize *sun* and *moon.* Capitalize *earth* only when it refers to our planet or when it is used with other capitalized terms. Never capitalize *earth* when it is preceded by the article *the* or when it refers to land surface, or soil.

Did water once flow on Mars as it does on Earth?

The earth has many land forms carved by water.

Buildings, Bridges, and Other Landmarks

▶ **Capitalize the names of specific buildings, bridges, monuments, and other landmarks.**

Vietnam Memorial Golden Gate Bridge

World Trade Center Space Needle

Flora found a clock shaped like the Taj Mahal.

Planes, Trains, and Other Vehicles

▶ **Capitalize the names of specific airplanes, trains, ships, cars, and spacecraft.**

Type of Vehicle	Name
Airplanes	*Enola Gay, Spirit of St. Louis*
Trains	*Southwest Chief, City of New Orleans*
Ships	USS *John F. Kennedy, Pinta*
Cars	Malibu, Civic
Spacecraft	*Columbia, Mars Pathfinder*

CAPITALIZATION

2 Practice and Apply

A. CONCEPT CHECK: Places and Transportation

For each sentence, write the words that should be capitalized.

Second Time Around

1. From souvenirs of a trip to the bahamas to a model of the ss *clermont*, secondhand treasures abound.
2. Across the united states, from new England to the west coast, rummagers flock to flea markets.
3. Where else can you find a lamp in the shape of the eiffel tower?
4. Do you need a miniature model t Ford to complete your collection?
5. Are you looking for a velvet painting of mount rushmore for your wall?
6. Try visiting the Historic National Road Yard Sale, which runs more than 800 miles along u.s. 40 from baltimore, maryland, to st. louis, missouri.
7. Attend the annual rummage sale in north hill, located in the northern blue ridge mountains.
8. Take a stroll from maple street to oak boulevard and try a local garage sale.
9. A model of the Rolls Royce silver spirit may sell for a dollar.
10. A mobile of saturn, neptune, and mercury may have the down-to-earth price of fifty cents!

→ **For a SELF-CHECK and more practice, see the EXERCISE BANK, p. 334.**

B. WRITING: Postcard from a National Monument

Who Are These People?

Look up Mount Rushmore in a reference book or on the Internet. Learn where it is located, whose faces are on it, and other important information about it. Then write a five-sentence postcard to a friend describing the monument and including the facts you discovered. Use capitalization correctly.

Organizations and Other Subjects

1 Here's the Idea

Capitalize the names of organizations, historical events and documents, and months, days, and holidays.

Organizations and Institutions

Capitalize all important words in the names of businesses, governmental agencies, institutions, and other organizations.

Adams High School	Ralph's Foreign Car Repair, Inc.
Library of Congress	Guggenheim Museum
Federal Reserve System	Oberlin College

Do not capitalize words such as *school, company, church, college,* and *hospital* when they are not used as parts of proper names.

Abbreviations of Organization Names

Capitalize acronyms and abbreviations of the names of organizations and institutions.

UNICEF (United Nations International Children's Emergency Fund)

FTC (Federal Trade Commission)

ADA (American Dental Association)

PTA (Parent Teacher Association)

USC (University of Southern California)

Historical Events, Periods, and Documents

Capitalize the names of historical events, periods, and documents.

Historical Events, Periods, and Documents	
Events	Boston Tea Party, Revolutionary War, Gulf War
Periods	Great Depression, Sixties, Information Age
Documents	Mayflower Compact, Americans with Disabilities Act

The period of Reconstruction followed the Civil War.

CAPITALIZATION

Time Abbreviations and Calendar Items

Capitalize the abbreviations B.C., A.D., B.C.E., A.M., and P.M. In typeset material, time abbreviations are usually shown in small capital letters.

The Aztecs founded their capital in A.D. 1325.
The workshop begins at 8:00 A.M. and ends at 4:30 P.M.

A.D. goes before the date; B.C. goes after.

Capitalize the names of months, days, and holidays but not the names of seasons.

October	Wednesday	Labor Day
winter	Monday	Thanksgiving

Every February we celebrate Chinese New Year with a parade.

CHAPTER 10

Special Events, Awards, and Brand Names

Capitalize the names of special events and awards.

World Series	National Medal of Arts
Boston Marathon	Emmy Awards

Jim Morin won the Pulitzer Prize for Editorial Cartooning.

Capitalize the brand names of products but not common nouns that follow brand names.

Good Stuff spinach   Playpen Toys pacifiers

School Courses

Capitalize the titles of specific courses and courses that are followed by a number. Do not capitalize the general names of school subjects except languages.

Business Machines 101	Intermediate Word Processing
algebra	Japanese

Capitalize the names of school years only when they refer to a specific group or event, or when they are used in direct address.

The Freshman Bake Sale is held every spring.

Every fall, the juniors hold their toy drive.

You'd better start preparing, Sophomores.

2 Practice and Apply

A. CONCEPT CHECK: Organizations and Other Subjects

For each sentence, write the words that should be capitalized.

Toyland

1. Will this year's class trip find seniors visiting the senate and the house of representatives in the spring?
2. Does the senior trip committee need to raise money?
3. Then take a fundraising tip from Mr. Iwo, who teaches social studies at byron high school.
4. Iwo, a member of the marble collectors' society of America, conceived the Toys for Teens sale at the school.
5. Held in november, the sale featured a wide range of toys.
6. Exhibited over a saturday and a sunday from 9:00 a.m. to 6:00 P.M. was a collection of primitive toys that predate the industrial revolution.
7. There were also cast-iron fire engines made by the stanley company after world war II.
8. People could buy die-cast racing cars licensed by NASCAR.
9. In fact, toys ranging from General Toy Company's fashion dolls to nfl action figures were on sale.
10. The successful sale attracted early christmas and hanukkah shoppers as well as avid toy collectors.

➜ **For a SELF-CHECK and more practice, see the EXERCISE BANK, p. 335.**

CAPITALIZATION

B. PROOFREADING: Capitalization Errors

Find and correct 21 capitalization errors in the following passage.

Classroom Toys

(1) If they gave an Award for innovative use of toys, the students at worth high school would surely win it. **(2)** Freshman History students have recreated revolutionary war battles with tin soldiers and used Fabusoft software to simulate air campaigns in the persian gulf war. **(3)** In economics 1.1, Juniors have looked at the market for Fuzzy Babies Toys produced by marvo, inc., to study supply and demand concepts. **(4)** Some students have even formed the toy collectors society, which meets on tuesdays at 7:00 p.m. **(5)** If you attend the meetings, you might hear about a soldier doll that looks like General Colin Powell or action figures made by neato.

Real World Grammar

Publicity Poster

If you take part in activities at school or outside of school, you will sometimes need to create a publicity poster. The poster will require names, dates, and other words that should be capitalized. Once you have the basic information down, proofread the poster for errors in capitalization.

Hidden Treasures Flea Market

Sponsored by the Community service Club of ralph bunche high school

Capitalize names of organizations

Date: Saturday, november 15

Capitalize months

Time: 9:00 a.m. to 4:00 p.m.

Capitalize time abbreviations

Place: East Gym

Find just the right thing to dress up your room or your life!

- **Vintage clothing from the '60s, '70s, '80s, and '90s**
- **Posters, stickers, pins, pennants, bumper stickers**
- **Books, videos, CDs, and vinyl records**
- **Toys, games, trading cards, and other collectibles**

☆☆☆ SPECIAL FEATURED SECTIONS ☆☆☆

Books

Go tell it on the Mountain and other favorites you won't want to put down

Videos

The Wizard Of Oz and other timeless classics

Capitalize book and movie titles properly.

CDs and Tapes

favorite rap, R & B, rock, blues, jazz, and classical recordings

Don't capitalize titles unless they're used as part of a name

The President of our club is Vicki Sanchez.

Our faculty Sponsor is Mr. Robinson.

All proceeds will go to the Your Place Homeless Shelter.

Using Grammar in Writing

Names of organizations	Watch out for words like *club* and *school;* capitalize these words only when they are part of the name of a group.
Days, months, and time abbreviations	In addition to using capital letters, don't forget to punctuate the abbreviations A.M. and P.M. with periods.
Titles of published works	Remember, short words in a title are not necessarily unimportant words. Words like *Is, It,* and *All* should be capitalized in titles even when they are not the first words.
Personal titles	You may be tempted to capitalize titles like *chairperson* or *sponsor* because they seem important. When they appear apart from a person's name, however, they are ordinary nouns and should not be capitalized.

PRACTICE AND APPLY: Writing

Following are notes taken at a planning meeting for a school play. Create a publicity poster for the play, using the information shown and capitalizing it correctly.

PLAY TITLE: FAHRENHEIT 451
ADAPTED FROM THE NOVEL BY RAY BRADBURY

SANDRA LOPEZ, A JUNIOR, WILL PLAY CLARISSE AND TED ROSNER, A SOPHOMORE, WILL PLAY MONTAG.
MONTAG'S WIFE, MILDRED = PLAYED BY NAN WONG.
STUDENT DIRECTORS = NATE KEENE AND LISA FINCH.
FACULTY DIRECTOR= MARTHA LEE

FRI AND SAT, 7 IN THE EVENING
MAY 4 AND 5,
PARTRIDGE AUDITORIUM.
THE WELLSPRING DRAMA SOCIETY, JEFFERSON HIGH SCHOOL.

Mixed Review

A. Sentence Capitalization One collector of action figures sent the following e-mail message to another. Revise the message to capitalize all the letters in the message that should be capitalized in ordinary writing.

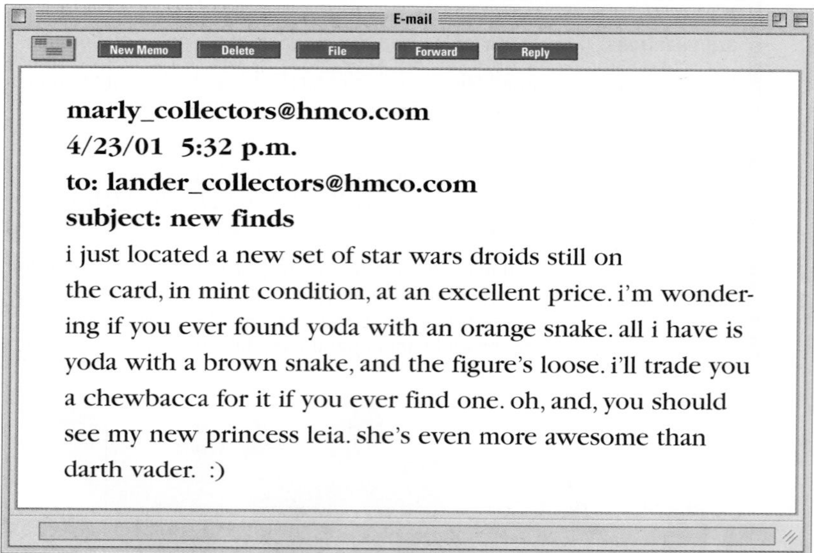

E-mail

New Memo | Delete | File | Forward | Reply

marly_collectors@hmco.com
4/23/01 5:32 p.m.
to: lander_collectors@hmco.com
subject: new finds

i just located a new set of star wars droids still on the card, in mint condition, at an excellent price. i'm wondering if you ever found yoda with an orange snake. all i have is yoda with a brown snake, and the figure's loose. i'll trade you a chewbacca for it if you ever find one. oh, and, you should see my new princess leia. she's even more awesome than darth vader. :)

B. Capitalization of Proper Nouns and Adjectives The following headlines contain some words that should always be capitalized and others that are normally shown in lowercase. Rewrite these headlines as complete sentences using proper capitalization and punctuation.

Example: RECORD CROWDS AT YOSEMITE
Answer: Record crowds visited Yosemite National Park.

1. FIRES RAGE; RED CROSS SAYS 500 DEAD
2. HURRICANE SLAMS CAROLINA COAST
3. 7 DIE AS MOUNT ST. HELENS ERUPTS
4. BLINDING ASH HALTS TRAFFIC ACROSS STATE
5. 52 U.S. HOSTAGES FLOWN TO FREEDOM
6. BRITAIN ANNOUNCES ARGENTINE SURRENDER
7. FLOODS RAGE IN CONNECTICUT; 8 BELIEVED DEAD
8. FOURTH OF JULY PARADE SNARLS CITY TRAFFIC
9. 2 UNIVERSITY PHYSICISTS TAKE NOBEL PRIZE
10. MOVIE DRAWS RECORD NUMBERS TO LEWISTOWN MALL

Mastery Test: What Did You Learn?

For each underlined group of words, choose the letter of the correct revision.

After receiving the call from reverend Bates about Mrs. Bates's death, (1) Dennis Rocker could almost hear her lovely irish voice (2) saying, "Care for my salt shakers when I'm gone." He (3) would treasure them as much as he did their long friendship that began with this letter.

dear Mr. Rocker, (4)

Lenny Bruce once said, "the liberals (5) can understand everything but the people who don't understand them." The same is true of collectors. I'm glad you enjoyed my story "A Pinch of Salt And Pepper." (6) The picture of my ivory shakers of the Leaning tower of Pisa (7) came out well. You'd probably also like my shakers shaped like union soldiers from the Civil War (8) and the Campbell's soup Kids. (9) Please stop by some Saturday in the Spring after 2:00 P.M. (10) I'd love to show my collection to you.

Sincerely yours,

Ida Mae Bates

1. A. Reverend
   B. mrs.
   C. bates
   D. Correct as is

2. A. Lovely
   B. Irish
   C. Voice
   D. Correct as is

3. A. When
   B. i'm
   C. he
   D. Correct as is

4. A. Dear
   B. mr.
   C. rocker
   D. Correct as is

5. A. lenny
   B. bruce
   C. The
   D. Correct as is

6. A. a
   B. Of
   C. and
   D. Correct as is

7. A. The
   B. leaning
   C. Tower
   D. Correct as is

8. A. Union
   B. Soldiers
   C. civil
   D. Correct as is

9. A. The
   B. campbell's
   C. Soup
   D. Correct as is

10. A. saturday
    B. spring
    C. 2:00 p.m.
    D. Correct as is

CAPITALIZATION

Student Help Desk

Capitalization at a Glance

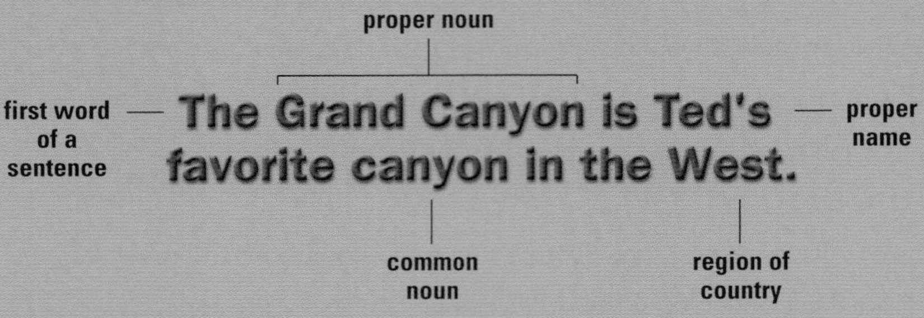

CHAPTER 10

Do Capitalize

Caps On!

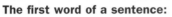

The first word of a sentence:
Building a collection is hard work.

The first word in every line of a traditional poem:
Love is not all: it is not meat nor drink
Nor slumber nor a roof against the rain; . . .
—Edna St. Vincent Millay, "Sonnet XXX" of *Fatal Interview*

The first word of the greeting in a letter:
My dearest, Darling nephew,

The first word and all important words in titles:
A Raisin in the Sun

Family words when used with names or in place of names:
The world's largest golf ball collection belongs to Mother.
She inherited some of it from Aunt Seretha.

Proper nouns that name people, places, and things:
The *Empire Builder* took them through the Badlands and the Rocky Mountains.

"If Anderson is C.E.O., and Wyatt is C.F.O., and you're C.O.O., then who am I, and what am I doing here?"

CAPITALIZATION

Don't Capitalize

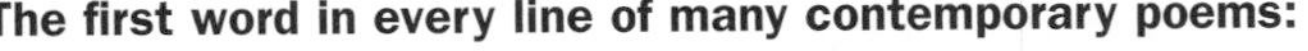

Caps Off!

The first words in partial questions that follow grammatically from a complete sentence:

Do you collect dolls? model airplanes? stuffed animals? frogs?

The first word in every line of many contemporary poems:

The song is gone; the dance
is secret with the dancers in the earth . . .

—Judith Wright, "Bora Ring"

Words after the first word of the greeting in a letter:

My dearest neighbor,

Articles, coordinating conjunctions, or prepositions shorter than five letters:

"By the Waters of Babylon"

Family words when used as ordinary nouns:

Jeb's uncle has an even larger collection.
He got some of it from his aunt, Maureen.

The common nouns that stand for people, places, or things:

The train took them through the desolate hills and the snowcapped mountains.

Chapter 11

Punctuation

Theme: In and Around the Ocean

Little Things That Mean a Lot

The fisherman in the picture above uses the same word to express three different thoughts about the shark that is circling his boat. Imagine that you are the fisherman. Then read each thought aloud. How do the punctuation marks make the same word express three different thoughts?

Punctuation marks may look small, but they add a world of meaning to your writing. This chapter offers guidelines for using punctuation to make your ideas clearer and easier for readers to understand.

Write Away: Punctuate It!

Think of a time when something exciting, dangerous, or frightening happened to you. Write a paragraph about this experience, using at least four different punctuation marks, such as periods, question marks, exclamation points, and quotation marks. Put your paragraph in your **Working Portfolio.**

Diagnostic Test: What Do You Know?

For each numbered section, choose the letter of the correct answer.

People have long wondered what happened to Atlantis? (1) Have you read about the ancient lost continent: some (2) people believe that volcanic eruptions, earthquakes, and tidal waves (3) caused it to sink into the sea. If this is true the (4) ruins of a magnificent civilization lie on the floor of the Atlantic Ocean. Plato, the ancient Greek philosopher wrote (5) that Atlantis was destroyed in about 10,000 B.C. He read about Atlantis in ancient records and wrote (6) about it. His works which are still read, (7) have helped to keep the legend of Atlantis alive. Many people believe in the legend however, (8) no one has proven that Atlantis actually existed! (9) "Atlantis is an island of the mind, said one historian. (10)

1. A. Atlantis!
   B. Atlantis.
   C. Atlantis,
   D. Correct as is

2. A. continent? Some
   B. continent. some
   C. continent; some
   D. Correct as is

3. A. volcanic, eruptions, earthquakes and tidal waves
   B. volcanic eruptions earthquakes and tidal waves
   C. volcanic eruptions, earthquakes, and, tidal waves
   D. Correct as is

4. A. If this is true: the
   B. If this is true. The
   C. If this is true, the
   D. Correct as is

5. A. Plato, the ancient Greek philosopher, wrote
   B. "Plato," the ancient Greek philosopher wrote
   C. Plato the ancient Greek philosopher wrote,
   D. Correct as is

6. A. records, and wrote
   B. records. And wrote
   C. records, wrote
   D. Correct as is

7. A. works which are still read
   B. works, which are still read,
   C. works, which are still read
   D. Correct as is

8. A. legend; however,
   B. legend—however,
   C. legend: however,
   D. Correct as is

9. A. existed."
   B. existed?
   C. existed.
   D. Correct as is

10. A. Atlantis is an island of the mind, "said one historian."
    B. "Atlantis is an island of the mind," said one historian.
    C. Atlantis is an island of the mind, said one historian.
    D. Correct as is

PUNCTUATION

LESSON 1 Periods and Other End Marks

1 Here's the Idea

End marks—periods, question marks, and exclamation points—are punctuation marks used at the end of sentences or of complete thoughts. Periods are also used in other ways.

Periods

▶ **Use a period at the end of all declarative sentences and most imperative sentences.**

The waters around Monterey Bay contain sharks. (DECLARATIVE)

Swim with caution. (IMPERATIVE)

When an imperative sentence expresses strong emotion or excitement, use an exclamation point.

Get out of the water!

▶ **Use periods at the end of most indirect questions.** An **indirect question** indicates that someone has asked a question, but the person's exact words are not shown.

The lifeguard asked whether any sharks had been spotted in the area. (INDIRECT)

Have any sharks been spotted in the area? (DIRECT)

Question Marks

▶ **Use a question mark at the end of an interrogative sentence or after a question that is not a complete sentence.**

INTERROGATIVE SENTENCE

Has the demand for shark fins resulted in overfishing?

INCOMPLETE QUESTION

The truth? Some shark species have been overfished.

Sometimes writers punctuate what looks like a declarative sentence with a question mark to indicate that the sentence should be read as a question.

DECLARATIVE	DECLARATIVE WITH A QUESTION MARK
Marla saw a shark.	Marla saw a shark?
The shark was startled.	The shark was startled?

CHAPTER 11

Exclamation Points

▶ **Use an exclamation point after a strong interjection, at the end of an exclamatory sentence, or after an imperative sentence that expresses strong emotion.**

An **interjection** is a word or group of words that expresses emotion or imitates a sound.

Wow! What sharp teeth he has! Get away!

For information about using end marks with direct quotations, see p. 279.

PUNCTUATION

Other Uses of Periods

▶ **Use a period at the end of most abbreviations or initials.**
If you're not sure how to punctuate an abbreviation, look it up in a current dictionary.

Periods with Abbreviations and Initials	
Personal names	E. B. White Sally K. Ride Kurt Vonnegut, Jr. José Estevez, Sr.
Titles	Mr. Mrs. Ms. Dr. Sen. Gov. Capt.
Parts of business names	Assocs. Bros. Co. Corp. Inc. Ltd.
Addresses	St. Rd. Blvd. Pkwy. Bldg.
Chronology	A.D. B.C.
Time of day	A.M. P.M.
Measurement (U.S.)	12 ft. 5 in.
Time	1 hr. 15 min.

Do not use periods with these abbreviations: metric measurements (cm, ml, kg, g, L), acronyms (NATO, UNICEF, NASA), abbreviations that are pronounced letter by letter (CIA, NBA, EPA, IRS, NAACP), state names in postal addresses (TX, CA, FL), or points on a compass (N, NE, S, SW).

Many abbreviations are not appropriate in formal writing and correspondence. Proofread your formal letters and writing assignments and make sure you've spelled out words you might abbreviate in casual writing.

Use a period after each number or letter in an outline or a list.

Outline	List
I. Dangerous sharks	The Most Dangerous Sharks
A. Great white shark	1. Great white shark
1. Size	2. Tiger shark
2. Habitat	3. Bull shark
B. Tiger shark	4. Oceanic whitetip shark

2 Practice and Apply

A. CONCEPT CHECK: Periods and Other End Marks

On a sheet of paper, write the last word of each sentence in the passage below and add the appropriate end mark.

Man-eating Monsters?

(1) Shark experts are often asked whether sharks are truly man-eating monsters **(2)** Although some species of sharks will attack and eat human beings, sharks are not the crazed killers portrayed in fiction and films **(3)** Phew **(4)** Isn't that a relief

(5) Are they potentially dangerous **(6)** You bet **(7)** Do they crave people sandwiches **(8)** Don't you believe it **(9)** Most sharks crave fatty food **(10)** In their eyes, humans are just light snacks **(11)** A large sea lion provides more calories for a lot less trouble **(12)** Why, then, do sharks sometimes attack people **(13)** Experts believe that most attacks are cases of mistaken identity **(14)** To a shark, a swimmer's flapping hands and feet may look like plump little fish swimming along **(15)** Watch out

➜ **For a SELF-CHECK and more practice, see the EXERCISE BANK, p. 335.**

B. REVISING: Periods

Rewrite the outline below, adding the seven missing periods.

Shark Facts

I Interesting shark facts

A Facts about anatomy

1 Some sharks grow ten inches per year

2 Whale sharks have about 300 rows of teeth

B Facts about behavior

LESSON 2 Comma Uses

1 Here's the Idea

Commas make writing clearer by separating words, ideas, and other elements in sentences.

Commas in a Series

In a series of three or more items, use a comma after every item except the last one.

The items in a series may be words, phrases, or clauses.

Rocks, snags, and **shoals** can be hazardous to boats.

The boat **hit a rock, took on water,** and **sank into the sea**.

We do not know **when the boat sank, where it was headed,** or **who was aboard**.

No commas are needed if the items in a series are joined by *and, or,* or *nor*.

The sea was dark **and** deep **and** menacing.

Use a comma after the introductory words *first, second,* and so on when they introduce items in a series.

You'll pass three landmarks on the way to the island: **first,** the lighthouse; **second,** Star Point; and **third,** Lil's Landing.

Use commas between two or more adjectives that modify the same noun.

A thick, damp fog blanketed the coastline.

How do you know when to add commas between adjectives?

Here's How **Adding Commas Between Adjectives**

The captain issued orders in a **low tense** voice.

1. First, switch the order of the adjectives and insert the word *and* between them.

   The captain issued orders in a **tense and low** voice.

2. Add a comma if the meaning of the sentence has not changed and if the word *and* sounds natural between the adjectives.

   The captain issued orders in a **low, tense** voice.

PUNCTUATION

In general, don't use commas after numbers and adjectives of size, shape, and age.

five small boats
a **round** nylon cushion
a **big** yellow moon
the **old** stone lighthouse

Commas with Introductory Elements

Use a comma after an introductory word or a mild interjection at the beginning of a sentence.

No, our crew was unable to call for help.

Eventually, a ship spotted us.

Hey, what's that in the water over there?

Use a comma after an introductory prepositional phrase that contains one or more additional prepositional phrases.

In the spring of 1930, marine science took a giant step forward.

For the first time in history, a scientist explored the ocean's depths.

A single prepositional phrase at the beginning of a sentence may be set off by a comma if it is followed by a natural pause when it is read out loud. Don't use a comma if the phrase is very short or if you would not pause after saying it.

At first they didn't know what they would find.

Use a comma after a verbal phrase at the beginning of a sentence.

To make the half-mile dive, scientists and engineers designed a deep-sea vehicle.

Use a comma after an introductory adverb or an adverb clause at the beginning of a sentence.

Fortunately, the vehicle worked well.

When scientist William Beebe made the first dive, he was amazed by what he saw.

Do not use a comma after a phrase or a clause that is the subject of a sentence.

To survive at such depths is difficult.

What he saw amazed him.

CHAPTER 11

Commas with Interrupters

Use commas to set off a parenthetical expression.
A parenthetical expression provides explanatory or supplementary information that is closely related to the sentence.

Beebe did**, of course,** keep a journal.

He took notes**, I believe,** on several previously unknown species.

Common Parenthetical Expressions

after all	furthermore	I suppose	nevertheless
by the way	however	in fact	of course
for example	I believe	moreover	therefore

Use commas to set off words of direct address.
Words of direct address are names, titles, terms of respect, and phrases used to address an individual directly.

PROFESSIONAL MODEL

"Thank you**, Captain Lowry,** for a job well done."

"It was nothing**, sir.**"

PUNCTUATION

Commas with Nonessential Material

Use commas to set off nonessential clauses and nonessential participial phrases. Both of these sentence parts add information to a sentence, but the information is not essential to the meaning of the sentence.

Advanced Lifesaving**, which is an excellent course,** prepares students to be lifeguards. (NONESSENTIAL CLAUSE)

Mrs. Lewis**, worried about her daughter's safety,** paced nervously on the shore. (NONESSENTIAL PARTICIPIAL PHRASE)

Use commas to set off nonessential appositives.
A **nonessential appositive** is a word or a phrase that adds information about a noun or pronoun.

Scientists transformed the H.M.S. *Challenger*, **a British warship,** into a floating laboratory.

An **essential appositive** is not set off with commas.

Rachel Carson's book ***The Sea Around Us*** helped raised public awareness of ocean pollution.

For more information on essential and nonessential material, see pp. 69 and 95.

❷ Practice and Apply

A. CONCEPT CHECK: Commas

Fourteen commas are missing from the sentences below. Write the word before each missing comma and add the comma.

England's Underwater Rowboat

1. On a warm day in 1620 King James I of England witnessed an amazing test.
2. Cornelis Drebbel a Dutch scientist demonstrated an underwater boat for the king.
3. Drebbel had in fact invented the first successful submarine.
4. To waterproof the wooden vessel Drebbel covered it with greased leather.
5. Because few sources of energy were available Drebbel relied on manpower to propel the vessel.
6. His sub was powered steered and controlled by a crew of oarsmen.
7. The Thames River which runs through the city of London was the test site for Drebbel's invention.
8. Fresh clean air was provided by tubes that floated on the surface of the river.
9. Apparently the sub was submerged by letting water into the hull.
10. Cruising at a depth of 16 feet Drebbel's vessel helped speed the development of the modern submarine.

➜ **For a SELF-CHECK and more practice, see the EXERCISE BANK, p. 336.**

B. PROOFREADING: Correcting Comma Errors

Rewrite the following paragraph, correcting comma errors and inserting commas where they are needed.

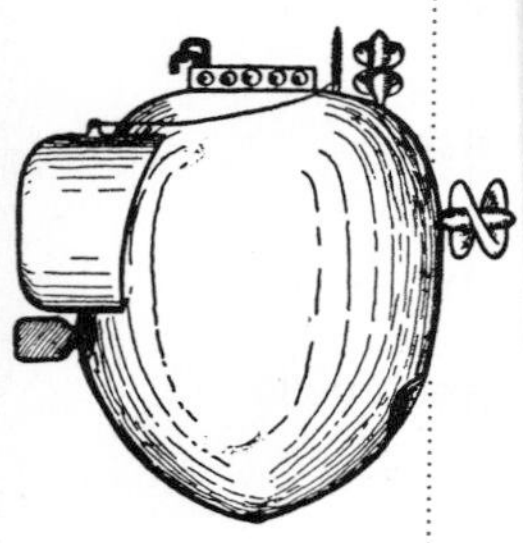

A Revolutionary Submarine

Not, surprisingly the *Turtle* was a slow submarine. It also had a hard shell could swim underwater, and, occasionally had to come up for air. Unlike its reptilian namesake, the *Turtle*, packed an explosive punch. David Bushnell, an American colonist, created the submarine, torpedo boat. Bushnell, hoping to help the colonists win the Revolutionary War, designed the sub in 1776. The one-person wooden vehicle was powered by pedals shaped, like an egg, and armed with a keg of gunpowder. Unfortunately the *Turtle's* first target H.M.S. *Eagle*, had a hard shell of its own. Yes the *Turtle* took an early retirement.

LESSON 3

More Comma Uses

1 Here's the Idea

Commas with Quotations

▶ **Use commas to set off the explanatory words (such as *he said* or *she asked*) of a direct quotation.**

Commas, like periods, always go inside closing quotation marks.

STUDENT MODEL

Mrs. Lewis called, "A boat has capsized!"

Her daughter Ida ran down from the house to the dock. "Tell me the location of the accident," **Ida calmly said.**

Mrs. Lewis pointed out at the ocean. "The boat tipped over," **she explained,** "about 100 yards due east of here."

Mrs. Lewis told her daughter that two people were in the boat.

Use a comma to set off explanatory words that come before or after a direct quotation.

Use commas to set off explanatory words in the middle of a direct quotation.

Indirect quotations do not need commas.

PUNCTUATION

Commas in Compound Sentences

▶ **Use a comma before the coordinating conjunction that joins the two independent clauses of a compound sentence.**

Ida Lewis jumped into her rowboat, **and** she headed due east.

Use a comma before the conjunctions *yet* and *for* when they join independent clauses.

Lewis feared the worst, **yet** she hoped for the best.

She was worried about the victims, **for** the water was cold.

Do not use a comma to separate the verb phrases of a compound predicate.

Lewis **jumped into her rowboat and quickly headed due east.**
COMPOUND PREDICATE

Make sure you use both a comma and a conjunction between independent clauses. Using a comma without a conjunction will result in a run-on sentence.

It was the middle of winter, *and* the water was extremely cold.

For more about run-on sentences, see p. 120.

Commas in Dates, Place Names, and Letters

In dates, use a comma to separate the day of the month from the year.

April 15, 2003 November 1, 1960

Don't use a comma when only the month and the year are given.

December 1945

When a date is part of a sentence, use a comma after the year.

On October 1, 1975, a ship was lost at sea.

Use a comma to separate the name of a city or town and the name of its state, province, or country.

Dallas, Texas Bancroft, Ontario Mexico City, Mexico

When an address is part of a sentence, use a comma after each item. Do not put a comma between the name of a state and the ZIP code, however.

Please forward my mail to 4795 Seaside Drive, Manisota, Florida 36006.

Use a comma after the salutation of a friendly letter and after the closing of a friendly or business letter.

Hello Aunt Lucy, Dearest Charlie, Dear Mrs. Oliver,

Love, Yours truly, Sincerely,

Commas with Names and Numbers

Use a comma between a personal name and an abbreviation that follows it, such as *Jr., Sr.,* or *M.D.* Also use a comma between a business name and an abbreviation, such as *Inc.*

Lara Johnson, M.D. Paradise Cruises, Inc.

When names and abbreviations are part of a sentence, set off the abbreviations with commas.

Paradise Cruises, Inc., has hired Lara Johnson, M.D., as its medical director.

Lara Johnson, M.D.
General Practioner

CHAPTER 11

Commas to Avoid Confusion

Use a comma to separate words or phrases that might be misunderstood when they are read.

Here are four ways commas can clear up confusion in your sentences.

1. Use a comma before the conjunction *but* or *for* when it may be mistaken for a preposition.

Confusing **The victims were grateful for the young woman** had saved their lives.	**Clear** **The victims were grateful,** for the young woman had saved their lives.

2. Use a comma after an introductory adverb that could be mistaken for a preposition.

Confusing **Inside the boat** was in good condition.	**Clear** **Inside,** the boat was in good condition.

3. Use a comma to separate a short introductory verbal phrase from the noun that follows it.

Confusing **While rocking the boat** almost capsized.	**Clear** **While rocking,** the boat almost capsized.

4. Use a comma to separate repeated words.

Confusing What an "old salt" **is is** an experienced sailor.	**Clear** What an "old salt" **is, is** an experienced sailor.

Use a comma to indicate the words left out of parallel word groups, or word groups that repeat the same structure.
In this situation, the comma takes the place of the verb.

The captain was old; the crew, young.

David ordered lobster, and Connie, softshell crabs.

In numbers of more than three digits, use a comma after every third digit from the right. ZIP codes, phone numbers, years, and house numbers are exceptions to this rule.

3,000 people   3491 Chestnut Ridge Road (NO COMMA)

PUNCTUATION

❷ Practice and Apply

A. CONCEPT CHECK: More Comma Uses

Write the word before each missing comma and place each comma correctly. Write *Correct* if no commas are needed.

Rhode Island Rescuer

1. It was a lazy day in September 1859. Off Lime Rock Rhode Island the breeze was light; the sea calm.
2. Captain Hosea Lewis leapt out of his rocking chair for he saw an alarming sight.
3. "Have a look out there" he called to his daughter. He added "Those boys bobbing in the water can't swim."
4. Ida Lewis scanned the sea with her eyes and located the problem.
5. Nearby four boys were clinging to their capsized sailboat.
6. Ida hurried to her boat for there was no time to lose.
7. Lewis made her first rescue but it would not be her last.
8. On March 29 1869 she saved two soldiers lost at sea.
9. While touring New England President Grant visited Lewis to thank her.
10. He laughed when he fell on some rocks and got his feet wet. "To see Ida Lewis" he said "I'd gladly get wet up to my armpits."

➜ **For a SELF-CHECK and more practice, see the EXERCISE BANK, p. 336.**

B. PROOFREADING: Mixed Review of Commas

Rewrite the letter below, adding commas where necessary.

Dear Joe

Well it's only noon here but we have already put in a full day. At 5:30 this morning my grandfather yelled "Wake up boy! We're going to the island." The boat race to Mackinac Island ended this morning and there was a lot of excitement around here. *Stars and Stripes,* which finished the 333-mile race in just under 20 hours set a new world's record. What a crowd showed up to cheer the winner! There must have been 1000 people at the harbor.

Drop me a line sometime in care of my grandfather. His name is William Benis M.D. His address is 300 West Bluff Street St. Ignace MI 49781.

Your friend

Bob

CHAPTER 11

LESSON 4

Semicolons and Colons

PUNCTUATION

1 Here's the Idea

A semicolon separates different elements within a sentence.
A colon indicates that an example or explanation follows.

Semicolons

Use semicolons to separate items in a series if any of the items contains commas.

The divers gathered at dawn; put on their tanks, masks, and wet suits; and jumped off the pier into the ocean.

Use a semicolon between independent clauses joined by a conjunction if either clause contains commas.

The deep sea once appeared to be cold, murky, and lifeless; but scientists have discovered strange fish living in this region.

Use a semicolon to join the independent clauses of a compound sentence if no coordinating conjunction is used.

Using a semicolon instead of a comma and a conjunction indicates a stronger relationship between the clauses. Don't use a semicolon unless the ideas in the clauses are closely related.

The storm struck with savage fury, but our house was not damaged at all.

The storm struck with savage fury; it demolished most of the coastal town.

Use a semicolon before a conjunctive adverb or a parenthetical expression that joins the clauses of a compound sentence.

Use a comma after the adverb or expression.

CONJUNCTIVE ADVERB

The weather was stormy; therefore, we postponed our sailing trip.

PARENTHETICAL EXPRESSION

Storms pose great risks for sailors; in fact, they can be deadly.

For a list of conjunctive adverbs, see p. 27.

Colons

Use a colon to introduce a list of items.

On a short sailing excursion, you should bring these items: a life jacket, a pair of sunglasses, and a tube of sunscreen.

Do not use a colon in the following situations: after a verb, in the middle of a prepositional phrase, or after *because* or *as*.

After a verb

Incorrect: The three longest rivers in the world **are:** the Nile, the Amazon, and the Yangtze.	**Correct:** These are the three longest rivers in the world: the Nile, the Amazon, and the Yangtze.

In the middle of a prepositional phrase

Incorrect: I have swum **in:** the Atlantic Ocean, the Pacific Ocean, and the Mediterranean Sea.	**Correct:** I have swum in the following bodies of water: the Atlantic Ocean, the Pacific Ocean, and the Mediterranean Sea.

After *because* or *as*

Incorrect: The ship was in danger **because:** a terrible storm was approaching.	**Correct:** The ship was in danger because a terrible storm was approaching.

▶ **Use a colon between two independent clauses when the second clause explains or summarizes the first.**

The captain was right: we should have waited out the storm.

▶ **Use a colon to introduce a formal or long quotation.**

Winston Churchill inspired the people of England with these words: "We shall not fail or falter; we shall not weaken or tire."

After a colon, capitalize the first word of a formal statement. If the statement is informal, it should begin with a lowercase letter.

Other Uses of Colons Use a colon in the following situations:

- **After the formal salutation of a business letter**
  Dear Madam:
- **After labels that signal important ideas**
  Beware: These waters contain sharks.
- **Between the hour and minute figures of clock time**
  12:15 P.M.
- **Between chapter and verse when referring to certain religious works, such as the Bible, the Qur'an (Koran), and the Talmud**
  Psalm 23:7

❷ Practice and Apply

A. CONCEPT CHECK: Semicolon and Colon

Write the word before each missing semicolon or colon in the paragraph below, and insert the appropriate punctuation marks.

Underwater Heat Vents

In 1993 a ship left the shores of Seattle, Washington it headed toward the waters off the coast of Oregon. Geologists had made an interesting discovery a series of seaquakes were occurring on the Juan de Fuca Ridge, an underwater mountain range. Seaquakes occur when areas of the earth's crust shift, collide, and pile up and they are often accompanied by volcanic eruptions. Periodically, sections of the ridge split open, releasing hot lava that heats up the surrounding water.

High ocean temperatures do not usually support life however, some primitive life forms like heat. Scientists aboard the ship were hoping to find at least three forms of life sea-bed microbes, simple plants, and tube worms. All three exist at the bottom of the food chain all three support higher forms of life. The scientists received their reward they found a volcanic chimney growing over a vent. The interior of the chimney reached more than 500 degrees nevertheless, it was crawling with life.

➜ **For a SELF-CHECK and more practice, see the EXERCISE BANK, p. 337.**

B. REVISING: Correcting Semicolon and Colon Use

Rewrite the following paragraph by adding, deleting, or replacing semicolons and colons. Use capitalization correctly.

Godzilla Spotted Near Seattle!

(1) Godzilla has been spotted near Seattle, however, there is no need for panic. **(2)** This Godzilla is no lizard it is an undersea volcanic chimney. **(3)** There's a reason why the chimney was named Godzilla; It is 15 stories high, almost as tall as the movie monster. **(4)** Other large chimneys dot the Juan de Fuca Ridge. **(5)** Three of them are named: Beard, Mongo, and Church. **(6)** If you want to visit any of these chimneys, you'll need to buy a few items: a submarine; diving gear; and an underwater robot. **(7)** A team of scientists organized an undersea expedition: to remove a chimney from the sea floor and bring it into a laboratory for study. **(8)** The team included Cindy Van Dover, a biologist, John R. Delaney, a geologist, and Marv Lilley, a geochemist.

PUNCTUATION

Dashes and Parentheses

1 Here's the Idea

Dashes and parentheses are used to set off information that interrupts the flow of sentences.

Dashes

▶ **Use dashes to show an abrupt break in thought. If the thought continues after the break, use a second dash.**

Your prize will be a cruise to Bermuda—**assuming you win the contest.**

Our room—**supposedly the best on the ship**—was tiny, hot, and noisy.

When writing dialogue, you can use a dash to show interrupted speech.

PROFESSIONAL MODEL

"I'm hiding from a passenger," whispered Tod. "Please don't tell my—"

"Oh, Tod," called Mrs. Wembly, "come and meet my niece."

—Elizabeth Botzow, "At Sea"

▶ **Use dashes to set off a long explanatory statement that interrupts the main thought of a sentence.**

Ocean currents—**the tendency of the oceans' waters to move in a certain direction**—puzzled early navigators.

▶ **Use a dash to set off an introductory list.**

Whales, dolphins, sea lions, exotic fish—all these ocean wonders await you at Seaside Aquarium.

Do not overuse dashes. Paragraphs filled with dashes are difficult to read and seem carelessly written.

Difficult: The lines at Seaside were long—it was a holiday—and many people had the day off. We were relaxed—we enjoyed our visit—however, the lines tried our patience.

CHAPTER 11

Parentheses

▶ **Use parentheses to set off nonessential explanatory material that is loosely related to the sentence.**

Nonessential material interrupts the flow of the sentence and is helpful but not important to its meaning.

> Although *The Sea Around Us* is somewhat dated **(it was first published in 1951)**, the book is still a fascinating source of information about the sea.

Use the chart below to help you punctuate and capitalize parenthetical information.

When the parenthetical information is . . .	
a complete sentence within another sentence	
The giant waves (they were terrifying!) tossed the ship as if it were a toy. 	• It begins with a lowercase letter unless the first word is a proper noun. • It ends without any punctuation or with a question mark or an exclamation point but NOT with a period.
a complete sentence that stands alone	
Amy had never been so seasick in her life. (She still gets queasy at the thought of eating chocolate mousse.)	• It begins with a capital letter. • It ends with a period, exclamation point, or question mark inside the parentheses.
a fragment within another sentence	
The captain (a very nice man) sent a pot of peppermint tea to our room.	• It begins with a lowercase letter. • It ends without any punctuation or with a question mark or an exclamation point but NOT with a period.

PUNCTUATION

- **Use parentheses to enclose numbers or letters in a list that is part of a sentence.**

  According to the drill instructions, we need to (1) make sure that everyone is wearing a life jacket, (2) prepare the life rafts, and (3) radio the Coast Guard.

- **In a research paper, use parentheses to identify the source of any quoted or paraphrased information you use.**

  Since ancient times, the sea has been thought of as "a thing of beauty and terror, a giver and taker of life" (Broad, 21).

2 Practice and Apply

CONCEPT CHECK: Dashes and Parentheses

For each item, write each word that should precede and follow a dash or the words that should be in parentheses. Add the appropriate punctuation.

The Man Behind the Map

1. Government official, inventor, scientist all these titles describe Benjamin Franklin.
2. Although everyone knows that Franklin took a scientific interest in electricity recall his kite experiments, few people know about his interest in the sea.
3. This interest grew out of one of his career positions that of Deputy Postmaster General of the Colonies.
4. Franklin noticed that British mail ships supposedly the fastest in the world took longer to cross the Atlantic than did American ships.
5. Puzzled, he asked Timothy Folger he was an American sea captain why.
6. Folger explained that British captains steered their ships into the Gulf Stream, whereas American ships "run along the side and frequently cross it." Carson, 134
7. The effects of the Gulf Stream were especially noticeable on the westward crossing of the Atlantic the trip from England to the colonies.
8. Sailing against the Gulf Stream one of the strongest currents in all the Atlantic slowed British ships.
9. Franklin hoping to improve mail service had a map of the current drawn up and sent to England.
10. Thus, he became the first person and doubtless the only postmaster to issue an official chart of the Gulf Stream.

➜ For a SELF-CHECK and more practice, see the EXERCISE BANK, p. 337.

Hyphens and Apostrophes

1 Here's the Idea

Hyphens

A hyphen connects the following kinds of words, which then function as a single unit.

Words to Hyphenate

Compound numbers from twenty-one to ninety-nine	thirty-five ships, ninety-two years
Spelled-out fractions	three-fifths of the crew
Certain compound nouns	time-out, brother-in-law
Compound adjectives used before a noun (but not after)	well-known fact (fact that is well known); 27-day ordeal
The prefixes *ex-*, *self-*, *great-*, *half-*, and *all-*; all prefixes used before proper nouns and proper adjectives	ex-captain, self-expression, great-grandmother, half-eaten, pre-Columbian
The suffixes *-elect* and *-style*	president-elect , English-style breakfast

Use a hyphen if part of a word must be carried down from one line to the next.

LITERARY MODEL

At last the rain came. It was sudden and **tremen-**
dous. For two or three moons the sun had been **gath-**
ering strength till it seemed to breathe a breath of fire on
the earth.

—Chinua Achebe, *Things Fall Apart*

Follow these rules to help you decide when and how to hyphenate a word at a line break.

Here's How **Hyphenating at Line Breaks**

- Hyphenate only words with two or more syllables.
- Divide words with hyphens only between syllables.
- Make sure there are two or more letters of the hyphenated word on each line.

PUNCTUATION

Apostrophes

Use an apostrophe to form the possessive case of a singular or plural noun.

To form the possessive of a singular noun, add an apostrophe and an *s* even if the singular noun ends in *s*.

Ed's journal a week's salary Columbus's journey

To form the possessive of a plural noun that ends in *s* or *es*, add only an apostrophe after the final *s*.

five countries' navies three years' time the Joneses' boat

To form the possessive of a plural noun that does not end in *s*, add an apostrophe and an *s*.

children's swimsuits people's choice

Some names are difficult to pronounce when an apostrophe and an *s* are added. In such cases, you may add the apostrophe alone.

Jesus' name Achilles' heel Odysseus' journey

If the names of two or more persons are used to show joint ownership, give only the last name the possessive form.

Hyacinth and Maria's party

If the names of two or more persons are used to show separate ownership, give each name the possessive form.

Peter's and Robert's sneakers

To form the possessive of an indefinite pronoun, add an apostrophe and *s*.

one's choices everybody's favorite each other's paper

Use an apostrophe to show where letters or words are missing in contractions.

you'll (you will) they're (they are) can't (cannot)

When writing dialogue that reflects regional dialects or accents, use an apostrophe to indicate missing letters.

Jo smiled and said, "How d'you do, Cap'n! Yer ship's a beaut'."

Use an apostrophe and *s* to form the plural of letters, numerals, and words referred to as words.

ABC's three A's two *5*'s *yes*'s and *no*'s

Use an apostrophe to show the missing numbers in a date.

class of '99 (1999) blizzard of '04 (2004)

CHAPTER 11

Don't use an apostrophe with plural possessive pronouns (*hers, its, theirs*) or in the plural of decades or temperatures (the Roaring '20s, the 1990s, temperatures in the 60s).

❷ Practice and Apply

A. CONCEPT CHECK: Hyphens and Apostrophes

Rewrite the words that are missing hyphens and apostrophes, adding the missing punctuation.

Mayday! Mayday!

1. Early on October 14, 1980, the teletype in Alaskas Coast Guard Rescue Coordination Center clattered out an ominous message.
2. There was a fire aboard the *Prisendam,* a 427 foot ocean liner.
3. Passengers and crew members lives were in danger.
4. The well equipped liner had a dozen life rafts that could accommodate twenty five people, and six lifeboats that could carry many more.
5. Many of its passengers were experienced voyagers, and the crew had run emergency drills to help ensure everyones safety.
6. However, even well trained passengers may panic during a real emergency, especially during predawn hours, when its difficult to see.
7. In just a few minutes time, the Coast Guards rescue operation was underway.
8. When the first helicopter arrived, about one tenth of the crew and passengers were still aboard the fiery ship.
9. Escape was theirs for the taking: the helicopters rescue basket hovered just above their heads.
10. If not for the fast acting Coast Guard, the *Prisendam* fire of 80 might have been one of the decades worst disasters.

➜ **For a SELF-CHECK and more practice, see the EXERCISE BANK, p. 338.**

B. WRITING: Adding Hyphens

Write the words below, inserting hyphens to show where each word would be divided if it appeared at the end of a line. Some words may be divided in more than one place.

1. marine
2. self-contained
3. laboratory
4. biological
5. estuary
6. monument

PUNCTUATION

LESSON 7

Quotation Marks

1 Here's the Idea

Use quotation marks to set off direct quotations and some titles.

Direct and Indirect Quotations

Use quotation marks at the beginning and end of a direct quotation.
The first word of a direct quotation is usually capitalized.

A **direct quotation** is the exact words of a writer or speaker.

The guide said, **"The giant squid is one of the largest creatures in the sea."**

Don't use quotation marks to set off an **indirect quotation.**

The guide said that the giant squid is one of the largest creatures in the sea.

CHAPTER 11

Punctuation and Capitalization with Dialogue

In dialogue, punctuate a speaker's words with a comma, a question mark, or an exclamation point.

Put end punctuation marks inside the closing quotation marks.

"Early sailors believed giant squid were sea monsters," our guide explained.

"Just how big is a giant squid?" asked Tyrell.

"Believe it or not, some may be 75 feet long!" said the guide.

Place a comma after explanatory words, such as *she said* and *he asked,* that appear at the beginning of a sentence.
Place a period, question mark, or exclamation point inside the quotation marks at the end of the sentence.

Tyrell asked, "Just how big is a giant squid?"

For more about how to place punctuation with quotation marks, see p. 279.

Enclose both parts of a divided quotation in quotation marks.
Do not capitalize the first word of the second part unless it begins a new sentence.

"I wonder," said Rebecca, "whether the giant squid is dangerous to humans."

"You wonder?" asked Tyrell. "Look at the size of those tentacles!"

- **Start a new paragraph and begin the paragraph with a set of quotation marks to show a change in speakers.**

"Don't be afraid," said Rebecca. "Although the giant squid is large, it doesn't usually come into contact with humans."

"I'm glad to hear that," Tyrell replied, "because that toothed tongue looks nasty."

- **Use single quotation marks to enclose a quotation within a quotation.**

"The guidebook says that Herman Melville called the giant squid 'a vast pulpy mass,'" said Tyrell.

- **Colons and semicolons at the close of a quotation should be placed outside the quotation marks.**

Rebecca said, "I'm staying on land"; however, she soon joined us in the boat.

PUNCTUATION

Punctuation of Excerpts

- **If a sentence that includes a quotation is a question or an exclamation, place the question mark or exclamation point outside the quotation marks.**

Wasn't it Edgar Allan Poe who called the sea a "wilderness of glass"?

- **When a quoted fragment (a short quoted excerpt that is not a complete sentence) is inserted in a sentence, do not capitalize the first word of the fragment unless it begins a sentence or is a proper noun.**

No comma is needed to set the quotation apart from the rest of the sentence.

A 16th-century Swedish cleric described giant squid as "horrible forms with huge eyes."

- **A direct quotation from an author's work may be several paragraphs in length. Begin each paragraph with quotation marks. Place quotation marks at the end of only the last paragraph.**

If you are quoting an excerpt of five or more lines, you can set it off from the rest of the text by indenting the excerpt ten spaces and double-spacing it. Do not use quotation marks if you set off an excerpt in this way.

Titles with Quotation Marks

Use quotation marks to set off the titles of chapters, magazine articles, short stories, TV episodes, essays, poems, and songs.

Titles with Quotation Marks	
Chapter titles	"Chapter 10: Rescued!"
Articles	"An Angry Public Backs Champ"
Short stories	"By the Waters of Babylon"
TV episodes	"Two on a Raft"
Essays	"Once More to the Lake"
Poems	"Fifth Grade Autobiography"
Songs	"The Star-Spangled Banner"

For information on setting titles in italics or underlining, see p. 272.

CHAPTER 11

2 Practice and Apply

A. CONCEPT CHECK: Quotation Marks

Rewrite the sentences below to correct errors in the use and placement of quotation marks, commas, and periods.

Batteries Not Included

1. Are you surprised to learn that, "a great majority of deep-sea fishes have light-generating capabilities?"
2. Richard Ellis explains in his book *Deep Atlantic* that "there are three ways whereby sea animals create living light:" by releasing energy to special organs, by ejecting glowing chemicals, and by hosting bacteria that glow.
3. Having learned how fish emit light, you might very well wonder "what purpose the light serves?"
4. According to Ellis, biologists have long been interested in living light, but there is, "No agreement as to its function or as to why so many different creatures should have developed," this ability.
5. In the chapter Bioluminescence, Ellis explains that the light may serve several purposes.

6. “Lights might be useful” he says “to attract potential mates.”
7. “Ellis continues “Light organs around the eyes of some species of lantern fishes probably function as headlights to illuminate prey items immediately before they are consumed”.
8. According to Ellis, one scientist even suggested lights may ‘serve as a sort of burglar alarm’ for fish under attack.
9. By flashing a light, a fish being preyed upon might attract “another predator to prey upon the first, thus protecting the prey”.
10. Ellis sums up our lack of understanding by saying ‘It is clear that we, like the bearers of the light organs, are in the dark.

➜ **For a SELF-CHECK and more practice, see the EXERCISE BANK, p. 339.**

B. WRITING: Dialogue

Do You See What I See?

Imagine that while walking home from school, you and a friend saw the strange sight pictured below. Write at least 10 lines of the conversation that you and your friend might have about it. Make sure you use quotation marks and other marks of punctuation correctly in the dialogue. If you need help getting started, you can begin with the line below.

“Do you see what I see?” I asked as my jaw dropped.

PUNCTUATION

LESSON 8

Ellipses and Italics

1 Here's the Idea

Ellipses

Use ellipsis points to indicate omission of a word, phrase, line, or paragraph within a quoted passage.

LITERARY MODELS

A small crowd . . . followed them as they walked the long, dusty, sunlit street.

—James Baldwin, *Go Tell It on the Mountain*

To show an omission within a sentence, use three dots (. . .) with a space between each dot.

Half a mile from home, at the farther edge of the woods, where the land was highest, a great pine tree stood, the last of its generation. . . . Sylvia knew it well. She had always believed that whoever climbed to the top of it could see the ocean.

—Sarah Orne Jewett, "A White Heron"

To show an omission at the end of a sentence, use an end mark after the ellipsis points.

CHAPTER 11

Italics

Use italics or underscoring to set off titles of books, movies, magazines, newspapers, TV series, plays, works of art, epic (long) poems, and long musical compositions.

Titles to Italicize	
Books	*The Old Man and the Sea*
Movies	*Mr. Roberts*
Magazines	*People, Time*
Newspapers	*The New York Times*
TV series	*Masterpiece Theater*
Plays	*A Raisin in the Sun*
Works of art	Rodin's *The Thinker*
Epic poems	*Aeneid*
Long musical compositions	*The Magic Flute*

For information on punctuating titles with quotation marks, see p. 270.

▶ **Use italics to indicate a word referred to as a word and to set off foreign words or phrases that are not common in English.**

Does anybody know what the word ***abyss*** means?

A word processing program allows you to italicize words by selecting the italic form of a font. When writing by hand or using a typewriter, underline words that should be italicized.

❷ Practice and Apply

A. CONCEPT CHECK: Italics and Punctuation Errors

Rewrite the sentences, underlining words and titles that should be italicized and adding missing commas and apostrophes.

The Inspiring Sea

1. From ancient epic poetry to the modern musical Titanic many works of art depict the perils of seafaring.
2. William Shakespeare describes the terrible beauty and power of the sea in his play The Tempest.
3. In The Wreck of a Transport Ship artist Joseph Turner captures the terror of sailors lost in a storm at sea.
4. Herman Melvilles epic novel Moby Dick describes a disastrous sea quest.
5. In the novel, Captain Ahab tries to conquer a great white whale; some would use the word nemesis to describe the captains unbeatable opponent.

➜ **For a SELF-CHECK and more practice, see the EXERCISE BANK, p. 339.**

B. PROOFREADING: Ellipses and Italics

Rewrite the paragraph below, adding italics where necessary and replacing the boldface text with ellipsis points.

Movie Review

To me, the word exciting should **not be thrown around lightly when describing a movie. It should** be used to describe only movies that truly keep me on the edge of my seat. Steven Spielberg's great action film Jaws is just such a movie. **The plot of the movie is simple: a shark attacks swimmers in a resort area, and the chase to capture the killer fish begins.** What makes the film so exciting is that the shark attacks look absolutely real, even though a mechanical shark was used in many scenes.

PUNCTUATION

Real World Grammar

Business Letter

When you're conducting research, you may need to write a business letter to a research institution or other organization to request information on your topic. The letter you write should be clear, courteous, and professional. Once you've completed a final draft of your letter, carefully proofread it to correct punctuation errors. Comma-use errors in particular can make your letter difficult to understand; as a result, you may not get the information you need.

March 1 2003 *add missing comma*

Frank–watch out for comma errors.

Add your address here.

Monterey Bay Aquarium Institute
P.O. Box 628
Moss Landing CA 95039 *comma goes between city and state*
Attention: Research Librarian

Dear Sir or Madam, *use colon for a business letter*

I am a sophomore at Washington High School in Newton *(add comma between city and state)* Pennsylvania. Currently, I am writing a research report about the dangerous *(place comma)* irreversible effects of global warming on ocean life? *(wrong end mark)* I have seen most of the Web site's *(not a possessive noun)* on this topic *(place comma)* but your site was the most helpful. I read many of the articles posted there; while I was scanning *(place comma)* the title of an unpublished article came to my attention: "Global Climate Change and Ocean-Related Processes." Would it be possible to get a copy of this article through your organization. *(wrong end mark)*

I would like to receive this article as soon as possible *(place comma)* for my paper is due in mid-April. I'll be happy to pay for photocopying, *(delete comma)* and postage. Thank you for your time. I appreciate your help, *(and — add conjunction to avoid run-on)* I look forward to hearing from you.

Sincerely *(place comma)*

Franklin Thomas

PRACTICE AND APPLY: Revising

Imagine that you have written the rough draft of the letter below. Revise the draft to correct punctuation errors. Add your address and the date above the recipient's address. Choose an appropriate closing for the letter.

Student Help Desk: Phrases

(Add your address)
(Add the date)

Ms. LaVonne Reiger
Channel 49
1090 West Woodbury Street
Pines, NY 94100

Dear Ms Reiger

I am writing for information about an organization you profiled on the October 19 edition of your television program titled Our Environment.The name of the organization was Whale Protectors, the person you interviewed from the organization was Dr Karen J Smith.

During the program you offered to send out a free packet—of information about protecting endangered whales—to anyone interested. It just so happens that I am working on a research report on this topic I would like to use your information in my research. My self addressed stamped, envelope is enclosed.Would you please also send me Whale Protectors mailing address if it is'nt included in the packet! Thank you, for your time.

(Add a closing)

PUNCTUATION

Mixed Review

A. Punctuation Follow the directions to rewrite each sentence or pair of sentences. Add correct punctuation.

1. The squid and the octopus are similar in many ways, but their body shapes are different. (Use *however* instead of *but.*)
2. The squid has an elongated body that ends in tentacles. The octopus has a large head resting on a ring of tentacles. (Use a semicolon to join the sentences.)
3. Both animals have beaks and well-developed eyes. Both animals have siphons. (Combine, using series commas.)
4. The animals use the siphons to expel water. The water is taken in through the mantle opening. (Combine, using *which.*)
5. Both the squid and the octopus are agile animals. Both the squid and the octopus are flexible animals. (Combine the sentences so that the adjectives are next to each other.)
6. They can be very difficult to catch. (Add a parenthetical expression, such as "in fact.")
7. Scientists have difficulty gathering mature specimens <u>because the adult squid and octopus are good at avoiding capture</u>. (Rewrite so the underlined clause begins the sentence.)
8. The octopus is difficult to catch for another reason. It can live at great depths. (Change punctuation to show that the second sentence explains the first.)
9. Marine scientists use indirect measuring techniques <u>to estimate the size of the squid and octopus populations</u>. (Rewrite so the underlined phrase begins the sentence.)
10. A. de C. Baker wrote, "The world population of squid must be extremely large, for they form the major part of the diet of the sperm and other toothed whales." (Rewrite as a divided quotation.)

B. Proofreading Rewrite the paragraph, adding correct punctuation.

Marine biologists divide the worlds oceans into two regions the benthic and the pelagic. The benthic region is the floor of the sea the pelagic region is the seawater. While many benthic organisms burrow in the seabed other benthic organisms live on the surface of the ocean floor. Pelagic organisms include whales seals turtles fish and plankton. The word plankton comes from the Greek word planktos which means "wandering." The name is appropriate for plankton drift through the water. In his article entitled Plankton Dr George D Ruggieri describes the importance of plankton to sea life. He describes the growth of microscopic plants as "the first and essential link in all the food chains in the sea."

Mastery Test: What Did You Learn?

For each numbered item, choose the letter of the correct answer.

> Beware. (1) Our wooden boats, docks, and bridges (2) may be under attack. The wood-eating gribble is just waiting to munch on them? (3) Although the crustacean is only two millimeters long; (4) it can cause mighty bridges to wobble and magnificent ships to sink. Boat-owners ask how this little monster can cause so much damage? (5) Noted science writer Jack Rudloe explains (6) that the gribble has extraordinarily sharp jaws. Its right jaw is like a small saw; and (7) its left jaw is like a metal file. There is a way to gribble-proof submerged wood (8) keep it well covered with paint. Any nick or scratch, that can expose the wood, (9) is an open invitation to gribbles. Rudloe warns "One (10) little scraped area where the surface is exposed, and they move in and take over."

1. A. Beware?
   B. Beware
   C. Beware!
   D. Correct as is

2. A. boats docks, and bridges
   B. boats docks and bridges
   C. boats, docks, and, bridges
   D. Correct as is

3. A. them.
   B. them,
   C. them—
   D. Correct as is

4. A. long.
   B. long,
   C. long:
   D. Correct as is

5. A. damage.
   B. damage,
   C. damage!
   D. Correct as is

6. A. writer, Jack Rudloe, explains
   B. writer, Jack Rudloe explains
   C. writer Jack, Rudloe explains
   D. Correct as is

7. A. saw: and
   B. saw, and
   C. saw; and,
   D. Correct as is

8. A. wood:
   B. wood;
   C. wood,
   D. Correct as is

9. A. scratch that can expose the wood,
   B. scratch that can expose the wood
   C. scratch, that can expose the wood
   D. Correct as is

10. A. Rudloe warns; "One
    B. Rudloe, warns "One
    C. Rudloe warns, "One
    D. Correct as is

Student Help Desk

Punctuation at a Glance

Period .

Question Mark ?

Exclamation Point !

Comma ,

Semicolon ;

Colon :

Dash —

(Parentheses)

Hyphen -

Apostrophe '

"Quotation Marks"

Ellipses . . .

Italics *abc*

CHAPTER 11

Titles & Punctuation
Treating Titles with Care

Use quotation marks to set off titles of	Use italics to set off titles of
• Book chapters	• Books
• Essays	• Epic poems
• Magazine articles	• Long musical compositions
• Poems	• Magazines
• Short stories	• Movies
• Songs	• Newspapers
• TV episodes	• Plays
	• TV series
	• Works of art

Punctuation with Quotation Marks

Inside or Outside?

Periods and commas	Semicolons and colons	Question marks and exclamation points
Rule: Always go inside quotation marks	**Rule:** Always go outside quotation marks	**Rule:** May go inside or outside depending on what they punctuate
Examples "I'm hungry," said Max. Tracy replied, "Me too." *	**Examples** Tracy calls raw fish "an exotic treat"; I prefer my fish cooked. My aunt calls these novels "some of the best literature ever written": *Wuthering Heights, Jane Eyre,* and *Arrowsmith.*	**Examples** **Outside** Did you read the article "Fish for Breakfast"? Stop saying "I'm hungry"! **Inside** "How can you eat that?" Tracy asked. "That looks disgusting!" she cried.

I know it's hard to believe right now, Lawrence, but some day you'll thank me for asking you to punctuate your sentences correctly.
SIPRESS

PUNCTUATION

*

Q: How come commas and periods stay inside quotation marks?

A: They're too little to stay out by themselves.

The Bottom Line

Checklist for Punctuation

Have I . . .

____ ended every sentence with the appropriate end mark?

____ inserted commas correctly to set off or separate sentence parts?

____ placed semicolons and colons correctly?

____ used dashes and parentheses to set off information?

____ used a dictionary to check hyphenated words?

____ placed apostrophes correctly to create possessive nouns?

____ used quotation marks correctly?

____ italicized words and titles correctly?

Quick Fix Editing Machine

You've worked hard on your assignment. Don't let misplaced commas, sentence fragments, and missing details lower your grade. Use this Quick-Fix Editing Machine to help you catch grammatical errors and make your writing more precise.

Fixing Errors

Improving Style

1 Sentence Fragments

What's the problem? Part of a sentence has been left out.
Why does it matter? A fragment doesn't convey a complete thought.
What should you do about it? Find out what is missing and add it.

What's the Problem?	Quick Fix
A. A subject is missing. Fell off my roller skates.	**Add a subject.** **The wheels** fell off my roller skates.
B. A verb is missing. Having no wheels skating difficult.	**Add a verb.** Having no wheels **makes** skating difficult.
C. A helping verb is missing. The wheels been missing since this morning.	**Add a helping verb.** The wheels **have** been missing since this morning.
D. Both a subject and a verb are missing. On my porch with nothing to do.	**Add a subject and a verb to make an independent clause.** **I'm sitting** on my porch with nothing to do.
E. A subordinate clause is treated as if it were a sentence. Even though my roller skates were new.	**Combine the fragment with an independent clause.** **I'm not upset,** even though my roller skates were new. **OR** **Remove the conjunction.** ~~Even though~~ my roller skates were new.

For more help, see Chapter 5, pp. 114–127.

QUICK FIX

Run-On Sentences

What's the problem? Two or more sentences have been run together.

Why does it matter? A run-on sentence doesn't show where one idea ends and another begins.

What should you do about it? Find the best way to separate the ideas or to show the proper relationship between them.

What's the Problem?	Quick Fix
A. The end mark separating two complete thoughts is missing. My summer job is fun I work in a pizza parlor.	**Add an end mark to divide the run-on into two sentences.** My summer job is fun**!** **I** work in a pizza parlor.
B. Two complete thoughts are separated only by a comma. Customers don't always know what they want, I have to make suggestions.	**Add a conjunction.** Customers don't always know what they want, **so** I have to make suggestions. **OR** **Change the comma to a semicolon.** Customers don't always know what they want**;** I have to make suggestions. **OR** **Change the comma to a semicolon and add a conjunctive adverb.** Customers don't always know what they want**; therefore,** I have to make suggestions. **OR** **Make one of the independent clauses into a subordinate clause.** **Because** customers don't always know what they want, I have to make suggestions.

For more help, see Chapter 5, pp. 114–127.

3 Subject-Verb Agreement

What's the problem? A verb does not agree with its subject in number.

Why does it matter? Readers may regard your work as careless.

What should you do about it? Identify the subject and use a verb that matches it in number.

What's the Problem?	Quick Fix
A. A verb agrees with the object of a preposition rather than with its subject. The production of music video **shows are** hard work.	**Mentally screen out the prepositional phrase and make the verb agree with the subject.** The **production** ~~of music video shows~~ **is** hard work.
B. A verb agrees with a word in an appositive phrase that comes between the subject and the verb. Producers, the people in charge of putting together each **show, has** to be creative.	**Read the sentence without the phrase and make the verb agree with the subject.** **Producers,** the people in charge of putting together each show, **have** to be creative.
C. The verb doesn't agree with an indefinite-pronoun subject. **Everyone** in the audience **want** to see his or her favorite artists.	**Decide whether the pronoun is singular or plural, and make the verb agree with it.** **Everyone** in the audience **wants** to see his or her favorite artists.
D. A verb in a contraction doesn't agree with its subject. **It don't take** long for the viewers to lose interest.	**Use a contraction that agrees with the subject.** **It doesn't take** long for the viewers to lose interest.

For more help, see Chapter 7, pp. 154–175.

What's the Problem?	Quick Fix
E. A verb doesn't agree with the true subject of a sentence beginning with *here* or *there*. **There is** many possible formats for a video.	**Mentally turn the sentence around so that the subject comes first, and make the verb agree with it.** **There are** many possible **formats** for a video.
F. A singular verb is used with a compound subject containing *and*. The producer and the **bandleader talks** it over.	**Use a plural verb.** **The producer and the bandleader talk** it over.
G. A verb doesn't agree with the nearest part of a compound subject containing *or* or *nor*. Neither **the band members nor the lead singer have arrived** yet.	**Make the verb agree with the nearest part.** Neither the band members nor the **lead singer has arrived** yet.
H. A collective noun referring to a single unit is treated as plural (or one referring to individuals is treated as singular). The **band are** always **getting** in trouble for being late.	**If the collective noun refers to a single unit, use a singular verb.** The **band is** always **getting** in trouble for being late.
I. A singular subject ending in *s, es,* or *ics* is mistaken for a plural. **Politics have** nothing to do with it.	**Watch out for these nouns and use singular verbs.** **Politics has** nothing to do with it.

For more help, see Chapter 7, pp. 154–175.

Pronoun Reference Problems

What's the problem? A pronoun does not agree in number or gender with its antecedent, or the antecedent is unclear.

Why does it matter? Lack of agreement can cause confusion.

What should you do about it? Find the antecedent and make the pronoun agree with it, or rewrite the sentence to make the antecedent clear.

What's the Problem?	Quick Fix
A. A pronoun doesn't agree with an indefinite-pronoun antecedent. **Everyone** who visits a "cybermall" ends up spending **their** money.	**Decide whether the indefinite pronoun is singular or plural, and make the pronoun agree with it.** **Everyone** who visits a "cybermall" ends up spending **his or her** money.
B. A pronoun that refers to a compound subject containing *or* or *nor* doesn't agree with the nearest part. Neither **the manager nor the customers** actually leave **his** home.	**Find the nearest simple subject and make the pronoun agree with it.** Neither the manager nor the **customers** actually leave **their** homes.
C. A pronoun doesn't have an antecedent. On the home page **it** says that service is given with a smile.	**Rewrite the sentence to eliminate the pronoun.** **Spendit's home page** says that service is given with a smile.
D. A pronoun's antecedent is vague or indefinite. The mall guarantees that **they** are always in a good mood.	**Change the pronoun to a specific noun.** The mall guarantees that **the clerks** are always in a good mood.
E. A pronoun could refer to more than one noun. Roz and Sue are my favorite "cyberclerks"; **she** thinks that a good mood is the only mood there is!	**Substitute a noun for the pronoun to make the reference specific.** Roz and Sue are my favorite "cyberclerks"; **Roz** thinks that a good mood is the only mood there is!

For more help, see Chapter 8, pp. 176–205.

Incorrect Pronoun Case

What's the problem? A pronoun is in the wrong case.

Why does it matter? Readers may regard your work as sloppy, especially if your writing is supposed to be formal.

What should you do about it? Recognize how the pronoun is being used, and replace it with the correct form.

What's the Problem?	Quick Fix
A. A pronoun that follows a linking verb is not in the nominative case. The best music student **is her.**	**Use the nominative case after a linking verb.** The best music student **is she.** **OR** **Reword the sentence.** **She is** the best music student.
B. A pronoun used as the object of a preposition is not in the objective case. The teacher asked Danni to play **for** Ben and **I.**	**Use the objective case as the object of a preposition.** The teacher asked Danni to play **for** Ben and **me.**
C. The wrong pronoun case is used in a comparison. Very few people are as patient as **us.**	**Mentally complete the comparison and use the appropriate case.** Very few people are as patient as **we [are].**
D. *Who* or *whom* is used incorrectly. When we want good music, though, it's Danni **who** we listen **to.**	**Use *who* if the pronoun is a subject, *whom* if it is an object.** When we want good music, though, it's Danni **whom** we listen **to.**
E. A pronoun followed by an appositive is in the wrong case. **Us kids make** a great team.	**Mentally screen out the appositive to test for the correct case.** **We ~~kids~~ make** a great team.

For more help, see Chapter 8, pp. 176–205.

6 *Who* and *Whom*

What's the problem? A form of the pronoun *who* or *whoever* is used incorrectly.

Why does it matter? The correct use of *who, whom, whoever,* and *whomever* in formal situations gives the impression that the speaker or writer is careful and knowledgeable.

What should you do about it? Decide how the pronoun functions in the sentence to determine which form to use.

What's the Problem?	Quick Fix
A. *Whom* is incorrectly used as the subject of a sentence or clause. I don't know **whom is giving** me a ride.	**Use *who* as the subject of a sentence or clause.** I don't know **who is giving** me a ride.
B. *Who* is incorrectly used as the object of a preposition. Please tell me **who** to go **with.**	**Use *whom* as the object of a preposition.** Please tell me **whom** to go **with.**
C. *Who* is incorrectly used as a direct object. **Who** did you say I **should ask?**	**Use *whom* as a direct object.** **Whom** did you say I **should ask?**
D. *Whomever* is incorrectly used as the subject of a sentence or clause. **Whomever wants** a ride should tell me now.	**Use *whoever* as a subject.** **Whoever wants** a ride should tell me now.
E. *Whoever* is incorrectly used as an object. You can ride with **whoever** you **like.**	**Use *whomever* as an object.** You can ride with **whomever** you **like.**
F. *Who's* is incorrectly used as the possessive form of *who*. **Who's car** is this anyway?	**Use *whose* to show possession.** **Whose car** is this anyway?

For more help, see Chapter 8, pp. 176–205.

7 Confusing Comparisons

What's the problem? The wrong form of a modifier is used to make a comparison.

Why does it matter? Incorrectly worded comparisons can be confusing and illogical.

What should you do about it? Use wording that makes the comparison clear.

What's the Problem?	Quick Fix
A. ***Both -er* and *more* or *-est* and *most* are used in making a comparison.**	**Eliminate the double comparison.**
My new schedule is **more crazier** than last year's schedule.	My new schedule is **crazier** than last year's schedule.
It is the **most hardest** I've ever had.	It is the **hardest** I've ever had.
B. The word *other* or *else* is missing in a comparison where it is logically needed.	**Add the missing word.**
My classes are harder **than anybody's.**	My classes are harder **than anybody else's.**
C. A superlative form is used where a comparative form is needed.	**If you're comparing two things, use the comparative form.**
I compared my schedule with Rich's to see whose was **worst.**	I compared my schedule with Rich's to see whose was **worse.**
D. A comparative form is used where a superlative form is needed.	**If you're comparing more than two things, use the superlative form.**
Of all my classes, geometry is the **harder** by far; it will probably kill me.	Of all my classes, geometry is the **hardest** by far; it will probably kill me.

For more help, see Chapter 9, pp. 206–225.

8 Verb Forms and Tenses

What's the problem? The wrong form or tense of a verb is used.

Why does it matter? Readers may regard your work as careless or find it confusing.

What should you do about it? Change the verb to the correct form or tense.

What's the Problem?	Quick Fix
A. The wrong form of a verb is used with a helping verb. It was snowing, and a plane full of passengers **had** not yet **took** off.	**Use a participle form with the helping verbs *have* and *be.*** It was snowing, and a plane full of passengers **had** not yet **taken** off.
B. A helping verb is missing. Irritated passengers **trying** to leave the plane.	**Add a helping verb.** Irritated passengers **were trying** to leave the plane.
C. An irregular verb is treated as though it were a regular verb. None of the passengers actually **leaved,** however.	**Look up the correct form of the irregular verb and use it.** None of the passengers actually **left,** however.
D. A past participle is used incorrectly. The passengers **begun** to get restless.	**Use the past form of the verb.** The passengers **began** to get restless. **OR** **Change the verb to the past perfect form by adding a helping verb.** The passengers **had begun** to get restless.
E. Different tenses are used in the same sentence without a good reason. The passengers were furious, and most will plan to sue the airline.	**Use the same tense throughout the sentence.** The passengers were furious, and most **planned** to sue the airline.

For more help, see Chapter 6, pp. 128–153.

9 Misplaced and Dangling Modifiers

What's the problem? A modifying word or phrase is in the wrong place, or it doesn't modify any other word in the sentence.

Why does it matter? The sentence can be confusing or unintentionally funny.

What should you do about it? Move the modifier closer to the word it modifies, or add a word for it to modify.

What's the Problem?	Quick Fix
A. The adverb *only* or *even* is not placed close to the word it modifies. **Even Tom** was trying to videotape the galloping horses.	**Move the adverb to make your meaning clear.** Tom was **even trying** to videotape the galloping horses.
B. A prepositional phrase is too far from the word it modifies. However, **in motion** it is very hard to film horses, even with a steady hand.	**Move the phrase closer to the word or words it modifies.** However, it is very hard to film horses **in motion,** even with a steady hand.
C. A participial phrase is too far from the word it modifies. **Running around the corral,** Tom videotaped his favorite horse.	**Move the phrase closer to the word or words it modifies.** Tom videotaped his favorite horse **running around the corral.**
D. A verbal phrase does not relate to anything in the sentence. **Having distracted the horse,** the video session went well.	**Reword the sentence, adding a word for the phrase to refer to.** **Having distracted the horse, the trainer** made sure that the video session went well.

For more help, see Chapter 5, pp. 114–127, and Chapter 9, pp. 206–225.

QUICK FIX

10 Missing or Misplaced Commas

What's the problem? Commas are missing or are used incorrectly.

Why does it matter? Sentences in which commas are used incorrectly can be hard to follow.

What should you do about it? Determine where commas are needed and add or omit them as necessary.

What's the Problem?	Quick Fix
A. A comma is missing before the conjunction in a series. Bill's family regularly eats tuna, salmon and trout.	**Add a comma.** Bill's family regularly eats tuna, salmon, and trout.
B. A comma is placed after a closing quotation mark. "I don't understand why Bill doesn't eat any of the fish he catches himself", says Sue.	**Always put a comma before a closing quotation mark.** "I don't understand why Bill doesn't eat any of the fish he catches himself," says Sue.
C. A comma is missing after an introductory clause. Although Bill goes fishing often he throws back all the fish he catches.	**Find the end of the clause and add a comma.** Although Bill goes fishing often, he throws back all the fish he catches.
D. Commas are missing around a nonessential phrase or clause. He enjoys fishing in the Cedar River which is close to his house and then buying dinner at a supermarket.	**Add commas to set off the nonessential phrase or clause.** He enjoys fishing in the Cedar River, which is close to his house, and then buying dinner at a supermarket.
E. A comma is missing from a compound sentence. Bill thinks he's being kind to the fish by throwing them back but the fish might not agree.	**Add a comma before the conjunction.** Bill thinks he's being kind to the fish by throwing them back, but the fish might not agree.

For more help, see Chapter 11, pp. 246–279.

QUICK FIX

11 Using Active and Passive Voice

What's the problem? The overuse of the passive voice makes a piece of writing weak.

Why does it matter? The active voice engages readers' attention better than the passive voice.

What should you do about it? Rewrite sentences, using the active voice.

What's the Problem?	Quick Fix
A. The passive voice makes a sentence dull. **Snakes** at the bottom of the pit **were sighted** by terrified tourists.	**Revise the sentence, using the active voice.** Terrified **tourists sighted** snakes at the bottom of the pit.
B. The passive voice takes the emphasis away from the performer of an action. The **tourists were warned** by a nervous guide that the snakes could escape from the pit.	**Change the voice from passive to active.** A nervous **guide warned** the tourists that the snakes could escape from the pit.
C. The passive voice makes a sentence wordy. Some of the tourists **were being terrified** by the slithering snakes.	**Change the voice from passive to active.** The slithering snakes **were terrifying** some of the tourists.

Note: The passive voice is appropriate when you want to

- **emphasize the receiver of an action or the action itself**

The snake pit **was closed** shortly after the incident.

- **make a statement about an action whose performer need not be specified or is not known**

No snakes **have been seen** in the area since then.

12 Improving Weak Sentences

What's the problem? A sentence repeats ideas or contains too many ideas.

Why does it matter? Empty and overloaded sentences are dull and confusing.

What should you do about it? Make sure every sentence has a clearly focused idea.

What's the Problem?	Quick Fix
A. An idea is repeated.	**Delete the repeated idea.**
Darren always gets picked for team games because he is an excellent athlete **and he plays sports well.**	Darren always gets picked for team games because he is an excellent athlete. ~~and he plays sports well.~~
B. Too many loosely related ideas are included in a single sentence.	**Divide the sentence into two or more sentences, using subordinate clauses to show relationships between ideas.**
Darren comes from a competitive family, and everybody in the family loves to play sports, including baseball, basketball, and tennis.	Darren comes from a competitive family in which everybody loves to play sports. They play baseball, basketball, and tennis.
C. Too much information is crammed into one sentence.	**Simplify the ideas and divide the sentence into two or more sentences.**
Darren hopes to get a football scholarship eventually, and he wants to go to a fine university—one at which he and other athletes can get a good education while they play football.	Darren hopes to get a football scholarship to a fine university. He wants to get a good education while he plays football.

13 Avoiding Wordiness

What's the problem? A sentence contains unnecessary words.

Why does it matter? Readers may be annoyed and confused by wordy sentences.

What should you do about it? Use concise terms and eliminate extra words.

What's the Problem?	Quick Fix
A. A single idea is unnecessarily expressed in two ways. After turning on the light switch **with my hand,** I sat on the **seat of the** chair.	**Delete the unnecessary words.** After turning on the light switch ~~with my hand~~, I sat on ~~the seat of~~ the chair.
B. A sentence contains words that do not add to its meaning. **Let me explain that** I heard a noise and discovered that an owl had flown in through the window.	**Delete the unnecessary words.** ~~Let me explain that~~ I heard a noise and discovered that an owl had flown in through the window.
C. A simple idea is expressed in too many words. We figured the owl was seeking shelter **out of the way of** the hailstorm.	**Simplify the expression.** We figured the owl was seeking shelter **from** the hailstorm.
D. A clause is used when a phrase would do. **While it was** peering at us from an attic rafter, the owl did not seem afraid.	**Reduce the clause to a phrase.** Peering at us from an attic rafter, the owl did not seem afraid.

QUICK FIX

14 Varying Sentence Beginnings

What's the problem? Too many sentences begin in the same way.

Why does it matter? Lack of variety in sentence beginnings makes writing dull and choppy.

What should you do about it? Reword the sentences so that they begin with prepositional phrases, verbal phrases, adverbs, or subordinate clauses.

What's the Problem?

Too many sentences in a paragraph start the same way.

Weather problems are one thing we all have in common. **Weather problems** surprise people on the East Coast and the West Coast and all those in between.

Weather problems can make people tough. **Weather problems** challenge people to come up with creative ways to cope.

Weather problems arise very suddenly. **Weather** can change your plans at a moment's notice.

Quick Fix

Start a sentence with a prepositional phrase.

Weather problems are one thing we all have in common. **From the East Coast to the West Coast,** weather surprises people.

OR

Start a sentence with a verbal phrase.

Dealing with weather problems makes people tough and inventive.

OR

Start a sentence with a subordinate clause.

Because weather problems arise very suddenly, they can change your plans at a moment's notice.

QUICK FIX

15 Varying Sentence Structure

What's the problem? A piece of writing contains too many simple sentences.

Why does it matter? Monotony in sentence structure makes writing dull and lifeless.

What should you do about it? Combine or reword sentences to create different structures.

What's the Problem?

A. Too many simple sentences are used.

Our student volunteers went to France. They met other students. These students were from all over the world.

B. Short sentences create a choppy effect.

The officials had other meetings. They were rushed. They promised to address the students' concerns later.

C. Repeated sentence patterns make writing dull.

The students organized a rally. They planned a parade. It attracted many officials.

For more help, see Chapter 4, pp. 90–113.

Quick Fix

Combine the sentences to form a compound sentence.

Our student volunteers went to France**, and** they met other students. ~~These students were~~ from all over the world.

Combine the sentences to form a complex sentence.

Because the hurried officials had other meetings, they promised to address the students' concerns later.

Combine the sentences to form a compound-complex sentence.

The students organized a rally**, and** they planned a parade **that** attracted many officials.

16 Adding Supporting Details

What's the problem? Unfamiliar terms aren't defined, and claims aren't supported.

Why does it matter? Undefined terms and unsupported claims weaken informative or persuasive writing.

What should you do about it? Add supporting details to clarify and elaborate statements.

What's the Problem?	Quick Fix
A. A key term is not defined. Because simplicity is attractive, ikebana has become popular.	**Define the term.** Because simplicity is attractive, ikebana, **the Japanese art of flower arrangement,** has become popular.
B. No reason is given for an opinion. Ikebana arrangements are beautiful.	**Add a reason.** Ikebana arrangements are beautiful **because they are based on principles of harmony and balance.**
C. No support is given for a fact. Floral customers are intrigued by ikebana.	**Add supporting facts and statistics.** **A survey of the Floral Club's 50,000 members** revealed that many people are intrigued by ikebana.
D. No supporting examples are given. Florists are learning more about ikebana.	**Add examples.** Florists are learning more about ikebana **by attending workshops and reading the publications of the Ikebana Association.**

17 Avoiding Clichés and Slang

What's the problem? Formal writing contains clichés or slang expressions.

Why does it matter? Clichés convey no new images to readers. Slang is not appropriate in formal writing.

What should you do about it? Reword sentences, replacing the clichés or slang with fresh expressions.

What's the Problem?	Quick Fix
A. A sentence contains a cliché. Brenda ran around the hospital lobby **like a chicken with its head cut off.**	**Replace the cliché with a description or explanation.** Brenda ran around the hospital lobby, **frantically seeking information about her grandmother's condition.**
B. Clichés don't accurately express the intended meaning. Getting to the hospital had been **like fighting World War III.** It was **harder to find than a needle in a haystack.**	**Replace the clichés with more appropriate images or explanations.** Getting to the hospital had been **like competing in a track meet.** It was **harder to find than she expected it would be.**
C. A sentence contains inappropriate slang. When Brenda didn't find her grandmother's room right away, **she went ballistic.**	**Replace the slang with more appropriate language.** When Brenda didn't find her grandmother's room right away, **her frustration turned to anger.**

QUICK FIX

18 Using Precise Words

What's the problem? Nouns, modifiers, and verbs are too general.

Why does it matter? Readers are engaged by writing in which specific words are used to show rather than tell.

What should you do about it? Replace general words with precise words.

What's the Problem?	Quick Fix
A. Nouns and pronouns are too general. The **committee** knew that the **event** was the most popular **one** of the school year.	**Use specific words.** The **dance committee members** knew that the **sophomore mixer** was the most popular **party** of the school year.
B. Adjectives and nouns are too vague. They planned to decorate the gym to resemble an **exotic locale.**	**Use more precise adjectives and nouns to paint a picture.** They planned to decorate the gym with **crepe-paper palm trees,** a **blue plastic lagoon,** and a **gigantic tin-foil moon.**
C. Adverbs are vague or are omitted when they would clarify the picture. **Slowly** they climbed ladders and hung stars above the tables.	**Use descriptive adverbs.** **Cautiously,** they climbed ladders and hung stars **high** above the tables.
D. Verbs tell about the action instead of showing it. As the committee **sat** back to admire their work, the balloons they had hidden among the rafters **fell** down.	**Use vivid verbs to show the action.** As the committee **relaxed** in folding chairs or **reclined** on the gym floor, admiring their work, the balloons they had hidden among the rafters began to come down. At first a few **loosened** and **drifted** toward them; then the whole lot **cascaded** over their weary bodies.

QUICK FIX

19 Using Figurative Language

What's the problem? A piece of writing is lifeless or unimaginative.

Why does it matter? Readers find such writing dull and can't form clear mental pictures of what is described.

What should you do about it? Add figures of speech, but don't weaken their impact by using too many or by combining them illogically.

What's the Problem?	Quick Fix
A. A description is dull and lifeless. On the girls' basketball team I was known for **my aggressiveness.** We often won because of our **very tall** center.	**Add a simile or metaphor.** On the girls' basketball team I was famous for **playing like a bulldog.** We often won because our center, **a tree who could shoot,** gave us an edge.
B. Too many figures of speech have been used. Neeta **ran like the wind** and **shot like a bolt of lightning** before **grinning like a Cheshire cat.**	**Replace one of the figures of speech with nonfigurative language.** Neeta **ran like the wind** and **shot quickly and accurately** before **grinning like a Cheshire cat.**
C. Figures of speech have been combined illogically. We shorter players could always pass to Neeta over the heads of the players on the other team, who scrambled around her **like ants around a giant** and who looked up for the ball **as if they were counting stars.**	**Choose a single figure of speech to emphasize.** We shorter players could always pass to Neeta over the heads of the players on the other team, who scrambled around her **like ants around a giant,** looking up for the ball.

QUICK FIX

20 Paragraphing

What's the problem? A paragraph contains too many ideas.

Why does it matter? A long paragraph discourages readers from continuing.

What should you do about it? Break the paragraph into smaller paragraphs and delete unnecessary material. Start a new paragraph whenever the speaker, setting, or focus changes.

What's the Problem?

A. Too many ideas are contained in one paragraph.

Ona's two suns beamed hotly upon Jadok's head as he warmed up in the school's hologym. Sweating hard, Jadok continued preparing for the 1,000-pound discus fling. Jadok had trained for this event while visiting his pal Carl last year.

Quick Fix

Start a new paragraph when the main idea changes.

Ona's two suns beamed hotly upon Jadok's head as he warmed up in the school's hologym. Sweating hard, Jadok continued preparing for the 1,000-pound discus fling.

Jadok had trained for this event while visiting his pal Carl last year.

B. Two characters speak in the same paragraph.

Jadok remembered joking, "My brother would laugh! He can fling about ten Earth yards, and he's only eight!" "Yeah, but that's on Ona," said Carl. "He wouldn't be able to fling at all on Earth."

Start a new paragraph when the speaker changes.

Jadok remembered joking, "My brother would laugh! He can fling about ten Earth yards, and he's only eight!"

"Yeah, but that's on Ona," said Carl. "He wouldn't be able to fling at all on Earth."

C. An unnecessary statement clutters a paragraph.

Jadok knew that, because of Earth's gravity, practicing on Earth would be perfect training for his sport. He's smart too. Flinging on Earth was taxing.

Delete the unnecessary information.

Jadok knew that, because of Earth's gravity, practicing on Earth would be perfect training for his sport. ~~He's smart too~~. Flinging on Earth was taxing.

What's the Problem?

The writing isn't broken into logical paragraphs.

Have you seen images of people walking on the moon? They appear to be moving with more bounce in their steps than we do. Why is this? Simply put, the earth has a greater mass than the moon, so the earth's gravitational pull is stronger than the moon's. That is why it is harder to leap into the air on the earth than it is to leap from the surface of the moon (once you get there!). It is a little-known fact that the force of gravity is not equally strong everywhere on the earth's surface. This can be seen in the level of the ocean above a submerged mountain. The mass of the mountain attracts water toward it, creating a slight rise in the level of the sea around it. The "bump" can be detected in photographs taken from satellites. Gravity, a force that still holds some mystery even for scientists, affects each one of us every day.

Quick Fix

Set off the introduction in its own paragraph.

Have you seen images of people walking on the moon? They appear to be moving with more bounce in their steps than we do. Why is this?

Start a new paragraph to introduce the first main idea.

Simply put, the earth has a greater mass than the moon, so the earth's gravitational pull is stronger than the moon's. That is why it is harder to leap into the air on the earth than it is to leap from the surface of the moon (once you get there!).

Start a new paragraph to introduce another main idea.

It is a little-known fact that the force of gravity is not equally strong everywhere on the earth's surface. This can be seen in the level of the ocean above a submerged mountain. The mass of the mountain attracts water toward it, creating a slight rise in the level of the sea around it. The "bump" can be detected in photographs taken from satellites.

Set off the conclusion in its own paragraph.

Gravity, a force that still holds some mystery even for scientists, affects each one of us every day.

Student Resources

Exercise Bank

1 The Parts of Speech

1. Nouns (links to exercise on p. 8)

→ 1. *Life:* common, singular; *safari:* common, singular; *perspective:* common, singular; *humans:* common, plural; *animals:* common, plural
2. *camps:* common, plural; *Kenya's:* proper, singular; *parks:* common, plural; *fences:* common, plural

Write the nouns in these sentences, identifying each as common or proper and as singular or plural.

1. Elephants are the largest land-dwelling animals in existence.
2. Only some varieties of whales are greater in size.
3. During the 19th century an African elephant named Jumbo became something of a celebrity.
4. After 17 years in the London Zoo, Jumbo was bought by P. T. Barnum and exhibited in his circus in America.
5. Wild elephants can still be seen in parts of Africa and Asia, although hunters have killed many for their tusks.

2. Personal Pronouns (links to exercise on p. 10)

→ 1. his, Malcolm; their, Malcolm and his family **2.** They, Malcolm and his family; her, grandmother

Write each pronoun and identify its antecedent.

1. With his powerful body and huge teeth, an adult male gorilla can appear threatening.
2. In fact, though, the creature is milder than he looks.
3. Gorillas sometimes pound their chests in a display of aggression.
4. They use the display to scare away humans and other gorillas.
5. At other times, they use it to maintain order in the group.
6. When a female gives birth to an infant, she cares for it intensively.
7. An infant is helpless for the first three months of its life.
8. The baby rides on its mother's back and sleeps in her nest at night.
9. Gorillas build their sleeping nests on the ground or in trees.
10. If you travel deep into the Ugandan forest, keep your eyes and ears open for signs of gorilla life.

3. Other Kinds of Pronouns (links to exercise A on p. 13)

➜ **1.** *they:* personal; *few:* indefinite **2.** *which:* relative

Write each pronoun and indicate what kind it is.

1. Everyone has seen chimpanzees clowning in human clothes.
2. That is how many of us imagine chimpanzees.
3. Ask yourself how much you know about chimpanzees' behavior.
4. Did you know chimps usually walk on all fours but can carry themselves upright if they choose?
5. Chimps eat fruits, berries, leaves, and seeds that they gather.
6. Some of their diet consists of small animals, which they stalk and kill.
7. They need not be taught everything by humans; chimps themselves are good at using tools.
8. A chimp can feed itself ants and termites by pushing a stick into the insects' nest and pulling some of them out.
9. Who would think chimps could talk to us?
10. Chimps, who are highly intelligent, can learn sign language and communicate with humans.

4. Verbs (links to exercise on p. 16)

➜ **1.** *want:* action **2.** *seems:* linking

Write each verb or verb phrase and identify it as linking or action. Circle the auxiliary verbs.

1. Squids are mollusks that live in oceans and coastal waters.
2. The smallest squid measures less than an inch in length.
3. The giant squid, however, can be more than 60 feet long!
4. A squid's head is short and compact; its body is long and tubular.
5. Eight arms and two tentacles surround the squid's mouth.
6. Rows of suckers run along the ends of the tentacles.
7. Although some squids drift in the current, others swim rapidly.
8. Some squids are even luminescent; they have special organs that can produce light.
9. Squids are eaten by sperm whales, fish, and people.
10. Enormous giant squids may have been responsible for some sea-monster sightings.

5. Adjectives (links to exercise A on p. 18)

➜ **1.** *An, enjoyable: way; a, new: country; a: horse* **2.** *a, unique, horseback: ride*

Write each adjective in these sentences, along with the word it modifies.

1. Wolves have remarkable coats, which are thick and luxurious.
2. The short, dense fur of the inner layer of the coat is light in color.
3. The outer layer of the coat is made of long hairs, which repel moisture and keep the inner fur dry.
4. The long hairs are referred to as guard hairs; the inside layer of the coat is called the underfur.
5. Long, thick guard hairs grow across the broad shoulders.
6. Short fur grows on the muzzle and down the powerful legs.
7. In cold climates, thick fur protects wolves from bitter temperatures.
8. To keep warm, a wolf curls into a tight ball with the nose under the furry tail.
9. The fur has special properties that keep the warm breath of the wolf from forming hard ice on the fur.
10. A wolf can enjoy a comfortable sleep when the mercury is very low.

6. Adverbs (links to exercise A on p. 22)

➜ **1.** Quite, often, anywhere **2.** crazily

Write each adverb in these sentences.

1. The platypus is a very strange mammal.
2. Almost all mammals give birth to live babies.
3. The platypus, however, actually reproduces by laying eggs.
4. The platypus's feet are completely webbed, like those of a duck.
5. Its broad, flat tail rather resembles that of a beaver.
6. The claws on its feet help it to dig burrows quickly.
7. Platypuses generally live on the banks of streams.
8. Their diet consists almost exclusively of worms, small shellfish, and other animals that live at the bottom of streams.
9. Once people hunted the platypus for its fur.
10. Now such hunting is illegal.

7. Prepositions (links to exercise A on p. 25)

➜ **1.** (for) students **2.** (in) other countries

Write the prepositional phrases in these sentences. Circle the prepositions.

1. With its peculiar shape and features, the camel does not look like a triumph of nature.

RESOURCES

2. Because of its odd features, the camel is well suited to its desert habitat.
3. Among camels' unusual physical attributes, the best known may well be their humps.
4. These humps—the Arabian camel has one of them, and the Bactrian camel has two—store food in the form of fat.
5. By means of its huge feet, which spread flat when it walks, the camel avoids sinking in loose desert sand.
6. The camel's eyes are protected from sand by long, curly lashes, while hair inside its ears keeps them sand free too.
7. In addition to its value to desert travelers as a beast of burden, the camel is a source of milk and meat.
8. The camel's hair is soft and warm, and Arabs weave it into cloth for clothing, blankets, and tents.
9. Camels can be difficult on account of their bad disposition.
10. In spite of these drawbacks, camels remain the most useful domestic animals for people of the desert.

8. Conjunctions (links to exercise A on p. 28)

→ **1.** or **2.** because

Write the conjunctions and conjunctive adverbs in the following sentences.

1. Penguins look clumsy on land, but they are graceful swimmers.
2. These birds live either on the continent of Antarctica or on landmasses that border the cold seas of the Southern Hemisphere.
3. Although the penguin's stubby wings are totally unsuited for flying, they function as paddles when the penguin swims.
4. Penguins have thick layers of fat under their skin and short, dense feathers; consequently, they can thrive in cold climates.
5. Penguins are fish eaters and spend much of their lives in the water, although they lay their eggs on land.
6. Female emperor penguins lay single eggs on the Antarctic ice; otherwise, they have no role in hatching the eggs.
7. The male penguins keep the eggs warm until they hatch, and the males feed the newly hatched babies.
8. The females then return to care for the young so that the males can hunt for food.
9. When the males return with food, both they and the females form a circle around the tightly grouped young to keep them warm.
10. Young penguins that neither starve nor fall to predators become self-sufficient in six months.

2 The Sentence and Its Parts

1. Simple Subjects and Predicates (links to exercise A on p. 39)

➜ **1.** Maria Fernanda Cordoso, runs **2.** She, owns

Write the simple subject and simple predicate of each sentence.

1. A professor once tested an elephant's memory.
2. He marked two wooden boxes with different symbols.
3. The box with a square on it contained food.
4. The box with a circle was empty.
5. He then gave the boxes to an elephant.
6. The elephant eventually learned the symbol for food.
7. Months later, the test was repeated with the same elephant.
8. Again and again, the animal chose the correct box.
9. The elephant must have remembered the symbol for food.
10. Otherwise, it would not have chosen the correct box every time.

2. Complete Subjects and Predicates (links to exercise A on p. 41)

➜ **1.** Crazy tests of endurance / swept the nation during the 1920s. **2.** "Shipwreck" Kelly / sat atop an Atlantic City flagpole for 49 days.

Write each sentence, drawing a line between the complete subject and the complete predicate.

1. Pop culture in the late 1950s and early 1960s reflected Americans' fear of the atom bomb.
2. Antibomb slogans appeared on bumper stickers.
3. Bob Dylan bitterly criticized leaders in his song "Masters of War."
4. Stanley Kubrick won rave reviews for his antibomb comedy *Dr. Strangelove.*
5. TV's *The Twilight Zone* featured cautionary tales about nuclear war.
6. One famous episode shows the aftermath of a nuclear attack.
7. A lonely survivor seeks companionship in the company of books.
8. Another episode depicts a desperate search for food and water.
9. President Kennedy had warned Americans about the need for community bomb shelters.
10. War between the United States and the Soviet Union seemed imminent.

3. Compound Sentence Parts (links to exercise A on p. 43)

➜ **1.** people; walk, jog **2.** Dave Kunst; took, ran

Write the sentences below, underlining each simple subject once and each verb twice.

1. Charles Lindbergh was born in Michigan but spent his childhood in Minnesota.
2. Airplanes and aviation fascinated him from an early age.
3. He became a pilot and flew a mail route between Chicago and St. Louis.
4. In 1926 he heard about a contest and entered it.
5. He could win $25,000 and make aviation history by successfully completing a solo trans-Atlantic flight.

4. Kinds of Sentences (links to exercise A on p. 45)

➜ **1.** interrogative **2.** declarative

Identify each sentence as declarative, imperative, interrogative, or exclamatory.

(**1**) Have you ever eaten in that diner? (**2**) The servers call out orders in "hash house Greek." (**3**) Hash house Greek is old-time restaurant slang. (**4**) Order beef stew there sometime. (**5**) They call it bossy in a bowl. (**6**) I am not kidding! (**7**) What do they call milk? (**8**) They call it moo juice. (**9**) Try the nervous pudding for dessert. (**10**) Nervous pudding is gelatin, of course!

5. Subjects in Unusual Positions (links to exercise A on p. 48)

➜ **1.** you, can get **2.** (You), come

Write the simple subjects and simple predicates in these sentences. Be sure to include all parts of verb phrases.

1. How did starch make football history?
2. Here are the facts.
3. There was a starch company in Decatur, Illinois, in 1920.
4. Among its employees was George Halas.
5. Would he organize and coach a football team for the A. E. Staley Manufacturing Company?
6. Believe it.
7. From Chicago came an offer.
8. Move the Decatur Staleys to that city.
9. What did Halas and the team do?
10. Into the pages of football history marched Halas and his Chicago Bears.

6. Subject Complements (links to exercise A on p. 50)

➜ 1. *fashionable:* predicate adjective 2. *Harlem:* predicate nominative

Write each subject complement and identify it as a predicate adjective or a predicate nominative.

1. Gum was a chewy treat even in ancient times.
2. The discovery in Sweden of a 9,000-year-old wad of chewed tree sap is proof.
3. Would 9,000-year-old gum taste stale?
4. Gum remains popular almost everywhere in the world.
5. In the Czech Republic, *žvýkačka* is the word for gum.
6. The word appears quite appropriate.
7. "Cud chewing" is the word's literal meaning.
8. In Turkey, gum is big business.
9. To the citizens of Singapore, gum factories might seem scandalous.
10. Gum is illegal there!

7. Objects of Verbs (links to exercise A on pp. 52–53)

➜ 1. *Francis A. Johnson:* indirect object; *credit:* direct object
2. *world:* indirect object; *patience:* direct object

Each sentence below contains at least one object. Write each object, identifying it as a direct object, an indirect object, or an objective complement. Identify each objective complement as a noun or an adjective.

1. Throw a few thousand of your friends a party.
2. Make your party memorable.
3. For a snack, serve everyone a burrito from California's La Costeña and Burrito Real restaurant.
4. The editors of *The Guinness Book of Records* consider at least one of the restaurant's burritos quite extraordinary.
5. In fact, they named the restaurant's 4,456-pound burrito the largest in the world.
6. Don't forget dessert.
7. Offer your guests a special treat.
8. Order them a cake from EarthGrains in Alabama.
9. This bakery once created a 128,000-pound cake that many considered a delicacy.
10. Of course, a cake like that might give you the world's largest stomachache!

3 Using Phrases

1. Prepositional Phrases (links to exercise A on p. 68)

→ 1. *in any bird record book*: adverb phrase; *belongs*
2. *of approximately two inches*: adjective phrase; *length*

Write each prepositional phrase and tell whether it is an adverb phrase or an adjective phrase. Also identify the word or words that the prepositional phrase modifies.

1. You'll surely find bats at the baseball park.
2. However, you wouldn't expect the kind with wings.
3. Yet that's exactly what the New York Mets encountered at their 1998 Florida training camp.
4. The stadium had become home to more than 30,000 bats.
5. As a protected species, the bats couldn't be harmed.
6. Yet both players and fans didn't want the bats inside the stadium.
7. One night, park management put screening around the park.
8. When the bats returned from hunting, they found the park closed.
9. Far from their home, the bats needed new lodging.
10. Local builders provided new accommodations when they erected a bat house near the stadium.

2. Appositives and Appositive Phrases (links to exercise A on p. 70)

→ 1. The Wright brothers, Wilbur and Orville, owned a bicycle shop in Dayton, Ohio, in the late 1800s. 3. The book was written by the German engineer Otto Lilienthal.

Add the appositive or appositive phrase in parentheses to each sentence. If the appositive is nonessential, set it off with commas.

1. Our solar system is located in the Milky Way. (a huge spiral galaxy)
2. At the center of the solar system is the sun. (our local star)
3. Circling it are the planet and eight other planets. (Mercury)
4. Our planet is special in several ways. (the third from the sun)
5. We depend on the presence of the gas in its atmosphere. (oxygen)

3. Verbals: Participles (links to exercise A on p. 72)

➜ **1.** *Appreciated for their color and grace*: past participle **2.** *Often bursting with color*: present participle

Write the participle or the participial phrase from each sentence. Indicate whether the participle is a present participle or a past participle.

1. Imagine a spring without the delightful sounds of singing birds.
2. Honored in 1999 as one of the most influential people of the 1900s, Rachel Carson warned of such a spring.
3. Worried about the overuse of chemical pesticides, such as DDT, this environmentalist wrote about their effects in *Silent Spring.*
4. Sprayed on farm fields and forestland, DDT killed useful as well as harmful insects.
5. Lasting a long time, it was absorbed by plants.
6. Animals eating the plants also absorbed the DDT.
7. It soon became apparent that animals exposed to DDT were in danger.
8. The alarm sounded by *Silent Spring* was finally heard.
9. Responding to it, governments restricted the use of DDT.
10. As a result, we can still enjoy chirping birds.

4. Verbals: Gerunds (links to exercise A on p. 74)

➜ **1.** *communicating with others*: object of a preposition
2. *Honking during migration:* subject

Write the gerund or gerund phrase that appears in each sentence. Indicate whether it is a subject, a direct object, an indirect object, a predicate nominative, or an object of a preposition.

1. Ancient Greek mythology offers a story about one of the first disasters in the history of flying.
2. Daedalus, the designer of the labyrinth, probably never dreamed of becoming a prisoner in it.
3. Yet after displeasing King Minos of Crete, he and his son, Icarus, were imprisoned there.
4. Now his challenge was escaping the confines of the labyrinth.
5. Soon Daedalus began to consider making two pairs of feather-and-wax wings.
6. The wings made leaving the labyrinth and Crete possible.
7. They put on the wings and gave flying a try.
8. Soaring too high, however, led to Icarus' death.

9. When he got too close to the sun, he began to notice the melting of the wax in his wings.
10. Instead of gaining freedom, he plummeted to his death.

5. Verbals: Infinitives (links to exercise A on p. 76)

→ **1.** *to form a honeybee colony:* adverb **2.** *to lay eggs*: noun

Write each infinitive or infinitive phrase and tell whether it functions as a noun, an adjective, or an adverb.

1. You have probably heard some of the words to live by known as proverbs.
2. In some proverbs our winged friends, birds, are used to make a point.
3. For example, maybe you have been told not to count your chickens before they hatch.
4. This proverb reminds you not to assume you have something before you actually get it.
5. Have you been asked to remember that the early bird catches the worm?
6. To reach a goal, you need to start working right away.
7. According to one proverb, you are likely to find that birds of a feather flock together.
8. To be comfortable, people often associate with others who have the same interests.
9. As another proverb has it, chickens come home to roost.
10. Therefore, you are likely to experience the consequences of earlier actions.

6. Placement of Phrases (links to exercise A on p. 79)

→ **1.** For many inventors, combining a car and an airplane into one vehicle was a long-time dream. **2.** Ford and other automobile manufacturers produced prototypes of flying cars called "flying flivvers."

Rewrite these sentences to eliminate misplaced and dangling modifiers. If a sentence has no errors in modifier placement, write *Correct.*

1. By running fast down a hill, a hang glider can be launched.
2. The pilot by a harness is attached to the glider.
3. After being launched like a large bird with wings extended, a glider pilot rides the air currents.
4. Using the control bar, the glider's speed can be adjusted.
5. The pilot also uses the control bar to steer the glider.

4 Clauses and Sentence Structure

1. Kinds of Clauses (links to exercise A on p. 94)

→ 1. None
2. which became popular in the early 1900s

Write the subordinate clause in each sentence below.

1. Some of the world's most important inventions were developed before history was written.
2. These include basic tools, such as the lever, that people use to move and lift objects.
3. The wheel, which many consider humanity's most important invention, has made many other inventions possible.
4. Another development that was important was the ability to make fire.
5. Although you may not think of pottery as an invention, the ability to make containers is considered essential for civilization.
6. More recent inventions help us to travel faster, communicate better, and live longer than people did before.
7. Automobiles make it possible for people to travel to places where they could never otherwise have gone.
8. Antibiotics help us fight illnesses that were formerly incurable.
9. Inventions that range from the pen and pencil to the telephone and computer help people exchange messages.
10. Thomas Edison, who invented the electric light bulb and the phonograph, made people's lives easier and more pleasant.

2. Adjective and Adverb Clauses (links to exercise A on p. 97)

→ 1. Long before the Wright brothers flew the first airplane, was testing
2. who was a French physicist, Louis Sébastien Lenormand

Write the adjective and adverb clauses in the following sentences. After each clause, write the word or words that it modifies.

1. Several devices, which are among the world's most important, are known as simple machines.
2. You may not think of these as machines at all, but they are the foundations of all machines that have ever been invented.
3. The simplest is the inclined plane, a sloping surface that helps us move heavy objects up and down.
4. If a road going up a mountain is an example of an inclined plane, a road winding around a mountain exemplifies another simple machine, the screw.

5. An everyday example of a wedge, which is really two inclined planes that meet at an edge, is an ax or a knife.
6. With a lever, one can easily lift a heavy load, as a small child can lift an adult on a seesaw.
7. When you open a kitchen drawer, you may find an example of a lever—a bottle opener.
8. Anyone who has rolled a suitcase on wheels knows the importance of the wheel and axle, another simple machine.
9. The sixth simple machine is the pulley, which reduces the effort needed to lift or pull a heavy load.
10. When you use any complex machine, from a pair of scissors to a ski lift, you are using some combination of these six simple machines.

3. Noun Clauses (links to exercise A on p. 99)

→ 1. *who invented the first eyeglasses*: direct object
2. *whoever wore them*: indirect object

Write the noun clause in each sentence. Indicate whether the clause functions as a subject, a direct object, an indirect object, a predicate nominative, or an object of a preposition.

1. Remarkable inventions throughout the ages have helped human beings expand what they know of the universe.
2. That is why we are able to keep learning more and more about the world around us.
3. Few people know which individuals invented the space shuttle, but NASA was credited with the invention in 1977.
4. Whoever worked on the space shuttle was no greater an inventor than Roger Bacon, an Englishman who may have invented the magnifying glass around 1250.
5. That the two-lens microscope was invented as long ago as 1590 may come as a surprise to you.
6. The name Fahrenheit is probably familiar to whoever has read a thermometer.
7. The reason is that Gabriel Daniel Fahrenheit invented the mercury thermometer in 1714 and developed the temperature scale that most of us use in the United States.
8. Any book on space travel will tell whoever reads it that Robert H. Goddard invented the liquid-fueled rocket engine in 1926.
9. Whoever is interested in oceanography has heard of Jacques Yves Cousteau, coinventor of the Aqua-Lung.
10. What more we learn about the universe will depend on inventors like these.

4. Sentence Structure (links to exercise A on p. 103)

➜ **3.** compound **4.** complex

Identify each sentence as simple, compound, complex, or compound-complex.

1. Some inventions entertain us.
2. Radio and television have entertained us for many years, and now VCRs and CD players entertain us as well.
3. The piano was invented by Bartolomeo Cristofori in Italy around the year 1709.
4. In the 1890s several inventors developed the moving-picture projector, without which we would have no movies today.
5. Vladimir K. Zworykin is sometimes credited with the invention of television, but there were others, including Philo T. Farnsworth and John Baird, who contributed to the invention.
6. If you can't imagine life without video games, you should thank the U.S. inventor Nolan Bushnell, who invented the video game Pong.
7. Pong is a simulation of table tennis.
8. It features two "racquets" that hit a ball back and forth while sound effects simulate the ball's hitting the racquets.
9. Credit for some modern inventions is given to corporations rather than individuals.
10. Sony, a Japanese corporation, was the inventor of the videotape cassette; and RCA, a U.S. corporation, is credited with the invention of the compact disc.

5 Writing Complete Sentences

1. Sentence Fragments (links to exercise A on p. 119)

➜ Last summer, Lisa, Ruben, and Eva decided to start their own business. They earned money by helping others get organized.

Rewrite the following paragraph, eliminating the fragments.

According to experts, an Asian breed of gray wolf may be the ancestor of all domestic dogs. Regardless of their breed. Although some scientists think that dogs began evolving from wolves more than 100,000 years ago. The fossils of modern dogs are not nearly that old. Found in southwestern Asia. The oldest fossils are only 11,000 to 12,000 years old. Most domesticated dogs have changed a great deal. And no longer resemble primitive dogs very much. However, in some remote areas wild dogs still have characteristics of primitive dogs. As an example of a modern dog that resembles a primitive dog. Take a look at the dingo, which is a wild dog of Australia. The dingo has these primitive characteristics. A short ginger-colored coat, pointy ears, and a foxlike snout. Dogs can thank their wolf ancestors. For many of their inherited behavioral traits too. For example, by "hanging out" together. Dogs are exhibiting wolf-pack behavior. Dogs that enjoy chasing cats are using their hunting skills. Even though their food most likely comes from the supermarket.

2. Run-On Sentences (links to exercise A on p. 121)

➜ **2.** Entrepreneurs are people who start their own businesses; Using the Internet, some teenagers are doing exactly this.
6. Unlike most adults, many teenagers have been using computers all their lives, so they have an advantage when it comes to dreaming up computer-related businesses.

Write R for each run-on and S for each correctly written sentence. Then correct the run-ons using techniques from the lesson.

1. A shooting star is not really a star it is a meteor.
2. A meteor is a glowing trail this trail is produced by a meteoroid's passing through the earth's atmosphere.
3. Meteoroids are chunks of metal or rock racing through space sometimes they enter the earth's atmosphere.
4. Friction causes them to heat up in our atmosphere the heat is responsible for the bright streaks that we call meteors.
5. Usually meteoroids burn up in the atmosphere, sometimes they hit the earth, they are known as meteorites.
6. If you don't know these terms, don't worry as recently as the 19th century, people didn't even believe there were meteorites.
7. In 1998 a meteoroid streaked into the earth's atmosphere and exploded over a back yard near Portales, New Mexico.
8. It left behind a black meteorite that was as large as a basketball and weighed 37 pounds.
9. This was a rare occurrence most meteoroids do not fall in populated areas.
10. In fact, few people ever see newly fallen meteorites they usually land in the ocean or unpopulated areas.

6 Using Verbs

1. The Principal Parts of a Verb (links to exercise A on p. 133)

➜ **1.** became **2.** began

Indicate which principal part of a verb each underlined word is.

1. Many people are still reading the detective fiction of Agatha Christie.
2. Over the years, fans have purchased more than 100 million copies of her works.
3. But many readers have not learned about the huge success of Christie's stories on stage and screen.
4. Her most successful play, *The Mousetrap,* ran for more than 21 continuous years at one London theater, setting a world record.
5. Successful adaptations of her fiction into films include *Murder on the Orient Express* and *Death on the Nile.*
6. Christie led a relatively quiet life.
7. As a child, she had received her education at home from her mother.
8. She began to write detective stories while she was working as a nurse during World War I.
9. In 1930 she married an archaeologist.
10. She traveled with him on expeditions to Iraq and Syria for several months every year.

2. Verb Tense (links to exercise A on p. 137)

➜ **1.** ranks **2.** have argued

Choose the better tense of the verb in parentheses.

1. Many readers (will recognize, had recognized) O. Henry as the author of many cleverly plotted short stories.
2. This writer, whose real name was William Sydney Porter, (live, lived) in New York City the last eight years of his life.
3. Before that, he (has spent, had spent) a large part of his short life in Texas.
4. After working on a Texas ranch, he (moved, had moved) in with a family friend in Austin.
5. O. Henry (married, has married) in 1887 and later settled in a small house at 409 East Fifth Street in Austin.
6. The house (has been restored, had been restored) recently and is now the O. Henry Museum.

7. The museum contains a lot of O. Henry's personal belongings that the curators (collect, have collected) over the years.
8. About 15,000 fans (visit, visited) the O. Henry Museum every year.
9. During his life O. Henry (writes, wrote) about Texas in a collection of stories called *The Heart of the West.*
10. Once you have finished reading that book, you (will read, will have read) some of the best stories about Texas ever written.

3. Progressive and Emphatic Forms (links to exercise A on p. 139)

➜ **1.** did manage **2.** was attending

Write the progressive or emphatic form of the verb in parentheses, using the correct tense.

1. The African-American writer Gwendolyn Brooks (compose) poetry almost all her life.
2. By the time she finally published her first book of poetry at the age of 28, she (write) for some time.
3. Her second volume of poetry, *Annie Allen,* was based on ideas she had gathered while she (grow) up in Chicago.
4. Although Brooks is primarily a poet, she (write) a novel, *Maud Martha*, in 1953.
5. By 1960 critics (praise) the poems collected in *The Bean Eaters* as her best verse.
6. Brooks continued to publish poetry throughout the '60s, '70s, and '80s, but she (have) other accomplishments.
7. She (serve) as poet laureate of Illinois when she was named poetry consultant to the Library of Congress in 1985.
8. Though she was 73 years old, she (accept) a professorship of English at Chicago State University in 1990.
9. Brooks (inspire) young poets all her life, and many consider her a personal hero.
10. Her fans hope that Brooks (create) poetry well into the 21st century.

4. The Voice of a Verb (links to exercise A on p. 142)

➜ **2.** developed **3.** was signed

Write each verb in parentheses using the correct tense and the correct voice—active or passive.

1. Readers and critics alike (enjoy) Kurt Vonnegut's satirical fiction for five decades.
2. Vonnegut (study) biochemistry at Cornell University.

3. Vonnegut (join) the U.S. Army in World War II.
4. Vonnegut (capture) by the Germans during the war.
5. His captors (assign) him to a work group in Dresden, Germany.
6. Dresden (firebomb) by Allied planes near the end of the war.
7. Vonnegut and his fellow prisoners (hide) in an underground meat locker.
8. Everything but the cellars (destroy) by the bombs.
9. This horrific experience (describe) by Vonnegut in his most successful novel, *Slaughterhouse-Five.*
10. Numerous plays, works of nonfiction, and short stories (write) by Vonnegut.

5. Shifts in Tense, Form, and Voice **(links to exercise A on p. 145)**

➜ 1. Sandra Cisneros grew up for the most part in Chicago, but her father occasionally moved the family to Mexico.
3. Because she felt lonely as a child, Cisneros read books for comfort.

Some of the following sentences contain awkward uses of verb tenses or voices. Revise those sentences to correct the problems. If a sentence contains no such problems, write *Correct.*

1. Although Langston Hughes was born in Joplin, Missouri, he lives most of his life in Harlem in New York City.
2. For many years literary historians have identified Hughes with the Harlem Renaissance, a black arts movement of the 1920s, because he contributed his energy and talent to it.
3. The poet Arna Bontemps recognized Hughes's achievements and was calling Hughes and his contemporary Countee Cullen the "twin stars of the black Awakening in literature."
4. Hughes's long literary career began with his poem "The Negro Speaks of Rivers," which he has written the summer after his high school graduation.
5. Even though a number of his poems had appeared in black periodicals, Hughes did not receive national attention until his "discovery" by the popular white poet Vachel Lindsay.
6. Hughes was working as a busboy in a hotel restaurant when he had slipped three of his poems beside Lindsay's plate.
7. Lindsay was impressed with Hughes's poems, and he helps to bring Hughes to the notice of a wider public.
8. The publicity gave Hughes the attention he will need, as well as finances to finish college.

9. By the end of the 1920s, Hughes had graduated from college and published his first two books of poetry.
10. Ironically, Hughes's reputation as a poet ultimately surpassed Lindsay's, and Hughes is remembered in the future as one of the great American poets of the 20th century.

6. The Mood of a Verb (links to exercise A on p. 147)

➜ **1.** indicative **2.** imperative, indicative, indicative, imperative

Identify each verb or verb phrase in the following sentences as indicative, imperative, or subjunctive. Then rewrite five of the sentences, changing the mood of a verb.

1. "We passed that farmhouse an hour ago."
2. "Look at the map and locate the intersection of Route 40 and Jolly Lane."
3. "There is no Jolly Lane on the map."
4. "Give me the map!"
5. "If I were you, I'd ask for directions."
6. "If there were a gas station, I would."
7. "Look, another farmhouse—pull in there!"
8. "I wish we had never left home."
9. "Well, ask at the farmhouse where a gas station is."
10. "No, I insist that we look for a gas station ourselves."

7 Subject-Verb Agreement

1. Agreement in Number (links to exercise A on p. 157)

➜ **1.** undergoes **2.** have

For each sentence, write the correct form of the verb in parentheses.

1. A stunt person's essential equipment (includes, include) a calculator, paper, and a pencil.
2. Good stunt persons (has, have) also used dummies.
3. A stunt dummy (has, have) the same weight and height as the stunt person.
4. Before the person (performs, perform) a stunt, the dummy does it.
5. Perhaps a character (plans, plan) to jump from a helicopter.
6. First, crew members (pushes, push) the dummy out of the helicopter.
7. If the dummy (hits, hit) the safety air bag on target, the person will do the stunt next.

8. Dar Robinson (is, are) considered the best stuntman who ever worked.
9. Stunt people usually (earns, earn) about $500 per day.
10. Robinson (was, were) once paid $250,000 for a single stunt!

2. Phrases Between Subject and Verb (links to exercise A on p. 159)

→ **2.** are **3.** has

For each sentence, write the verb form that agrees with the subject.

1. Special effects in a movie (is, are) referred to as FX.
2. A film about blizzards (uses, use) salt, plastic, or shredded paper for snow.
3. An icicle, a larger formation, (is, are) made from plastic.
4. A wind machine placed in different positions (blows, blow) snow into actors' faces or into drifts.
5. Computers in the studio (creates, create) snow and ice FX too.
6. *Twister,* a disaster movie, (combines, combine) computer imagery with footage of real tornadoes.
7. No actor in this film ever (goes, go) near an actual storm.
8. A film such as *The Hunt for Red October* (suggests, suggest) an underwater submarine by combining models, a smoke machine, and creative lighting effects.
9. The actors in *Hard Rain* probably (was, were) wishing for a similar setup.
10. This film, about a flood, (features, feature) no scene without some form of moving water.

3. Compound Subjects (links to exercise A on p. 161)

→ **1.** are **2.** work

For each sentence, write the verb form that agrees with the subject.

1. Lon Chaney and Boris Karloff (is, are) known for playing some of the most frightening monsters ever seen on film.
2. Neither computer graphics nor any modern effects (appears, appear) in the movies these actors made in the 1920s and 1930s.
3. Both *The Hunchback of Notre Dame* and *The Phantom of the Opera* (features, feature) the silent-movie star Lon Chaney.
4. Chaney's own makeup techniques and materials (remains, remain) a well-kept secret even today.
5. A 70-pound "hump" and an eggshell pasted over an eye (was, were) used to create a realistic hunchback.

4. Indefinite-Pronoun Subjects (links to exercise A on p. 163)

➜ **2.** know **4.** consists

For each sentence, write the verb form that agrees with the subject.

1. Nobody (predicts, predict) all the Oscar winners correctly.
2. Every year, several of the awards (is, are) surprises.
3. Many (feels, feel) that no movie should win too many awards.
4. Some (thinks, think) the awards should be better distributed.
5. But some (doesn't, don't) mind if a good film wins a lot of awards.
6. Anyone who wins a big award (expects, expect) to receive applause.
7. Most (seems, seem) happy when a charming film wins.
8. Few (has, have) challenged *Forrest Gump*'s best-film award or Tom Hanks's best-actor award for his work in that movie.
9. But many (questions, question) the giving of major awards to violent films.
10. Some (wonders, wonder) whether violence should be rewarded.

5. Other Problem Subjects (links to exercise A on p. 166)

➜ **1.** is **2.** has

For each sentence, write the verb form that agrees with the subject.

1. Mathematics (comes, come) in handy when you research facts about movies.
2. Four and a half million dollars (is, are) what Macaulay Culkin earned for *Home Alone 2: Lost in New York.*
3. Charlie Chaplin's *City Lights* (has, have) a single scene that was reshot 342 times.
4. Two hundred four (is, are) the number of films in which the fictional character Sherlock Holmes has appeared.
5. The cast of extras in *Gandhi* (numbers, number) 300,000.
6. The film audience in China (chooses, choose) from over 152,000 different movie theaters.
7. *Jaws* (was, were) the first movie to earn over $100 million.
8. According to some sources, 180 million dollars (is, are) what the film *Waterworld* cost.
9. Eighty years (was, were) the age of the oldest Oscar winner ever, Jessica Tandy.
10. Eighty-five hours (is, are) the running time of the U.S. film *The Cure for Insomnia!*

6. Special Sentence Problems (links to exercise A on p. 169)

➜ **1.** Does, Buster Keaton **2.** is, character

Write the correct verb form in parentheses. Then write the subject with which the verb agrees.

1. There (is, are) few comic actors as popular as Robin Williams.
2. Williams is the actor who (is, are) known for playing an extraterrestrial on TV's *Mork and Mindy.*
3. Williams (is, are) a hilarious housekeeper in *Mrs. Doubtfire.*
4. Into a family's home (comes, come) Williams dressed as a 50-year-old woman.
5. On display in *Patch Adams* (is, are) many of Williams's comic talents.
6. (Isn't, Aren't) a funny nose and a clown suit enough to cheer up hospital patients?
7. Dramatic roles (is, are) another aspect of Williams's career.
8. (Doesn't, Don't) Williams portray a sensitive high school teacher in *Dead Poets Society?*
9. He plays an eccentric psychologist who (helps, help) a brilliant young man in *Good Will Hunting.*
10. There (is, are) many fans who enjoy watching Williams be himself.

8 Using Pronouns

2. Nominative and Objective Cases (links to exercise A on p. 181)

➜ **2.** he, N **3.** he, N

Write the correct form of the pronoun in parentheses. Identify the form as nominative (N) or objective (O).

1. Although some historians believe that a King Arthur of Britain actually existed, they know little about (he, him).
2. We know a number of stories about Arthur through the writings of Sir Thomas Malory; it was (him, he) who wrote *Le Morte d'Arthur* around the year 1469.
3. Later authors—such as Mark Twain, T. H. White, and John Steinbeck—also wrote about the legendary king. Malory's original work gave (they, them) many ideas.
4. In Mark Twain's hilarious novel *A Connecticut Yankee in King Arthur's Court,* the main character and (us, we) travel back in time to the days of King Arthur.

5. In the first part of *The Once and Future King,* T. H. White wrote about Arthur's childhood and the magician Merlin's education of (him, he) and his foster brother Kay.
6. The book tells about a contest that Arthur and Kay enter. The competition between (he, him) and Kay, which also involves other knights, is to pull a sword out of a stone.
7. Whoever does it will be the future king of England. "Who will it be, Kay?" Arthur asks. "Will it be you or (I, me)?"
8. Arthur says, "It looks like the winner will be (I, me)!"
9. In *The Acts of King Arthur and His Noble Knights,* John Steinbeck wrote about the knights of the Round Table and the battles between (they, them) and other knights.
10. The book also tells how King Arthur met the beautiful Princess Guinevere and fell in love with (her, she).

3. The Possessive Case (links to exercise A on p. 184)

➜ **3.** their **4.** their

For each sentence, choose the correct word in parentheses.

1. *The Guinness Book of Records* is a well-known compilation of statistics and record-breaking events, but many people do not know the story of (it's, its) origin.
2. Sir Hugh Beaver of Ireland got the idea for the book when friends couldn't forget (him, his) arguing whether the golden plover was Europe's fastest game bird.
3. The argument may sound trivial; however, three years later, (their, theirs) dispute flared again, and still no one had the answer.
4. Beaver thought other people must have similar disagreements, so he decided to produce a book that would make settling (our, ours) disputes possible.
5. The first edition, published in 1955, shot to the top of the British bestseller list; many people bought (there's, theirs) as soon as it appeared in bookstores.
6. (Mine, my) is always nearby.
7. (Your, Yours) appears well used too.
8. Was (your, you're) copy a gift?
9. According to the book, the fastest birds on land are ostriches. (Their, They're) running speed can reach 37 miles per hour.
10. (Our, Ours) fruitless searching for answers to such odd questions is over, thanks to Sir Hugh Beaver.

4. Using *Who* and *Whom* (links to exercise A on p. 187)

➜ **1.** Who **2.** whom

Choose the correct pronoun in parentheses.

1. The *Ramayana* is an epic poem of India, supposedly written by the poet Valmiki, (who, whom) lived during the 200s B.C.
2. By (who, whom) was it translated from the original Sanskrit?
3. The author of the Hindi version was (who, whom)?
4. In the *Ramayana,* Rama is the son of a king, by (who, whom) he is made to leave the country.
5. Sita is the beautiful woman (who, whom) Rama marries.
6. The main conflict of the story is between Rama and Ravana, an evil king (who, whom) kidnaps Sita.
7. (Who, Whom) do you think wins this battle?
8. (Who, Whom) helps Rama rescue his wife?
9. It is said that Valmiki made the *Ramayana* delightful for (whoever, whomever) hears it.
10. The *Ramayana* remains immensely popular today, and (whoever, whomever) reads it discovers an exciting traditional tale of India.

5. Pronoun-Antecedent Agreement (links to exercise A on p. 190)

➜ **1.** its **2.** his or her

Write the correct pronoun given in parentheses.

1. Whether you read the full-length story or an abbreviated version of *Gulliver's Travels,* you are sure to find (it, them) fascinating.
2. Jonathan Swift wrote the book as a satire, but the groups he satirized may not have realized he was making fun of (it, them).
3. The book tells of Gulliver's wild adventures and describes (it, them) in highly entertaining ways.
4. During Gulliver's first adventure, he finds himself in a land called Lilliput, where he discovers, to (his, your) surprise, that the inhabitants are only six inches tall.
5. In the description of these miniature people and their emperor, Swift makes fun of (him, them) and all other people who take themselves too seriously.
6. On his second voyage Gulliver ends up in a land where every person is a giant. There, a young girl adopts him as (his, her) pet.
7. Neither Gulliver nor the fantastic characters he meets seem aware of (its, their) unusual lives.
8. At one time, Gulliver finds himself in a city where the residents spend most of (your, their) time making up ridiculous scientific theories.

9. Gulliver also visits other imaginary lands; these extraordinary places have (its, their) purposes in Swift's clever satire.
10. A talking horse and other odd characters play (his, their) part in Gulliver's final adventure.

6. Indefinite Pronouns as Antecedents (links to exercise A on p. 193)

➜ **1.** . . . their musicians. **2.** . . . their guitars louder.

Find and correct the errors in agreement in these sentences. Write *Correct* if a sentence contains no error.

1. Many of America's cities have summer festivals, but few have more than Chicago.
2. It seems clear that everyone can find a summer festival that appeals to them in the "Second City," where the possibilities include the blues festival and the gospel festival.
3. Both of these festivals draw its share of music lovers.
4. Everyone who performs brings their own talent to the festival.
5. Few of the concertgoers can keep his or her feet still when the music gets going.
6. Perhaps the most famous festival is Taste of Chicago, where many have their own favorite food booths.
7. Each of the restaurants has their own specialty.
8. All of the food is selected for their appeal to the public.
9. Most of the restaurants provide samples of their most famous foods.
10. Some of the restaurants make half their annual food sales at Taste of Chicago.

7. Other Pronoun Problems (links to exercise A on p. 196)

➜ **1.** We **2.** she

Choose the correct pronoun in parentheses.

1. At an early age Rupert started taking piano lessons from his mother, and soon he played as well as (she, her).
2. (Us, We) cousins enjoyed listening to Rupert learn new pieces, and he rarely needed encouragement to play for us.
3. When Rupert's mother came home from work in the evening, the two of them, Rupert and (her, she), would sometimes practice duets together.
4. Though he had a lot of fun playing with his mother, Rupert soon decided that he wanted a teacher who had more experience than (she, her).

5. Rupert's mother had great respect for her former piano teachers, Samantha and Jabi Bean; and since she had less time than (them, they) to teach Rupert, she was glad to have him learn from them instead.
6. When Rupert went to the Beans' house for the first time, he was delighted to discover that they were as enthusiastic about playing the piano as (he, him).
7. Rupert enjoyed meeting the other students, but he was intimidated because he had not been playing as long as (them, they).
8. After two months of taking lessons from the Beans, Rupert was overjoyed to learn that he was going to be included in a recital, and he invited (we, us) relatives to attend.
9. The night of the recital, Rupert found out that he would be playing first. Judit, one of the other students, told him, "When you've taken lessons as long as (me, I), you'll be able to choose when you play."
10. Rupert's mother made sure that his most avid fans, his father and (she, her), had good seats for his premiere, and they cheered wildly when he finished his piece.

8. Pronoun Reference (links to exercise A on pp. 198–199)

➜ **1.** A recent magazine article explains that Reggae Sunsplash began as an annual music festival in Jamaica. **2.** The article says that the popular festival now tours Europe and the United States.

Rewrite the following sentences to correct instances of indefinite, ambiguous, and general pronoun reference.

1. An old reference book may be out-of-date, but you have fascinating firsthand information about what life was like at the time of its publication.
2. For example, in *The Wonder Book of Knowledge,* published in 1927, they refer to "the new science of radio."
3. The book provides a history of adding machines, but they did not know about computers then.
4. In the article on an up-to-date farm, a photograph depicting "a modern grain binder" shows a machine on a farm, which is being pulled by a team of horses.
5. In the section on airships, it says, "This record breaking machine developed a speed of over 250 miles per hour," under a picture of a navy racing plane.
6. The book describes a new device that could reproduce music and other sounds on a record, which it calls a "talking machine."

7. Photographs of what was then a modern fire engine or a modern motion-picture camera are interesting because they look like quaint antiques.
8. Some of the sections of the book do not focus on technology, but rather on natural processes and historical events; therefore, they are not in the least outdated.
9. For instance, in one section you learn how bees make honey, and another describes the building of the Panama Canal.
10. *The Wonder Book of Knowledge* is interesting to look at, which can help you realize that today's reference materials will probably be viewed by future generations as quaint and old-fashioned.

9 Using Modifiers

1. Using Adjectives and Adverbs (links to exercise A on p. 210)

➜ **1.** *named:* adjective; *shiny:* adjective; *sparkling:* adjective; *American River's:* adjective; *south:* adjective **2.** *His:* adjective; *lucky:* adjective; *eventually:* adverb; *bad:* adjective; *his:* adjective; *kindly:* adjective

Write the modifiers (except *a, an,* and *the*) in these sentences, identifying each as an adjective or an adverb.

1. A hundred years ago, the forerunners of today's personal checks were issued not just by banks but by mines, railroads, and other commercial enterprises.
2. Most checks were both beautiful and functional.
3. They featured finely wrought engravings of gold mines, spouting geysers, and redwood forests.
4. An endorsed check was as good as cold cash in the stores and saloons of the Old West.
5. Some people today collect these checks for their historical interest, their artistic quality, or their expected increase in value.
6. Some like to map the travels of the checks around the western territories by the endorsements on their backs.
7. Other collectors specialize in checks from specific states, mines, banks, or ghost towns.
8. Wells Fargo is one bank that issued many checks in the 1800s.
9. The in-house historian of the bank collects early checks printed by the Women's Cooperative Printing Union of San Francisco.
10. That co-op, founded in 1868 by the activist Agnes B. Peterson, employed women workers when other companies did not.

2. Problems with Modifiers (links to exercise A on p. 214)

➜ **1.** any **2.** badly

For each sentence, choose the correct modifier.

1. Everyone knows how (convenient, conveniently) vending machines are for buying snacks.
2. You can use (these, them) machines to buy anything from an apple to the junkiest junk food.
3. But did you know how long (these, them) machines have been around?
4. The first recorded vending machine worked (good, well) nearly 2,000 years ago.
5. (That, That there) machine dispensed holy water when a coin dropped into it struck a lever.
6. Vending machines have been improved (great, greatly) since then.
7. Now you can hardly (ever, never) tell the difference between their performance and that of humans.
8. (Those, Them) machines can recognize the right coin by testing its size, weight, and electric and magnetic properties.
9. Some even cook, though how (good, well) they cook is debatable.
10. Some vending machines, known as ATMs, (even, evenly) dispense money.

3. Using Comparisons (links to exercise A on p. 217)

➜ **1.** faster **4.** less freely

Choose the correct form of comparison for each sentence.

1. One of the (large, largest) archaeological digs to date is in North America, at Oak Island, Nova Scotia.
2. The island, named for its red oak trees, is one of the (small, smallest) islands in Nova Scotia's Mahone Bay.
3. The hope of finding treasure draws (great, greatest) numbers of people, seeking untold riches.
4. (Many, Most) pirates, such as William Kidd and Blackbeard, are rumored to have buried treasure on Oak Island.
5. The (better, best) historical records, however, fail to support the claim that Oak Island is the site of buried treasure.
6. Between 1795 and 1987, fifteen expeditions went to Oak Island, each with (great, greater) hopes than the group before.
7. The (few, fewer) pieces of evidence that have been found are three links of a gold chain, a quill pen, and a scrap of parchment.
8. Skeptics say that there is (little, less) hope of finding the famous riches on Oak Island.

9. This does not discourage those who are prepared to enter into one of the (most costly, costly) treasure hunts of all time.
10. The excavation of Oak Island continues, with each expedition digging (deep, deeper) than the last.

4. Problems with Comparisons (links to exercise A on p. 219)

➔ **1.** biggest **2.** any other

Choose the correct form of comparison for each sentence.

1. It used to be that the (biggest, most biggest) money to be made in entertainment was in movies.
2. Today, television is more profitable than (any, any other) kind of entertainment.
3. That's due partly to the (greater, more greater) number of TV networks today and the advent of cable.
4. Another reason is that TV shows, especially situation comedies, are much (cheaper, more cheaper) to make than movies.
5. Half-hour sitcoms are also (easier, more easier) to syndicate than hourlong shows.
6. Syndication is (more lucrative, most lucrative) than one-time use.
7. The sitcom *Seinfeld* has earned more money than (any, any other) entertainment product in history.
8. Syndicated even before its prime-time run was over, it outearned the (highest-earning, most highest-earning) movie of all time.
9. The Carsey-Werner TV production company is worth more than (any, any other) movie production company.
10. With total earnings of well over $1 billion, it's even (richer, more richer) than Steven Spielberg's company, DreamWorks SKG.

10 Capitalization

1. People and Cultures (links to exercise A on p. 230)

➔ **1.** J. Pérez, Native American **2.** Mr. Pérez, Marta Ríos, M.D.

For each sentence, write the words that should be capitalized.

(1) Ophelia Johnson, ph.d., and dr. Frederick Johnson, jr., are my aunt and uncle. **(2)** Recently i noticed that aunt ophelia and uncle fred have developed a passion for beads. **(3)** Their interest in beads began when my cousin Jeff, a methodist seminary student, went to Ireland to learn gaelic. **(4)** My aunt and uncle visited cousin Jeff there and then went to England. **(5)** In England they learned about african beads and saw a british collection amassed by a. j. arkell. **(6)** A museum guide explained that Arkell began collecting beads when he was stationed in several sudanese districts in Africa. **(7)** In the 1930s muslims from Africa would go on the haj, a sacred pilgrimage to Mecca. **(8)** In Mecca they traded beads with indian and other islamic peoples. **(9)** Years later, professor Arkell became a curator at a museum of egyptian antiquities. **(10)** My aunt and uncle returned from England with mauritanian powder-glass beads and tuareg necklaces.

2. First Words and Titles (links to exercise A on p. 233)

➜ **1.** Parting, *Romeo, Juliet* **2.** It's

For each sentence, write the words that should be capitalized.

1. Have you read *The Cat in the hat* and *The pilgrim's progress?*
2. Do you prefer a poster for *Star wars* to the painting *Starry night?*
3. If you don't know *The Rite of spring* but you know the theme music of *the Simpsons,* you probably need to learn more about the arts.
4. In 1930 Arnold Bennett wrote, "good taste is better than bad taste, but bad taste is better than no taste."
5. so who's to judge what is good or bad?
6. Is it the book reviewer for the *Post* or a critic for *TV guide?*
7. It helps to outline the sources of opinion:
   I. experts
      A. critics
      B. scholars
8. Another resource is *the dictionary of Cultural Literacy.*
9. In the introduction, the authors write, "to become part of cultural literacy, an item must have lasting significance."
10. Examples of entries on a single page are ones for the opera *carmen,* the movie *casablanca,* and the song "casey jones."

3. Places and Transportation (links to exercise A on p. 236)

➜ **1.** Bahamas, SS *Clermont* **2.** United States, New, West Coast

For each sentence, write the words that should be capitalized.

(1) I vow I'm going to start a west coast group to help children of bargain hunters. **(2)** My parents own a novelty store on west aspen street, just north of the coyote river. **(3)** Every summer my family heads north toward vancouver, british columbia, or east to the great plains on buying trips. **(4)** One year we even took a cruise around the mediterranean sea and went shopping in europe. **(5)** Mom and Dad bought models of the rock of Gibraltar and the parthenon. **(6)** In palermo, sicily, they even found a door knocker in the shape of mount etna. **(7)** During a storm in the strait of messina, I was sure that our ship, the *atlantis searcher,* would sink from the weight of all our souvenirs. **(8)** My dream vacation is to visit cape canaveral on the eastern side of florida, watch a space-shuttle launch, and not buy anything! **(9)** But I know that wherever we vacationed, even on the space station *mir,* my parents could probably find treasures to bring home. **(10)** If we colonized a planet such as mars, my folks would probably spend their time bargaining to buy rocks at the right price.

4. Organizations and Other Subjects (links to exercise A on p. 239)

➔ **1.** Senate, House, Representatives **2.** Senior Trip Committee

For each sentence, write the words that should be capitalized.

(1) The Massachusetts institute of technology (mit) is serious about toys. **(2)** Mit's media laboratory is researching the role that computers will play in designing toys of the future. **(3)** Can you imagine enrolling in Technology and toys 101? **(4)** The freshman class of a.d. 2010 might sign up for it and other computer-science courses as well. **(5)** Some may enroll with the hope of receiving the national inventor of the year award for a cutting-edge toy. **(6)** At first, Bandai company's Tamagotchi and the giga pets of Tiger Electronics, inc., seemed innovative. **(7)** However, virtual pets have had to compete with electronic games on the internet. **(8)** At the end of the next millennium, will high-tech toys inspire the nostalgia that cracker jack novelties do today? **(9)** Will mattel's barbie software be as collectible as dolls from world war I? **(10)** Will the Smithsonian institution have a wing for nintendo games and computer chips?

11 Punctuation

1. Periods and Other End Marks (links to exercise A on p. 250)

➔ **1.** monsters. **3.** Phew!

Write the last word of each sentence, adding the correct end mark.

1. Is it safe to surf in shark territory
2. Ask Eric Larsen
3. He was riding the waves off Monterey when he felt a blinding pain
4. Larsen wondered what could possibly be wrong
5. Suddenly, he felt himself being dragged beneath the waves

6. Oh, no! A shark had seized him
7. Larsen frantically beat the predator with his fists
8. Miraculously, the shark surrendered and swam away
9. Larsen was badly bitten but lived to tell his tale
10. What is the moral of his story Never surf with sharks

2. Comma Uses (links to exercise A on p. 254)

➜ **1.** 1620, **2.** Drebbel, scientist,

Write the word before each missing comma, adding the comma. Write *Correct* if no commas are needed in a sentence.

1. In 1954 the actors Kirk Douglas Peter Lorre and James Mason took an imaginary trip beneath the waves.
2. They starred in *20,000 Leagues Under the Sea,* an underwater fantasy movie.
3. Based on a novel by Jules Verne the movie was a huge hit.
4. At the center of the tale is mad vengeful Captain Nemo.
5. Professor Aronnax a naturalist from the Paris Museum of Natural History takes a wild ride in Nemo's submarine the *Nautilus.*
6. During their long trip in the depths of the sea the men have many adventures.
7. First they sink a warship; second they battle a giant squid.
8. Finally the men explore the seafloor.
9. Thrilled by the sight of ancient grottoes Aronnax cries out in wonder.
10. Although the tale was factually inaccurate it helped generate public interest in the sea.

3. More Comma Uses (links to exercise A on p. 258)

➜ **1.** Rock, Island, sea, **2.** chair,

Write the word before each missing comma, adding the comma. Write *Correct* if no commas are needed in a sentence.

1. Danny Ferrington grew up in Enterprise Louisiana during the 1950s.
2. His father was a cabinetmaker; his mother a homemaker.
3. As a child Ferrington liked music and enjoyed working with wood.
4. His mother recalling his passion for woodworking said "We knew he had a gift."
5. Ferrington attended college but he did not receive a degree.
6. Worried Ferrington settled for a low-paying job in a guitar repair shop.

7. At the Old Time Pickin' Parlour which paid him only $2 an hour Ferrington learned to make guitars.
8. Today he is famous for his handmade guitars are among the best.
9. Musicians searching for unique guitars flock to his Los Angeles California shop.
10. "Each of his guitars" says Linda Ronstadt "is a unique creation."

4. Semicolons and Colons (links to exercise A on p. 261)

➜ **1.** Washington; **2.** discovery:

Write the word before each missing semicolon or colon, adding the the correct punctuation mark.

1. In February of 1945, three powerful leaders met in Yalta, a seaside resort in Soviet Russia and they discussed the future of the postwar world.
2. Attending the conference were Franklin D. Roosevelt, president of the United States Winston Churchill, prime minister of Great Britain and Joseph Stalin, premier of the Soviet Union.
3. World War II was not yet over nevertheless, the "Big Three" were confident that Germany would soon surrender.
4. The Big Three were concerned about Germany they didn't want this nation to start a third world war.
5. The Allied leaders planned to divide postwar Germany into four zones one controlled by the United States, one by Great Britain, one by Russia, and one by France.
6. The war with Japan was also on the agenda unlike Germany, Japan was not on the brink of surrender.
7. The Soviet Union was at war with Germany it had not, however, declared war on Japan.
8. Roosevelt wanted the Soviet Union to join the war against Japan in return, Stalin wanted the United States to support its recovery of former territories.
9. Roosevelt and Stalin struck a bargain Russia would declare war on Japan if the United States would support the Soviet Union's plans.
10. The Yalta agreements were presented as proof of Allied unity but Roosevelt and Churchill did not, in reality, trust Stalin.

5. Dashes and Parentheses (links to exercise A on p. 264)

➜ **1.** scientist—all **2.** (recall his kite experiments)

Insert dashes, parentheses, or commas wherever necessary.

1. Ricky, Lucy, Fred, Ethel these were once the most famous names on American TV.

2. *I Love Lucy* the show in which these characters appeared was a 1950s megahit.
3. By the end of the show's first season it premiered late in 1951, about 11 million TV sets were tuned to *I Love Lucy* every Monday night.
4. If you consider the total number of TVs in U.S. households at that time about 15 million sets you will understand just how much Americans really did love Lucy.
5. Comedian Lucille Ball she was such a riot played the role of Lucy Ricardo.
6. Desi Arnaz Ball's Cuban-born real-life husband played Ricky Ricardo.
7. Ball and Arnaz supposedly one of the happiest couples in Hollywood shocked their fans when they later divorced.
8. Ball went on to star in three shows of her own: a *The Lucy Show,* b *Here's Lucy,* and c *Life with Lucy.*
9. She also starred in *Wildcat* a Broadway show and the movie *Mame.*
10. In 1989 Lucille Ball star of stage, film, and TV died at the age of 77.

6. Hyphens and Apostrophes (links to exercise A on p. 267)

➜ **1.** Alaska's **2.** 427-foot

Rewrite the words that need hyphens or apostrophes, adding the missing punctuation.

1. Although about three quarters of the earths surface is covered by oceans and seas, peoples knowledge of the worlds waters is limited.
2. Water is not peoples natural habitat.
3. The human body has its needs, and they cant be ignored.
4. With todays diving gear, however, the underwater world can be yours to enjoy.
5. First and foremost, youll need breathing apparatus and oxygen tanks.
6. In addition, a wet suit will help you retain your bodys natural heat.
7. Its cold underwater: while it may be in the 80s on land, the temperature below may be a bone chilling 40 degrees.
8. Protect your eyes with a pair of high quality goggles.
9. If you dont have an underwater camera, you may want to borrow a friends.
10. Finally, for your own well being, dive with other people, and be aware of your partners locations at all times.

7. Quotation Marks (links to exercise A on pp. 270–271)

➔ **1.** Are you surprised to learn that "a great majority of deep-sea fishes have light-generating capabilities"?

Rewrite this paragraph, adding quotation marks, other punctuation, and paragraph divisions where appropriate.

My sister loves poetry; I don't. So when I had to write a poem for my English class, I knocked on her door and screamed Help She opened her bedroom door and said Is the house on fire No I answered just my brain. I have to write a poem, and I don't know what to say. Is it supposed to rhyme she asked My English teacher always says Poems don't have to rhyme I explained Just then, her phone rang. It was Gary, her boyfriend. Listening to my sister argue with him, I came up with a great idea for a poem. When she hung up, I announced that my poem was almost finished. You're almost done my sister cried in amazement Let me see that Sure I replied, handing over the poem. About all you did was copy down what I said to Gary she said angrily. I guess she didn't like my little poem, The Big Breakup Now I love poetry; my sister doesn't.

8. Italics (links to exercise A on p. 273)

➔ **1.** From ancient epic poetry to the modern musical *Titanic,* many works of art depict the perils of seafaring.

Write and underline the words that should be italicized in these sentences. If a sentence needs no italics, write *Correct.*

1. When someone says the word sports, my brother's eyes light up.
2. Jeb pores over the sports section of the Los Angeles Times daily.
3. I often use the word obsession to describe my brother's fascination with sports.
4. After school, he thumbs through his collection of Sports Illustrated magazines.
5. On summer evenings, you can find him looking up sports statistics in his Complete Baseball Record Book.
6. Come September, he studies a book called Football Pro.
7. When the snow falls, he rents Space Jam at the video store and reads his basketball books.
8. His bedroom walls are plastered with posters of sports stars, and over his bed hangs a copy of the painting Baseball at Night.
9. Each week, he studies TV Guide and circles the time of every televised sporting event.
10. The only time I get to watch my favorite TV series, Biography, is when it happens to be about the life of some sports star.

Guidelines for Spelling

Forming Plural Nouns

To form the plural of most nouns, just add *-s.*

prizes **dreams** **circles** **stations**

For most singular nouns ending in *o,* add *-s.*

solos **halos** **studios** **photos** **pianos**

For a few nouns ending in *o,* add *-es.*

heroes **tomatoes** **potatoes** **echoes**

When the singular noun ends in *s, sh, ch, x,* or *z,* add *-es.*

waitresses **brushes** **ditches** **axes** **buzzes**

When a singular noun ends in *y* with a consonant before it, change the *y* to *i* and add *-es.*

army—armies **candy—candies** **baby—babies**
diary—diaries **ferry—ferries** **conspiracy—conspiracies**

When a vowel *(a, e, i, o, u)* comes before the *y,* just add *-s.*

boys—boys **way—ways** **array—arrays**
alloy—alloys **weekday—weekdays** **jockey—jockeys**

For most nouns ending in *f* or *fe,* change the *f* to *v* and add *-es* or *-s.* Since there is no rule, you must memorize such words.

life—lives **calf—calves** **knife—knives**
thief—thieves **shelf—shelves** **loaf—loaves**

For some nouns ending in *f,* add *-s* to make the plural.

roofs **chiefs** **reefs** **beliefs**

Some nouns have the same form for both singular and plural.

deer **sheep** **moose** **salmon** **trout**

For some nouns, the plural is formed in a special way.

man—men **goose—geese** **ox—oxen**
woman—women **mouse—mice** **child—children**

For a compound noun written as one word, form the plural by changing the last word in the compound to its plural form.

stepchild—stepchildren **firefly—fireflies**

If a compound noun is written as a hyphenated word or as two separate words, change the most important word to the plural form.

brother-in-law—brothers-in-law **life jacket—life jackets**

Forming Possessives

If a noun is singular, add *'s.*

mother—my mother's car **Ross—Ross's desk**

Exception: The **s** after the apostrophe is dropped after *Jesus'*, *Moses'*, and certain names in classical mythology (*Zeus'*). These possessive forms, therefore, can be pronounced easily.

If a noun is plural and ends with **s**, just add an apostrophe.

parents—my parents' car **the Santinis—the Santinis' house**

If a noun is plural but does not end in **s**, add *'s.*

people—the people's choice **women—the women's coats**

Spelling Rules

Words Ending in a Silent *e*

Before adding a suffix beginning with a vowel or *y* to a word ending in a silent **e**, drop the **e** (with some exceptions).

amaze + -ing = amazing **love + -able = lovable**
create + -ed = created **nerve + -ous = nervous**

Exceptions: *change + -able = changeable; courage + -ous = courageous*

When adding a suffix beginning with a consonant to a word ending in a silent **e**, keep the **e** (with some exceptions).

late + -ly = lately **spite + -ful = spiteful**
noise + -less = noiseless **state + -ment = statement**

Exceptions include *truly, argument, ninth, wholly,* and *awful.*

When a suffix beginning with ***a*** or **o** is added to a word with a final silent **e**, the final **e** is usually retained if it is preceded by a soft **c** or a soft *g.*

bridge + -able = bridgeable **peace + -able = peaceable**
outrage + -ous = outrageous **advantage + -ous = advantageous**

When a suffix beginning with a vowel is added to words ending in **ee** or **oe**, the final silent **e** is retained.

agree + -ing = agreeing **free + -ing = freeing**
hoe + -ing = hoeing **see + -ing = seeing**

Words Ending in *y*

Before adding a suffix to a word that ends in *y* preceded by a consonant, change the *y* to *i.*

easy + -est = easiest **crazy + -est = craziest**
silly + -ness = silliness **marry + -age = marriage**

Exceptions include *dryness, shyness,* and *slyness.*

However, when you add *-ing,* the *y* does not change.

empty + -ed = emptied but **empty + -ing = emptying**

When adding a suffix to a word that ends in *y* and is preceded by a vowel, the *y* usually does not change.

play + -er = player **employ + -ed = employed**
coy + -ness = coyness **pay + -able = payable**

Exceptions include *daily* and *gaily.*

Words Ending in a Consonant

In one-syllable words that end in one consonant preceded by one vowel, double the final consonant before adding a suffix beginning with a vowel, such as *-ed* or *-ing.* These are sometimes called 1+1+1 words.

dip + -ed = dipped **set + -ing = setting**
slim + -est = slimmest **fit + -er = fitter**

The rule does not apply to words of one syllable that end in a consonant preceded by two vowels.

feel + -ing = feeling **peel + -ed = peeled**
reap + -ed = reaped **loot + -ed = looted**

In words of more than one syllable, double the final consonant (**1**) when the word ends with one consonant preceded by one vowel and (**2**) when the word is accented on the last syllable.

be•gin´ per•mit´ re•fer´

In the following examples, note that in the new words formed with suffixes, the accent remains on the same syllable.

be•gin´ + -ing = be•gin´ ning = beginning
per•mit´ + -ed = per•mit´ ted = permitted

In the following examples, the accent does not remain on the same syllable; thus, the final consonant is not doubled.

re•fer´ + -ence = ref´ er•ence = reference
con•fer´ + -ence = con´ fer•ence = conference

Prefixes and Suffixes

When adding a prefix to a word, do not change the spelling of the base word. When a prefix creates a double letter, keep both letters.

dis- + approve = disapprove
ir- + regular = irregular
anti- + trust = antitrust
re- + build = rebuild
mis- + spell = misspell
il- + logical = illogical

When adding ***-ly*** to a word ending in ***l***, keep both ***l***'s. When adding ***-ness*** to a word ending in ***n***, keep both ***n***'s.

careful + -ly = carefully
final + -ly = finally
sudden + -ness = suddenness
thin + -ness = thinness

Special Spelling Problems

Only one English word ends in ***-sede:*** supersede. Three words end in ***-ceed:*** *exceed, proceed,* and *succeed.* All other verbs ending in the sound of ***seed*** (**sēd**) are spelled with ***-cede.***

concede	**precede**	**recede**	**secede**

In words with *ie* and *ei,* when the sound is long **e** (ē), the word is spelled ***ie*** except after **c** (with some exceptions).

i **before** ***e***	**thief**	**relieve**	**piece**	**field**	**grieve**	**pier**
except after ***c***	**conceit**	**perceive**	**ceiling**	**receive**	**receipt**
Exceptions:	**either**	**neither**	**weird**	**leisure**	**seize**

Commonly Misspelled Words

abbreviate
accidentally
achievement
amateur
analyze
anonymous
answer
apologize
appearance
appreciate
appropriate
argument
associate
awkward
beginning
believe
bicycle
brief
bulletin
bureau
business
calendar
campaign
candidate
certain
changeable
characteristic
column
committee
courageous
courteous
criticize
curiosity
decision
definitely
dependent
description
desirable
despair
desperate
development
dictionary
different
disappear
disappoint
discipline
dissatisfied
efficient
eighth
eligible
eliminate
embarrass
enthusiastic
especially
exaggerate
exceed
existence
experience
familiar
fascinating
February
financial
foreign
fourth
fragile
generally
government
grammar
guarantee
guard
height
humorous
immediately
independent
indispensable
irritable
judgment
knowledge
laboratory
license
lightning
literature
loneliness
marriage
mathematics
minimum
mischievous
mortgage
necessary
nickel
ninety
noticeable
nuclear
nuisance
obstacle
occasionally
occurrence
opinion
opportunity
outrageous
parallel
particularly
permanent
permissible
persuade
pleasant
pneumonia
possess
possibility
prejudice
privilege
probably
psychology
pursue
realize
receipt
receive
recognize
recommend
reference
rehearse
repetition
restaurant
rhythm
ridiculous
sandwich
schedule
scissors
seize
separate
sergeant
similar
sincerely
sophomore
souvenir
specifically
strategy
success
surprise
syllable
sympathy
symptom
temperature
thorough
throughout
tomorrow
traffic
tragedy
transferred
truly
Tuesday
twelfth
undoubtedly
unnecessary
usable
vacuum
vicinity
village
weird
yield

Commonly Confused Words

Good writers master words that are easy to misuse and misspell. Study the following words, noting how their meanings differ.

accept, except — *Accept* means "to agree to something" or "to receive something willingly." *Except* usually means "not including."
Did the teacher *accept* your report?
Everyone smiled for the photographer *except* Jody.

adapt, adopt — *Adapt* means "to make apt or suitable; to adjust." *Adopt* means "to opt or choose as one's own; to accept."
The writer *adapted* the play for the screen.
After years of living in Japan, she had *adopted* its culture.

advice, advise — *Advice* is a noun that means "counsel given to someone." *Advise* is a verb that means "to give counsel."
Jim should take some of his own *advice.*
The mechanic *advised* me to get new brakes for my car.

affect, effect — *Affect* means "to move or influence" or "to wear or to pretend to have." *Effect* as a verb means "to bring about." As a noun, *effect* means "the result of an action."
The news from South Africa *affected* him deeply.
The band's singer *affects* a British accent.
The students tried to *effect* a change in school policy.
What *effect* did the acidic soil produce in the plants?

all ready, already — *All ready* means "all are ready" or "completely prepared." *Already* means "previously."
The students were *all ready* for the field trip.
We had *already* pitched our tent before it started raining.

all right — *All right* is the correct spelling. *Alright* is nonstandard and should not be used.

all together, altogether — *Altogether* means "completely." *All together* means "as a group."
The news story is *altogether* false.
Let's sing a song *all together.*

a lot — *A lot* may be used in informal writing. *Alot* is incorrect.

among, between are prepositions. *Between* refers to two people or things. The object of *between* is never singular. *Among* refers to a group of three or more.

Texas lies *between* Louisiana and New Mexico.
What are the differences *among* the four candidates?

anywhere, nowhere, somewhere, anyway *Anywhere, nowhere, somewhere,* and *anyway* are all correct. *Anywheres, nowheres, somewheres,* and *anyways* are incorrect.

I don't see geometry mentioned *anywhere.*
***Somewhere* in this book is a map of ancient Sumer.**
***Anyway,* this street map is out of date.**

borrow, lend *Borrow* means "to receive something on loan." *Lend* means "to give out temporarily."

Please *lend* me your book.
He *borrowed* five dollars from his sister.

bring, take *Bring* refers to movement toward or with. *Take* refers to movement away from.

I'll *bring* you a glass of water.
Would you please *take* these apples to Pam and John?

can, may *Can* means "to be able; to have the power to do something." *May* means "to have permission to do something." *May* can also mean "possibly will."

We *may* not use pesticides on our community garden.
Pesticides *may* not be necessary, anyway.
Vegetables *can* grow nicely without pesticides.

capital, capitol, the Capitol *Capital* means "excellent," "most serious," or "most important." It also means "seat of government." *Capitol* is a "building in which a state legislature meets." The *Capitol* is "the building in Washington, D.C., in which the U.S. Congress meets."

Proper nouns begin with *capital* letters.
Is Madison the *capital* of Wisconsin?
Protesters rallied at the state *capitol.*
A subway connects the Senate and the House in *the Capitol.*

choose, chose *Choose* is a verb that means "to decide or prefer." *Chose* is the past tense form of *choose.*

He had to *choose* between art and band.
She *chose* to write for the school newspaper.

desert, dessert *Desert* (des´ ert) means "a dry, sandy, barren region." *Desert* (de sert´) means "to abandon." *Dessert* (des sert´) is a sweet, such as cake.

The Sahara in North Africa is the world's largest *desert*.
The night guard did not *desert* his post.
Alison's favorite *dessert* is chocolate cake.

differ from, differ with *Differ from* means "to be dissimilar." *Differ with* means "to disagree with."

The racing bike *differs* greatly from the mountain bike.
I *differ with* her as to the meaning of Hamlet's speech.

different from is used to compare dissimilar items. *Different than* is nonstandard.

The hot sauce is much *different from* the yogurt sauce.

farther, further *Farther* refers to distance. *Further* refers to something additional.

We traveled two hundred miles *farther* that afternoon.
This idea needs *further* discussion.

fewer, less *Fewer* refers to numbers of things that can be counted. *Less* refers to amount, degree, or value.

***Fewer* than ten students camped out.**
We made *less* money this year on the walkathon than last year.

good, well *Good* is always an adjective. *Well* is usually an adverb that modifies an action verb. *Well* can also be an adjective meaning "in good health."

Dana felt *good* when she finished painting her room.
Angela ran *well* in yesterday's race.
I felt *well* when I left my house.

imply, infer *Imply* means "to suggest something in an indirect way." *Infer* means "to come to a conclusion based on something that has been read or heard."

Josh *implied* that he would be taking the bus.
From what you said, I *inferred* that the book would be difficult.

its, it's *Its* is a possessive pronoun. *It's* is a contraction for *it is* or *it has.*

Sanibel Island is known for *its* beautiful beaches.
***It's* great weather for a picnic.**

kind of, sort of Neither of these two expressions should be followed by the word *a.*

What *kind of* horse is Scout?

What *sorts of* animals live in swamps?

The use of these two expressions as adverbs, as in "It's kind of hot today," is informal.

lay, lie *Lay* is a verb that means "to place." It takes a direct object. *Lie* is a verb that means "to be in a certain place." *Lie,* or its past form *lay,* never takes a direct object.

The carpenter will *lay* the planks on the bench.

My cat likes to *lie* under the bed.

lead, led *Lead* can be a noun that means "a heavy metal" or a verb that means "to show the way." *Led* is the past tense form of the verb.

***Lead* is used in nuclear reactors.**

Raul always *leads* his team onto the field.

She *led* the class as president of the student council.

learn, teach *Learn* means "to gain knowledge." *Teach* means "to instruct."

Enrique is *learning* about black holes in space.

Marva *teaches* astronomy at a college in the city.

leave, let *Leave* means "to go away from." *Leave* can be transitive or intransitive. *Let* is usually used with another verb. It means "to allow to."

Don't *leave* the refrigerator open.

She *leaves* for Scotland tomorrow.

Cyclops wouldn't *let* Odysseus' men *leave* the cave.

like as a conjunction before a clause is incorrect. Use *as* or *as if.*

Ramon talked *as if* he had a cold.

loan, lone *Loan* refers to "something given for temporary use." *Lone* refers to "the condition of being by oneself, alone."

I gave that shirt to Max as a gift, not a *loan.*

The *lone* plant in our yard turned out to be a weed.

lose, loose *Lose* means "to mislay or suffer the loss of something." *Loose* means "free" or "not fastened."

That tire will *lose* air unless you patch it.

My little brother has three *loose* teeth.

majority means more than half of a group of things or people that can be counted. It is incorrect to use *majority* in referring to time or distance, as in "The majority of our time there was wasted."

Most of our time there was wasted.

The *majority* of the students study a foreign language.

most, almost *Most* can be a pronoun, an adjective, or an adverb, but it should never be used in place of *almost,* an adverb that means "nearly."

***Most* of the students enjoy writing in their journals.** (pronoun)

***Most* mammals give birth to live young.** (adjective)

You missed the *most* exciting part of the trip. (adverb)

***Almost* every mammal gives live birth.** (adverb)

of is incorrectly used in a phrase such as *could of.* Examples of correct wordings are *could have, should have,* and *must have.*

I *must have* missed the phone call.

If you had played, we *would have* won.

principal, principle *Principal* means "of chief or central importance" and refers to the head of a school. *Principle* is a "basic truth, standard, or rule of behavior."

Lack of customers is the *principal* reason for closing the store.

The *principal* of our school awarded the trophy.

One of my *principles* is to be honest with others.

quiet, quite *Quiet* refers to "freedom from noise or disturbance." *Quite* means "truly" or "almost completely."

Observers must be *quiet* during the recording session.

We were *quite* worried about the results of the test.

raise, rise *Raise* means "to lift" or "to make something go up." It takes a direct object. *Rise* means "to go upward." It does not take a direct object.

The maintenance workers *raise* the flag each morning.

The city's population is expected to *rise* steadily.

real, really *Real* is an adjective meaning "actual; true." Really is an adverb meaning "in reality; in fact."

***Real* skill comes from concentration and practice.**

She doesn't *really* know all the facts.

seldom should not be followed by *ever,* as in "We seldom ever run more than a mile." *Seldom, rarely, very seldom,* and *hardly ever* are correct.
I *seldom* hear traditional jazz.

set, sit *Set* means "to place" and takes a direct object. *Sit* means "to occupy a seat or a place" and does not take a direct object.
He *set* the box down outside the shed.
We *sit* in the last row of the upper balcony.

stationary, stationery *Stationary* means "fixed or unmoving." *Stationery* means "paper for writing letters."
The wheel pivots, but the seat is *stationary.*
Rex wrote on special *stationery* imprinted with his name.

than, then *Than* is used to introduce the second part of a comparison. *Then* means "next in order."
Ramon is stronger *than* Mark.
Cut the grass and *then* trim the hedges.

their, there, they're *Their* means "belonging to them." *There* means "in that place." *They're* is the contraction for *they are.*
All the campers returned to *their* cabins.
I keep my card collection *there* in those folders.
Lisa and Beth run daily; *they're* on the track team.

way refers to distance; *ways* is nonstandard and should not be used in writing.
The subway was a long *way* from the stadium.

whose, who's *Whose* is the possessive form of *who. Who's* is a contraction for *who is* or *who has.*
***Whose* parents will drive us to the movies?**
***Who's* going to the recycling center?**

your, you're *Your* is the possessive form of *you. You're* is a contraction for *you are.*
What was *your* record in the fifty-yard dash?
***You're* one of the winners of the essay contest.**

Index

A

B

C

D

E

F

G

H

I, J, K

L

M

INDEX

Q

RESOURCES

R

S

T

U, V

W, X, Y, Z

Acknowledgments

For Literature and Text

Alfred A. Knopf and Writers House: "The Study of History," from *Collected Stories* by Frank O'Connor. Originally appeared in The New Yorker. Copyright © 1957 by Frank O'Connor. Copyright © 1981 by Harriet O'Donovan Sheehy, Executrix of the Estate of Frank O'Connor. Reprinted by permission of Alfred A. Knopf, Inc., and by arrangement with Harriet O'Donovan Sheehy, Executrix of the Estate of Frank O'Connor, c/o Writers House, LLC as agent for the proprietor.

Elizabeth Barnett, Literary Executor: *Excerpt from Sonnet XXX of Fatal Interview* by Edna St. Vincent Millay, from *Collected Poems* by Edna St. *Vincent Millay* (HarperCollins). Copyright © 1931, 1958 by Edna St. Vincent Millay and Norma Millay Ellis. Reprinted by permission of Elizabeth Barnett, Literary Executor.

Beacon Press: Excerpt from "The Sun" from *House of Light* by Mary Oliver. Copyright © 1990 by Mary Oliver. Reprinted by permission of Beacon Press, Boston.

Brandt & Hochman Literary Agents: "Searching for Summer," from *The Green Flash* by Joan Aiken. Copyright © 1969 by Joan Aiken. Reprinted by permission of Brandt & Hochman Literary Agents, Inc.

Felicity Bryan: From "Lalla," from *Love Stories* by Rosamunde Pilcher. Copyright © Rosamunde Pilcher. Reprinted by permission of Felicity Bryan, Oxford, England.

Don Congdon Associates: Excerpt from "There Will Come Soft Rains" by Ray Bradbury. First published in *Collier's,* May 6, 1950. Copyright © 1950 by Crowell-Collier Publishing Company, renewed 1977 by Ray Bradbury. Reprinted by permission of Don Congdon Associates, Inc.

"A Sound of Thunder" by Ray Bradbury. First published in *Collier's,* June 28, 1952. Copyright © 1952 by Crowell-Collier Publishing, renewed 1980 by Ray Bradbury. Reprinted by permission of Don Congdon Associates, Inc.

Nicholas Gage: Excerpt from "The Teacher Who Changed My Life" by Nicholas Gage, *Parade,* December 17, 1989. Reprinted from *A Place for Us* by Nicholas Gage. Copyright © 1989 by Nicholas Gage. Reprinted by permission of the author.

Harper's Magazine: Excerpt from "The Leap" by Louise Erdrich, *Harper's Magazine,* March 1990. Copyright © 1990 by Harper's Magazine. All rights reserved. Reproduced from the March 1990 issue by special permission of Harper's Magazine.

Henry Holt and Company: Excerpt from "Birches" by Robert Frost, from *The Poetry of Robert Frost,* edited by Edward Connery Lathem. Copyright © 1944 by Robert Frost. Copyright 1916, © 1969 by Henry Holt & Company. Reprinted by permission of Henry Holt and Company, LLC.

Estate of Robert Nemiroff: From "On Summer" by Lorraine Hansberry. Copyright © 1960 by Robert Nemiroff as Executor of the Estate of Lorraine Hansberry, © 1988 Robert Nemiroff. All rights reserved. Used by permission of the Estate of Robert Nemiroff.

Random House: From *I Know Why the Caged Bird Sings* by Maya Angelou. Copyright © 1969 by Maya Angelou. Published by Random House, Inc.

Universal Press Syndicate: Taken from the ROGER EBERT column by Roger Ebert © 1990 The Ebert Company. Dist. By UNIVERSAL PRESS SYNDICATE. Reprinted with permission. All rights reserved.

Art Credits

vi Illustration by Daniel Guidera; **vii** Starfoto/Mauritius/H. Armstrong Roberts; **viii** © Jon Eisberg/Getty Images; **ix** Illustration by Daniel Guidera; **x** © Philip Gould/Corbis; **xi, xii** © Getty Images; **xiii, 1** Illustrations by Daniel Guidera.

Illustrations by Daniel Guidera

1, 6, 7, 8, 11, 14, 20, 24, 29, 34, 35, 38, 40, 47, 51, 54, 57, 62, 63, 83, 88, 96, 112, 117, 118, 120, 126, 127, 131, 138, 152, 160, 174, 175, 179, 181, 185, 188, 192, 197, 205, 209, 215, 224, 228, 231, 238, 241, 244, 245, 246, 249, 268, 278.

Cover © Ryan Aldrich/McDougal Littell

CHAPTER 1 **2–3** © Getty Images; **4 background** © James Balog/Getty Images; **foreground** Tabletop by Sharon Hoogstraten; **6** © Manoj Shah/Getty Images; **9** Calvin and Hobbes © 1986 Watterson. Dist. by Universal Press Syndicate. Reprinted with permission. All rights reserved; **19 left** © George Hunter/Getty Images; **right** © SuperStock; **22** © Jon Eisberg/Getty Images; **27** © Robert Frerck/Getty Images; **30** Photo by Sharon Hoogstraten; **35** © The New Yorker Collection 1998 Roz Chast from cartoonbank.com. All rights reserved.

CHAPTER 2 **36** © Zig Leszczynski/Animals Animals; **43 bottom right** © Getty Images; **44** © 1997 Cindy Karp/Black Star; **46** AP/Wide World Photos; **53** Copyright 1999 by Kirby, Smith, Wilkins, www.roadsideamerica.com.

CHAPTER 3 **64 background** © Copyright MCMLXXXVIII Chris Sorensen. All rights reserved; **foreground** Photofest; **68** © Joe McDonald/Corbis; **72** © Luiz C. Marigo/Peter Arnold, Inc.; **75** © John R. MacGregor/Peter Arnold, Inc.; **76** © Werner H. Muller/Peter Arnold, Inc.; **84** Springtime (1885), Lionel Percy Smythe. Watercolor, 203–4″ x 15 1–4″, private collection. Photo by Christopher Newall; **86** © 1975 Tom McHugh, The National Audubon Society Collection/Photo Researchers, Inc.; **89** © Tribune Media Services, Inc. All rights reserved. Reprinted with permission.

CHAPTER 4 **90** Photo by Sharon Hoogstraten; **93** Peanuts reprinted by permission of United Feature Syndicate, Inc.; **100** AP Photo/University of Florida, Ray Carson; **107** Frank & Ernest reprinted by permission of Newspaper Enterprise Association, Inc.; **108 background** Photo by Sharon Hoogstraten; **foreground,** Yellow Vase (1990), Roy Lichtenstein. Copyright © 1990 Estate of Roy Lichtenstein/Gemini G.E.L.

CHAPTER 5 **114** Photo by Sharon Hoogstraten; **119** © Bob Daemmrich/Stock, Boston/PNI; **122, 124** © Getty Images

CHAPTER 6 **128 background** Tabletop by Sharon Hoogstraten; **foreground** © C. Bruce Forster/AllStock/PNI; **135** © 1987 FarWorks, Inc. All rights reserved. Reprinted by permission; **140** AP/Wide World Photos; **153** © 1999 King Features Syndicate, Inc. World rights reserved. Reprinted with special permission of King Features Syndicate.

CHAPTER 7 **154** © 1980 Warner/MPTV; **159** © Universal Studios/Photofest; **161** © The New Yorker Collection 1991 Jack Ziegler from cartoonbank.com. All rights reserved; **163** © Hollywood Pictures/Photofest; **165** © Paramount/Photofest; **169** © 1996 Warner Bros./Photofest; **170** © Tri-Star/Photofest.

CHAPTER 8 **176** © Bill Lisenby/Corbis; **182** © Phyllis Picardi; **186** Peanuts reprinted by permission of United Feature Syndicate, Inc.; **195** © Elmer Parolini/ www.CartoonStock.com; **199** AP/Wide World Photos; **201** Photograph © Jim Whitmer; **202** © Philip Gould/Corbis.

CHAPTER 9 **206** © Steve Shapiro/Black Star/PNI; **210** *Miners in the Sierras* (1851–1852), Charles Christian Nahl and Frederick August Wenderoth. Oil on canvas. National Museum of American Art, Smithsonian Institution, Washington, D.C./Art Resource, NY; **212–213** Photo by Sharon Hoogstraten; **215** © Corbis/Bob Rowan; **221** Courtesy Cluett, Peabody & Co., Inc.; **225** © The New Yorker Collection 1999 Danny Shanahan from cartoonbank.com. All rights reserved.

CHAPTER 10 **226 background** © J. Harrison/Stock Boston/PNI; **foreground** Photo by Sharon Hoogstraten; **229** Photo by Sharon Hoogstraten; **235** © Corbis/Kevin Fleming; **236** © Paul Damien/Getty Images; **245** © The New Yorker Collection 1994 Eric Teitelbaum from cartoonbank.com. All rights reserved.

CHAPTER 11 **250** © Corbis/Karl Weatherly; **258** © Getty Images; **264** © Corbis/ Bettmann; **267** © Rosanne Olson/AllStock/PNI; **271, 275** © Getty Images; **279** © 1999 David Sipress from cartoonbank.com. All rights reserved.

The editors have made every effort to trace the ownership of all copyrighted material found in this book and to make full acknowledgment for its use. Omissions brought to our attention will be corrected in a subsequent edition.